Beating Cancer with Faith, Optimism, and Humor

Fabiana Da Silva

To everyone who helped me through this dark time of my life. To Sarah Scarpim Wei, a brilliant young woman who represents all the traits an extraordinary student can have. Additionally, special thanks to the staff of EF Academy New York and student council of 2014. Finally, to Emily Aquina, director of activities, Jose Luis Pueyo, and Patch Rawanghet for promoting leukemia awareness in the school community. Thank you for fighting alongside me. I was never alone because of all of you.

Contents

Thanks

I would like to thank my parents from the bottom of my soul for everything they have done for me. They always made me believe in my recovery and supported me in this tough battle from beginning to end. A special thanks to my mom, who is my best friend and was my head nurse. She left her life in Brazil to help save my life back in New York. A special thanks to my father for being a friend and for being a clown. Thank you for being a very funny daddy who was able to make me smile even when I felt like crying. I do not come from a wealthy family, but I come from a family that gave me the greatest wealth that parents could give: great values. *Marta and Deroci, thank you very much for giving me the greatest treasures that parents can give: love, respect, and education.* It was from them that I learned that my color, race, and nationality do not define who I am. They taught me an important lesson: if you have a dream or a goal and a lot of determination, nothing and no one can stop you from achieving what you really wish.

A special thanks to my husband for supporting me through this difficult phase of our lives. Thanks for hanging in there while the storm was trying to scare us away and set us apart. Thanks for making me feel safe and pretty even when I felt I wasn't. Thank you for always believing that I was strong and that I would beat it. Most importantly, thank you for not running away when everything looked so bleak.

Special thanks to my mother-in-law and father-in-law who were there for me when I needed them the most. Thanks for bringing beautiful Christmas lights to my room; all the doctors always commented that they really felt the spirit of Christmas in my room. Thanks for bringing a homemade Christmas meal to my parents. I was so happy to know that in the middle of that storm, they were able to share a great moment with special people like you two. I guess that's what family is all about.

I would like to thank all my family members who have been praying and sending their good energy to me. A big thanks to all my friends from New York, from Brazil, and from all over the world.

I would like to thank all my friends and coworkers. I know they did their best to give me strength to fight this battle. I got so much support from all of my friends and numerous visits in a harsh and long winter.

I would like to express my gratitude for all the emails, cards, gift cards, phone calls, text messages, and messages from my social network. You are and will always be instrumental for my recovery. Today I can say that you truly know who your friends are when you go through tough times, and I am glad that most of my friends stayed from beginning to the end. I have no way to thank you, my friends, for everything you all did for me. Since we can find something positive in every bad situation, I would say that feeling your love and support was the best gift I could have received. I want you to know that the love that you shared with me gave me the strength to face all that I went through in a positive way. And every time I had a bad day, I knew that somewhere in the world, someone would be praying and sending good vibes to me.

I cannot finish this acknowledgment without thanking the excellent doctors who looked after me and the wonderful nurses who were part of this crazy and blessed journey. There were so many, but just to name a few: "Snow White", who always greeted me with a warm and beautiful smile; "Hope," who never allowed me to lose my hope; and "Mama Bear," who always treated me as if I were a daughter and not a patient. I was so lucky that I was surrounded by so many "Snow Whites," "Hopes," and "Mama and Papa Bears."

A special thanks to my friends Jenna Marcus, Jean Rivot, and Larissa Poma, who kindly worked with me in the creation of my "baby" book.

Introduction

My name is Fabiana Da Silva, and it is with much love that I am sharing how I overcame cancer with faith, optimism, and a smile. For those who don't know me, here is a brief introduction. I am thirty years old, and I have been living in New York for seven years. I am an only child of a wonderful couple, Marta and Deroci da Silva. I was born and grew up in Grajaú, a simple neighborhood in São Paulo, where I am proud to have lived in until I was twenty-four years old.

I came to the United States through an au pair program in 2008. I had a tough year because the family that chose me was very different from my own. There are many interesting and funny stories from my time there. That first year was also wonderful because I met friends that I will carry in my heart forever: Normita, Amy, Fabiolla, Olivia, Vanilda, and Kaira, among others.

At the end of my au pair year, I had a wonderful opportunity to earn my master of education in TESOL. Knowing that was a one-life-chance opportunity, I grabbed it with both arms, my brain, my heart, and my soul. I knew that with a master's degree from the US, I would get a good position when I returned to Brazil. I have yet to return permanently.

With much effort, in two years, I finished my master's degree, so the next step was to get a job, teach for a year, and then go back home. With a master's degree and with the experience of teaching abroad, I was sure I would get a great job in Brazil. The question was, How could I, a Brazilian teacher, find a job as an English teacher? Not even American teachers were able to work because of the recession. The response to this question was quick. As soon as I applied, I got two job proposals for two wonderful jobs. As soon as I made my choice, I started my professional career in the USA.

Not only did I get the job I wanted, but as soon as I finished my master's degree, I was invited by a teacher from one of my graduate school courses to teach one of the courses in the college as an adjunct professor. What an honor! I could not believe I was already teaching at an international school as well as teaching teachers how to teach English to ESL students. Life was (and still is) pretty good! It was at that moment that I realized that our life is full of ups and downs and that everyone can go through horrible moments, but we have to keep strong during a storm, because after the storm, the sun will always shine again, and wonderful moments will come. I love teaching English to English language learners. There is nothing more rewarding than seeing a student who wasn't able to say "hi" in the beginning of the semester able to complain about homework in a full sentence by the end of the semester.

After a few years of living and teaching in the USA, I met Richard Boyce. We dated for two years, and when we traveled to Florida, I knew he was the one. We were sitting on the beach, looking into each other's eyes and talking about our future. Time seemed to stop for us. The waves seemed to be dancing to some bossa nova sounds as we enjoyed the beautiful blue sky and each other's presence. At that moment, I felt he was the prince I had searched my entire life to find. We got married on May 4, 2013. We had some wonderful moments until December 4, 2013. Only seven months into our marriage, we were struck with the frightening diagnosis of cancer.

Chapter 1

Holy Headache!

On December 2, I was super excited about my trip to Brazil. I had planned the trip carefully, and in just five more days, I would be in Brazil. I could not believe I would be able to see my family again. Even though I loved living in New York, I still missed so many things about Brazil: my caring family, the delicious Brazilian food, the beautiful beaches, and, of course, our music, samba and *pagode*. Every time I heard it live at the beach, it always made my blood hotter and my pulse faster, and I felt excitement filling me. When we were at these concerts, nobody knew each other, but at that moment, we all became friends as we danced and sang together. I would have done anything to be able to live those moments again. Everything was set; I would be on my dream trip sooner than I thought! I would be able to leave the winter that I enjoyed only when I was inside my home sweet home, drinking a hot chocolate. Now I would have the chance to enjoy the season that I love the most: summer.

Since Christmas was just around the corner, I started buying lots of things for my family and friends, and since I can be spoiled too, I spent almost the entire month of November asking my parents for everything I missed and wanted to eat, from barbecue to *amorinha*, a Brazilian berry that tastes sour and kind of sweet at the same time. Also, I had already set up a lot of gatherings with my beloved friends. My family, friends, and I were all ready for all the parties we had planned together. That was the price I had to pay for living abroad; I would always miss my family and friends no matter where I decided to live in North America. However, I made sure that my visit home would be perfect. Everything was meticulously planned, so what could possibly go wrong? The ticket was already purchased, the presents were bought, and I would have a month to enjoy everything and everybody I had missed.

However, on Wednesday evening, December 3, I started to have a light headache that became stronger, stronger, and stronger until I started to cry like a hungry newborn baby throughout the whole night. My husband asked me if I wanted to go to the emergency room, but I did not want to. After all, it was just a headache! I woke up early the next morning, and I decided that despite not having slept all night, I would still go to work. Besides, the semester would end in only three more days, and the pain was not as strong as it had been during the night. What I didn't remember was that a few months ago, I had to go to the doctor because I had strong chest pains. Then I went to the doctor again because a "ball" popped up on my left eyelid. It was tiny compared to others, but for me, it looked like one eye was swollen compared to my normal-sized right eye. I kept asking Richard if he thought I would become an ogre or turn into the Hulk since the veins in my neck were protruding.

I decided to go to the administration building and talk to the secretaries who were also my friends. I showed my neck veins to them because I wanted to convince them that something was really off with me.

"Hey, girls, let me ask you a quick question. Can you please take a careful look at my neck? Tell me if you see anything weird in the veins of my neck. I think I'm turning into Fiona from *Shrek*. Please, take a look at this vein right over here."

My coworkers kindly took a look at it and said, "Fabi, you are funny! We don't see anything on your neck. But go to your doctor just to make sure that everything is all right."

Conclusion: no one knows more about your body than you do. So if you see anything unusual on your body, just run to the doctor and try to see different doctors to make sure you are well. Unfortunately, some diseases have symptoms not much different from a simple cold. So my advice is, if something hurts, you get a tiny lump, or if you are about to turn green, *do not wait!* Just go to the doctor!

According to the doctors that I had seen months earlier, I didn't have to worry about anything. My heart exam was great. I did the stress test, where I had to run on a treadmill (which I did wearing high heels!), and the doctors were surprised by my steady breathing. I ran for twenty minutes without stopping, and the more they increased the speed, the more I liked it. My primary doctor, with whom I had been doing my medical checkups for three years, came to the following conclusion: "Hey, Ms. DaSilva, you look great. You might be stressed out. You said you are working in different schools, taking a Spanish course, and dancing Zumba? You need to rest. A good massage will do it. Go to Brazil, and if these headaches continue, come back here."

On December 4, I worked the whole day, and as I was not feeling too much pain, I wondered whether or not I should go to the doctor again. I did not want to waste a lot of time sitting in a doctor's office. It was always the same blah, blah, blah: "Take an aspirin, and you'll be fine." I dutifully nodded in agreement, but inside me, I felt that I should insist on a follow-up and go back to the doctor. I was sure I had to go back to the doctor's office when my mom supported my concerns.

"Please go, Bi." (That's what she still calls me.) She continued, "We should never play around with our health."

Moms know it all!

Chapter 2

At the Doctor's Office

While I waited for the doctor, I observed every minute detail. Since I had been there so many times, the room was already familiar to me. Nothing seemed to have changed. The scary fluorescent white walls were still the same, and the flat-screen TV had a weird sign: "Please do not change the channel." It made me wonder if I really had to watch that silly program that somebody else had chosen. Besides, I had so many lessons to correct, and there I was, sitting in front of a TV and not paying attention to anything that was being said. My mind was too busy thinking about my amazing trip and everything I had to do before I traveled. Suddenly, the doctor interrupted my colorful thoughts about the beaches in Brazil and opened the door.

Doctor: Mrs. Da Silvaaaa! Here again? How are you feeling?

Me: Okay. How about you? (I had already been there so many times that it seemed like he was a close friend. I felt like saying, "Hey, pal, how are you doing?")

Doctor: Fine, thanks for asking. What brings you here today?

Me: Well, Doctor, I am feeling better now, but I had a horrible

5

headache last night. It wasn't like any pain I have felt before; it was a sharp one. I had the impression a knife was piercing my brain every five minutes. It was such a strong headache that it made me cry like a child who had lost her favorite stuffed animal.

Doctor: Hmm … I am really sorry to hear that. I'm going to prescribe you an over-the-counter painkiller.

Was he serious? Was that it? Just get a painkiller at a pharmacy?

Me (furious, about to explode like a pressure cooker): Doctor, I totally respect your opinion, but don't you think that maybe there might be something else going on with me? I come here almost every week with different symptoms. I already know your staff. At this point, the nurses know me so well that when I come in, they already call me by my first and last name. First, when I came here because of chest pain, you said it was nothing. Then I came here with basically a soccer ball on my left eyelid; again, according to you, it wasn't anything to worry about. Last week, when I came here because my neck veins were as thick as jungle vines, you also said it was not anything. Now I have this headache, which is not bad at the moment. Not to mention that I now realize that my blood cannot pass through my veins anymore. Take a look at this lump on my neck.

Doctor: Hmm, yeah. Let me hear your lungs just to verify that you are fine. From what I'm hearing here, everything sounds okay. Let's do an x-ray just to make sure you're really okay.

Chapter 3

And at the X-Ray Room

A friendly young man came to do my x-ray. He looked like a teenager to me, but I would say that he was in his early twenties.

X-ray technician: Is there any chance that you are pregnant? If there is, we cannot do this test because it can harm your baby.

Me: No. No chance at all. I have been married for only seven months, and we are planning to have one or two in three or four years, but let's go on with this exam because I have a lot of lessons to plan, comments to write, and I still need to finish packing. I'm traveling to Brazil in four days, and I have too much to pack.

X-ray technician: Are you serious? You're going to Brazil? That's so awesome! Isn't it summer there? I wish I could go to Brazil and run away from the cold winter in New York.

I was very happy that he had so many nice things to say about Brazil, but I was also excited to have that exam done and be free to go back home. Noticing that I did not engage in his conversation, he said, still in a cheerful voice, "Please, turn to our X-ray machine and hold your breath. There you go. You are all set."

Suddenly, I heard the x–ray guy. He did not sound cheerful

anymore; he actually sounded very shocked when he said, "Oh, wow! Doctor, can you please come here?"

Upon hearing the doctor's quick steps, I thought, *Oh, please, guys, give me a break! Do not start with any shenanigans! I am traveling on Sunday morning no matter what!* Little did I know what was about to come.

I left the room, ready to buy just the pills for a headache that I didn't even have anymore. At that point, I would be happy with whatever they prescribed me; I just needed to go already! Suddenly, I remembered: *Today is December 4, exactly seven months to the day that Richard and I are married. It's our seven "monthiversary"!* I thought about all the promises we had made to each other at that beautiful park in Bronxville when we were doing our photo shoot for our beautiful wedding. All I knew was that I needed to leave that Urgent Care soon to make a special dinner for Richard and me.

The x-ray guy and the doctor stared at me as if I were a ghost. They looked pretty scared, and one of them said, stuttering, "So … um … from what we see here … we can say that your lungs have a lot of fluid. You'll have to go to the emergency room tonight."

Me: Emergency room? Why do I have this liquid in my lungs, Doctor?

Doctor: I really do not know. I recommend you to go to the emergency room immediately.

Me: Oh, Doctor, I am so sorry. I am not sure I will have time for it tonight. I think I have already told you about my trip. Also, I just remembered that today is my seven-month anniversary, and I really need to go back home. Let's do like this. I will go to Brazil, and when I am back in the US, I promise I'll go straight to the emergency room.

It may have sounded crazy to them, but it made perfect sense to me at the time.

Doctor: Well, Mrs. Da Silva, you'd better go now, and then you will travel knowing what is going on.

I said jokingly to him and the x-ray guy: "Oh, I see what this is all about! I get it now! Someone seems to be a little bit jealous that I will be in a paradise and wants to stop me from traveling, right? I know how it is! I was telling you guys that I am going to Brazil, staying at the beach in nice warm weather, drinking coconut water, and listening to some joyful music. Of course, you guys got a little bit jealous since you are staying in the cold, dark winter days. So, I get it now; you're trying to sabotage my trip! Okay, you convinced me. I will stop by the emergency room very quickly, but I am already warning you that I will need to go home because I really have so much to get done that you cannot even imagine."

I took a picture of the x-ray that they had just taken. I have to confess that the x-ray looked confusing to me. I could see that one of my lungs was totally covered with some liquid, and the other lung looked fine. Without any medical experience, I assumed I had pneumonia. I knew it couldn't be anything that serious, but since I usually don't lose my sense of humor very quickly, I decided to send a message to my husband with the photo of the x-ray:

The message read: "Dear Richard, I am really sorry to inform you, but you married a woman who has only one and a half lungs. Look at the picture. I'm going to the emergency room, but I'll see you at home soon. Love you!"

$\mathscr{C}$hapter 4

In the Emergency Room

I felt tired after such a long day. When the doctor said I had to go to the emergency room, I first thought about driving back home, but I decided to be a big girl and drove to the closest emergency room. I had to walk for only about two minutes from the parking lot to the entrance of the hospital, but I felt like I had run miles and miles once I got to the front desk, I was so short of breath that I could barely say hi.

I was determined to do everything very fast. I started already telling the front desk lady everything that I was feeling so that she could share it with the doctor and I did not have to waste time repeating myself. It is amazing how even in a situation where we are not in control, we still think we can control everything. With the severity of the symptoms I had described, they quickly found a room where I would be seen by a doctor. I thought they were exaggerating or maybe I had gotten too precise in my descriptions and they thought it was something more serious than it was. I was sure there was no need to put me in a room just because I had a strong headache the night before. After all, I trusted my primary doctor a lot, and he had said that my "stress" would go away quickly once I got to Brazil.

Anyway, I did some blood tests. The technicians and nurses didn't tell me why they were running so many tests, but they kept saying that doctor would be able to let me know more. To be honest, I was already bored with all that busy work. I decided to give my mom a call to calm her down. I told her that the first doctor had sent me to the emergency room but that I was feeling fine and soon I would be out of that hospital.

When I started talking to the nurses, I began to realize that maybe I would not be leaving the hospital that night.

Nurse: Hi, dear. Are you feeling well?

Me (standing up and ready to go): I am feeling great! And soon I will have to leave.

Nurse: You can lie down on your bed so that you feel more comfortable. These pajamas are here for you.

Me: Pajamas? Oh, you're so sweet! Thank you so much, but I do not want to waste a second putting them on. Pretty soon I'll have to go, but I really appreciate your concern.

Nurse (insistent): Can you please put them on? It really facilitates doing your exams and blah, blah, blah …

After listening to her monotone talk, I got tired of her trying to convince me to put on that ugly outfit. I surrendered just so that she would stop talking. Little did I know it would be my outfit for several days.

Chapter 5

Almost a Fugitive?

I was in the hospital for just a couple of hours, but it seemed like I had been in prison forever. I was already impatient after waiting for so long, and the minutes were going by so slowly. I was hungry and wanted to be free again at any price. How long does it take to get the result of a blood work exam? I thought, *Well, since I'm here, and I am not really sure when I will be leaving, I'd better look for a vending machine because it is getting late. I am so hungry that I could eat a horse.* I just needed anything I could grab; organic fruits and veggies be damned!

I got my fancy black leather bag, put on my matching black high heels, and started walking around the hospital in my awful white and blue gown. Where would they have hidden those treasure machines that I needed so badly? I looked for those machines desperately, like a student who cheats and does not want to be caught by his favorite teacher. Suddenly, I heard someone running and screaming:

Nurse: Excuse me! You, right there! Please, stop!

Me: Are you talking to me?

Nurse: Where are you going?

(First, I felt like a kid stealing somebody else's lunch in the cafeteria. Then I thought to myself, *Hey, you can't talk to me like that! I am not a kid anymore!* There's got to be something positive about being a grown-up; I knew that paying bills wasn't one of them.)

Me: I'm just looking for a vending machine. I'm starving! It is 9:00 p.m., and the last time I ate was 11:00 a.m. I'm really hungry. I am sorry, but I really cannot take it anymore.

Nurse (with anger): You cannot eat!

Me: Who said so? Yes, I can! I haven't eaten the whole day. I am starting to get dizzy. I am so hungry I am about to faint here, and I really mean it!

Nurse: I'll check it out with your doctor, but I'm sure you cannot eat yet.

Me: Oh my goodness! Come on already! What the heck is going on? What is the big deal? Okay, I understand I had a strong headache last night, but it doesn't even hurt anymore. First, they insisted that I put on these weird pajamas. Now I find out I can't even eat? Why? I am feeling totally fine now. Why are you making such a big deal of it? Just let me go already!

Nurse: Why don't you lie down and cover yourself with this warm blanket that was just taken from the oven?

(It is true! The warm blankets the nurses offer us at the hospital are just magical. They have the power to calm us down, and we feel warm and protected.)

Me: Okay, I will have one, please. As we say in Brazil, well, if you are in hell, you'd better hug the devil.

$\mathscr{C}$hapter 6

The Lump

Since I had that "free time," I started to think about how I was so used to being busy all the time. I was so used to it that lying down in bed doing nothing for hours seemed a waste of time. I just loved my frenetic New Yorker lifestyle: I was teaching in two different schools—at an international high school, and I was also teaching a graduate course for teachers who wanted to delve into the ESL world. I was also teaching an online course for amazing teachers in Austria. I also worked for a Saturday school program where I helped some students catch up to their peers. I still had time to take my Spanish course and to go to my Zumba classes. Besides that, I always found time to take care of my husband and my hair (Hair? Yes! Some hair does require lots of time: one hour of hydration and at least one hour for brushing and styling it.) If you have hair similar to mine, this is all not news to you. This is the minimum you have to do in order to keep up a good relationship with your unruly hair.

Sometimes we have so much going on in our lives that we don't realize that silence is also beneficial so that we can be at peace with ourselves. I just could not stop thinking about my trip to Brazil. I had had so much fun planning every detail of it. I could not wait to be there with my family, but I knew I had to be patient. Soon, the doctors would confirm that was just a silly headache and I would be discharged and able to cook a wonderful meal to celebrate Richard and our seven months of marriage.

The doctor who was taking care of me came back saying that his work hours were done and he needed to go have dinner with his family. I thought, *I also want to have dinner with my family! And by the way, you're not helping me!* I was introduced to the doctor that would take care of me from that point on. He was about forty years of age, medium height, with gray and wavy hair—a mix of Bill Clinton and Michael Jackson. The new doctor came in to give me the verdict about if I could or could not eat.

Doctor: I heard you were walking around the hospital trying to buy some snacks.

The way he looked at me suggested I had been doing something illegal. He gave me an accusing look, the kid that teachers give when they realize that their students are trying to cheat right in front of them.

Me: Well, Doctor, I hope the other doctor has already explained to you that I am in a rush because I'm going to travel to Brazil this Saturday. Besides, today is my wedding anniversary, so I wanted to know if I can be discharged as soon as possible. Or if I am not going to be discharged immediately, I was wondering if I could at least get some warm food. I feel that if I don't eat something, I think I will start feeling sick.

Doctor: Mrs. Da Silva, you will have to have a very important test called PET scan for us to figure out why you have so much accumulation of fluid in your lungs. So, no food or drink until you have the exam.

Me: Okay, I will wait then!

The words the doctor said stuck in my mind: "very important

exam … excess of fluid in your lungs." I thought, *It cannot be anything serious! I have nothing to worry about. I do not smoke, and I do not even drink alcohol.* Okay, I will not lie to my readers; occasionally, I drink a glass of wine or champagne, or I have some caipirinha (a Brazilian national cocktail made with cachaça, lime, crushed ice, and some fruit that would make even the grumpiest person in the world have fun and relax). I am also not a saint! If you are over twenty-one, a margarita will not hurt you. I am Deroci's daughter, and he loves a cold beer; maybe that's where I learned to appreciate a cold drink.

Lying on that bed, I was thinking: *Where does this liquid come from?* Running my hands on my neck, I felt the lump that had been following me for days—the same lump I had already shown to two different doctors who assured me that it was nothing. I grabbed my phone and took some pictures to see if the scary lump was still there. Unfortunately, it was, and it looked stronger than ever! It was as if that little monster smiled at me, while I wanted to cry. For the first time, I realized that I was fighting something over which I had no control.

Looking at the photos, I started remembering numerous times I looked in the mirror and asked, "My God, what is this lump? How can the doctors say that all the symptoms and this lump is nothing? How can it be nothing if I can feel and see this lump that seems to be preventing my blood from circulating?"

More and more strange flashbacks/memories started coming to my mind while I lay there waiting for the frightening exam.

The First Memory

Me (very happy arriving from the supermarket): Hi, honey, how was your day?

Richard: It was okay. And yours?

Me: I had a wonderful day! I taught five classes, I had my

Spanish class, and after that, I went to the gym. My Zumba teacher rocked today. She is so energetic. Every time I finish her class, I am so pumped up that I could run a marathon. Now I am going to take a quick shower, and I will make a special dinner for us!

Richard: Cool! What's for dinner, hun?

Me: Oh, Richard, do not worry about the menu. You know how I am creative in the kitchen! I got it!

As soon as I was done with my shower that totally renewed my energy, I was a new "Fabi" and was ready to start my creative dinner. I looked at our ingredients and decided to create my dish that night. I decided to call it "dish a la Fabiana." A lot of onions, some spices, a hint of lemon, a lot of garlic, and some white rice with arugula and cranberry sauce would do it. Perfect!

Me: Dinner is ready, love! Oh, I forgot to let you know. Ollie, my friend who is a nurse, invited us to walk for breast cancer early tomorrow. Will you come with us? I'll go. It's always good to help people in some way.

Richard: Oh, that is pretty cool! Unfortunately, I will not be able to go, but if you go, make sure you make a good donation as well. Just walking will not help in the research of curing cancer.

Me (running to the bathroom): Ai, Love! I don't know what is going on, but I am feeling very weird. I am feeling so dizzy …

My vision was getting dark, and I saw a bunch of sparkling stars all over the place, just like when a character gets punched in the face in the cartoons. When I got in the bathroom, I saw that the yellow walls of our bathroom were spinning fast. I would have enjoyed that nightclub if we had some music on and I wasn't so dizzy. A few seconds later, I had to throw up the succulent steak that I had prepared with so much love. I wasn't frustrated about the steak going down the drain, but I did get upset when I looked at the mirror. I screamed, "Richard!"

Richard: What happened?

Me: Look at my face! Do you see what I see or is it just my sight?

(I became what I call Strawberry Woman. Honestly, I do not have anything better to describe my face. I just know my head looked like a giant strawberry! I was red like an apple, and I had some weird spots all over my face.)

Richard: Oh, my goodness! Your face is so red! You also have a lot of marks on your cheeks. How about drinking some water?

Me (shaking my redhead in disapproval and starting to get mad at him): Water? So you see my head is about to explode, and you think that water is going to solve it? Ah, you've got to be kidding, right? My head is hot and red. I have a bunch of weird flecks all over my face, and you think water is going to solve it.

Richard: I don't know. I am just trying to help you. Do you want me to call 911?

Me: No, no need to call 911. Maybe you are right about some water. Would you please get me a glass of water, hun? I'll go to bed now because tomorrow I am walking five kilometers to help fight cancer.

Hubby and Strawberry Woman

The Second Memory

Me (looking at myself in the mirror): Richardddddddddddd! Help me!

Richard: What is it now, *Dramiana* (a name he was now calling me)?

Me: I think that there is something going on with my body. Take a look at these veins in my neck!

Richard: It looks okay to me. What are you talking about?

Me (already trying to start a fight): Are you serious that it looks okay to you? Look at the size of my veins. They look so thick, and I have the impression that my blood is not going up or down.

Richard (trying to calm me down and giving me a new nickname): Dramy, calm down. Haven't you been to the doctor lately?

Me: Yes! But they just keep saying it is stress! Stress! Stress! I have never heard that stress gives lumps and thickens people's veins!

Richard: I think you need a good rest. Have you tried getting a second opinion? Did you try going to some other doctors?

Me: Oh my God! I think you are just not listening at all! I've been to two different doctors, and they always say I am stressed.

The Third Memory

Me: Richard! Help me!

Richard: Oh, God! What is it now, Fightiana?

It was funny how Richard was able to combine my name with whatever the flurry of the moment was.

Me: Richard, look what happened to my eye.

Richard: I don't see anything. It looks pretty normal to me. Why do you love creating diseases, huh? I think this is just a sty. I've never had one, but that's what it looks to me.

Me: But I've never seen a sty right in the middle of the eye from the outside. Maybe you're right, but to make sure that everything is okay, I will go to the doctor again.

Richard: You will be fine, Sweetyana. Don't worry. Everything will be just fine.

The next day, talking with the school receptionist, Cynthia, where I used to work:

Me: Girl, I'll have to take some time in my lunch, and maybe I need to use my other prep if the doctor takes me in.

Cynthia: Geez, of course, you can! It's totally okay, Fabi.

Me: I do not even know how to tell you this, but I think I'm becoming an ogress!

Cynthia: What do you mean, Fabi? Ogress?

Me: Ogress, like the wife of Shrek. Look right in my eye! You see?

Cynthia: I cannot see anything, Fabs!

I don't know why, but I always wanted to convince everyone that something was up with me. I wanted them to confirm that they could see what I could see, but the good thing is that they did not think I was crazy, and everyone always encouraged me to find a good doctor.

Me: Why can't you see it? It's so weird. I feel and I can see a ball in my eye. It is the size of a marble on the outside of my left eye, and I am so shocked that nobody can see it. Okay, let's try this then. Take a look at my neck on the right side; do you see a giant ball that is here?

Cynthia: Well, I'm not seeing anything, but if you are not feeling well, you should just go to the doctor. Don't worry about your classes; we will take care of them.

Memories with my Super Boss

I have to pause all these memories to explain that she is not just a boss but a friend and sister to me. She is beautiful, just like Xuxa, a famous show woman that would definitely be her doppelganger! Affectionately, I call her Xu. She is tall and blond and has hypnotizing blue eyes. She has such a huge heart that she is beautiful inside and out. We always had each other's back, and she always listened to my crazy stories, which I gladly told. So every time I realized that something was different with me, I would go talk to her:

Me: Kate, I am so glad I met you in the halls. I really need to talk to you.

Kate: What happened?

Me: Remember the story of a lump that I told you about three years ago, that it was just a bone that was sticking out because I was skinny? (I'm very observant. If my body had one little different hair or if my nail was growing differently, I always wanted to share with my friends, and Kate was certainly one of them.)

Kate: Yes. I do remember it. What is going on now?

Me (laughing): Now, seriously. I promise you that something is going on. Take a look here in my left eye.

Kate: Yes, it looks good to me.

Me: Does it?

Kate: Fabi, why are you saying it? I can't see anything.

Me: I really think I'm turning into a monster. My left eye is much bigger than the right one. Two weeks ago, I threw up after eating meat. Why meat? It's so weird to me. I have never felt sick eating meat. I am Brazilian; I have been eating barbecue basically since I was born.

Kate: Well, go to your doctor and do not worry about your classes. If you do not arrive on time, we will cover your classes without any problem. Okay?

Memories of Doctors That Could Have Diagnosed Me Since August 2013

After talking to Cynthia and Kate, I rushed to my super doctor's office. I'm certain I don't have to tell you what his diagnosis was, right? Stress! I couldn't believe that I had skipped my lunch to drive frantically for thirty minutes to his office, only to be seen for less than five. He only remarked that the results from my heart exam looked great. (I had visited him previously for chest pain, and since he hadn't asked for any tests, I went to a cardiologist on my own.)

According to Mr. Charlatan, I had no reason to worry about anything. I'll never forget his words: "Your heart is better than that of an Olympic runner!"

What more did I want to hear from a doctor? I was scared when I started feeling those pains because my grandfather had passed away in his sleep from a stroke. My dear grandfather, "Moreno" (his nickname because he was the only dark-skinned child among five lighter-complexioned siblings, and "Moreno" means dark skinned in Portuguese), had a heart attack and died when he was only fifty. So, hearing at thirty, from such a "reliable" doctor that my heart was healthier than an athlete's, was a compliment and a relief. This made me feel good. I was strong just like Wonder Woman!

My primary doctor for these past three years was very young. He always seemed to be in a rush, taking notes without really looking me in the eye. His hair, strictly parted and glistening with gel, always caught my attention. I was sure he spent lots of time combing it every morning in front of the mirror in his fancy Westchester home. No hair would dare to cross the wrong side of his head. He might have had a shrine for his hair, but he wasted little time actually figuring out what all my alarming symptoms added up to.

Dr. Quack Oncologist gave a routine, quick listen to my lungs. Afterward, he was ready to write my prescription for … spa sessions. Spa sessions? I repeated, shocked, "A day at the spa will alleviate all this pain?" But if a wise man, a doctor, was telling me that I only needed sessions at a spa, who was I to argue? Why would I question a man who had studied so much and had taken "such good care of me" for three years? I had no reason to doubt him. That was my big mistake: when it's your life on the line, don't be afraid to ask whatever you want, especially if your doctor's prescription seems absurd. Please speak up. Act! Have a hurricane tantrum if necessary, but I urge you, make yourself heard before it is too late. Make Doctor-Know-It-All understand that vomiting and having excruciating headaches and lumps may seem to be innocuous symptoms, but they shouldn't be overlooked. They may be pointing to something worse. Also, if your doctor specializes in oncology, they should be able to intuit the telltale signs of cancer at the mere mention of some of these symptoms. However, Dr. Quack Oncologist detected the need for a good massage and facial scrub.

This is how our conversation went:

Doctor: So, Ms. Da Silva, what's happening? I heard that you went to a cardiologist. I am glad to say that the results are great. Your heart is much better than that of an Olympic runner. Has anything changed in your life?

Me (all happy, showing the ring Richard had given me): I got married in May!

Doctor: So that must be it.

Me: What? My marriage?

Doctor: Yes! There is little more stressful than having to get along to have a happy life right after you get married. Marriage can be tough!

Me: Wow! I never knew this could interfere so much within my health. If I had known, I would have stayed single. (I said it in jest.)

Doctor: I'd like you to go to a spa, and if you are still in pain afterward, then you can come back.

Me: A spa? Hmm … I don't think I need to go to a spa because I'm going to Brazil, and I'll have plenty of relaxation in a few weeks.

Doctor: That's great! Sounds wonderful. See you when you return from Brazil.

Or so he thought.

Brazil! Brazil! ... Brazil?

Swimming in Brazil

My memories of my most recent date with Richard—was it a foreshadowing? Two weeks before my trip, Richard took me out for a special date. I thought it was romantic of him to have planned a date. It was just like the good old days when all we wanted was to be together and have fun with each other. We enjoyed each other's company when eating out, listening to really good, free jazz concerts in Catskills, cuddling up on our couch and watching my chick flicks, or talking about nonsense. We were happy with the simplicity of every moment we shared. Fancy restaurants, pricey vacations, and expensive diamonds didn't matter if our souls were not connected, and to have that connection, we didn't need a lot of money. All we needed was to be on the same page and share similar goals and dreams. After spending so many nights at the hospital, all I wished for was to wake up the next morning listening to his deep breathing and watching his chest rise up and down. The sound of his breath was priceless to me, and I could have this nowhere else in the world but home.

Since I had just gotten married, returning to Brazil would be bittersweet. I was ecstatic to be spending a month with my family in Brazil, but I was also sad that Richard and I would be apart for a month. I believe this is the price I have to pay for my dream of living abroad, to always feel *saudade* in both countries. Saudade has no real translation in English, but it conveys an indescribable painful feeling, and any person who lives abroad or who has lost a loved one knows exactly what I am talking about. The closest word to define it would be nostalgia, but this term is not even close to the real meaning of saudade in Portuguese. I guess I never expected that I would get married and actually end up staying here.

In any case, I was happy that he had surprised me with this date because I believe it's always healthy to get out with your "boo" to talk and break up the routine.

We went to see a movie that I had mentioned wanting to watch several times, *The Best Man Holiday*. Every time I saw the trailer in commercials, I would tell him how funny I thought the movie seemed. Maybe this was his strategy, to finally take me to watch it so I would no longer be a broken record, repeating how much fun we would have. I thought it was cute that he didn't tell me about it beforehand but had simply planned it out.

The night was cold. To say it was freezing would not fully describe the air's chill, so I'll just describe the temperature as North Pole Celsius. However, the cold weather could not prevent our date. Even though we were wrapped up in our winter coats, gloves, and hats, the harsh wind sliced our faces with its mere touch. Soon, we were so numb we couldn't feel or move our fingers. We had no reason to cry, but suddenly, involuntary tears started pouring from our eyes. Our cold breath came out in almost tangible puffs of white smoke, and for a moment, we looked like Jack and Rose from *Titanic*. I was glad we weren't stuck on that beautiful, "unsinkable" ship. At least that's what I was thinking. Little did I know that this was a mere ice cube compared to the iceberg Richard and I would soon be facing.

Even though the temperature was not in our favor, we weren't going to allow it to spoil our special moment. As soon as we got to the movie theater, instead of taking the elevator, as any tired thirty-year-old would do after a long day of work, my funny husband went for the stairs. You must be picturing a beautiful and romantic scene from *P.S. I Love You*: a beautiful, loving couple ascending the stairs, gazing at each other with unspeakable desire. Holding her, he feels only the beating of her heart and the warmth of her tiny, soft hand. Oh, please! Stop those crazy thoughts right now. Wake up! Remember that I'm writing the simple story of Fabiana and her husband going to the movies. So pull yourself away from act I of a sweet *Romeo and Juliet* love story and watch as the real Romeo in this story takes the stairs.

You must be asking yourself, "Okay, he was by your side. So what?" Of course not, my dear reader. My husband darted in front of me; no bullet could get that man. I remember clearly that he was faster than the Flash. I still don't know if he was trying to get me to race or just trying to run away from the cold, or maybe the cold had frozen his brain, and he had simply gone nuts. Although I might try to convert that weird scene into something more romantic, in reality, it was less a picturesque fairy tale and more of a surreal race because I started chasing after him. My dear reader, the more I ran, the farther he seemed. I even had the impression that I was running in slow motion, or even backward, but there was one odd detail: Strawberry Woman, the same alter ego that I had experienced at home some weeks ago, reappeared right on that staircase. Finally reaching the top of the stairs, I was angry about that unnecessary effort. Now, I was totally transformed into the Hulk. The only difference was that I wasn't green; I was red like a tomato, and my hair was disheveled. The messy hair was not a big deal at all, but something else was definitely a cause for concern: I couldn't speak I was so breathless, and the damn awful spots on my face had returned. I was breathing as if I had run five miles, complete with Darth Vader sound effects.

I started to bombard Richard with my usual complaints:

Fabiana: Richard, there's something happening to me … I'm not even able to run up the stairs anymore.

Richard: Oh, stop it, Fabi! Aren't you the one who is always bragging about how you have so much energy when you dance Zumba three times a week? You brag that you can run at least an hour on a treadmill every day. If you exercise so much during the week, do you expect me to believe you're out of breath just by running up these stairs for less than a minute? (He stared at me, puzzled.)

Fabiana: Sure, I exercise every day. I don't know what's going on with me, but I know I'm not myself anymore. With this little jog, I feel that my heart is beating like it's going to jump out through my mouth any minute, like I could have a heart attack.

From the skeptical look on Richard's face, I knew he was thinking I was just starting a new drama. "You'll be fine," he said and tried to comfort me by changing the subject. "Would you like some popcorn? How about some candy? Drinks?"

Since I didn't want him to come up with another one of his nicknames, such as "Whiniana," I just replied, "No, thanks. Let's just go in or we will be late for the movie. I've heard it's a great comedy, and I want to get some good seats. If we wait, we'll probably end up with those front loser seats so close to the screen, and after three hours with our heads leaning back, we'll have stiff necks."

Once inside the theater, we realized we weren't late. The lights were still on, and the loud trailers were still blasting. The crowd seemed joyful and excited about the movie. As soon as we walked in, I heard the crunch-crunch of people munching their popcorn. The buttery smell was so tempting.

It was getting close to Christmas, and everybody seemed in the mood for a romantic comedy to fill their hearts with the holiday spirit. The majority of the audience was young couples. Everybody seemed excited for the best comedy of the year.

My dear readers, about the movie we were watching: there was a rich football player, married with three beautiful children. Since I do not want to beat around the bush, I will spill the beans. From the beginning of the movie, I carefully observed the football player's wife, an odd-looking woman. During the movie, I kept thinking, *Jeez, this woman looks so different! I don't know what it is, but there is something about her that I don't quite get. She's so skinny; I can see her bones sticking out.* There was also something about her hair that I couldn't really explain. It just didn't seem right to me; it looked like that she was wearing a cheap wig, but why would the makeup artists forget to fix her hair? Was this a B- amateur movie? Maybe I was paying way too much attention to stupid details. However, I soon realized that a big reveal was being foreshadowed. The woman was getting sick; she was coughing up blood and fainting all the time for no reason. I will never forget the scene when she was decorating her Christmas tree and suddenly she just fainted in front of her kids, cutting herself with her Christmas decorations. How could we sing "fa-la-la" and wait for Santa to get his bloody cookies after that scene? It was getting harder and harder to keep up the Christmas mood.

Then suddenly, the woman's best friend, who has always been very busy, decides to visit her. She discovers that the wife has been diagnosed with cancer. The supposed best friend, embarrassed, apologizes several times for having been so absent when her friend needed her so much. Needless to say, my much-requested comedy turned into a total drama for which I was not ready. I think no one was really expecting that she would be sick. I am sure that the whole audience was as shocked as I was. At first, all I could hear was a deafening and brutal silence, and suddenly, some women in the audience, unable to hold in their feelings any longer, started to cry. And of course, genuine tears, not winter-induced ones, started falling desperately from my eyes too, and all I thought was, *Oh, my God, how can this young woman have such an awful disease?* Several jumbled thoughts kept coming to my mind: *Really? Cancer? She isn't going to die, is she? How did she get it? Who will take care of her three children if her husband is a busy football player?* I don't know why I was so worried about something that wasn't even real. I just couldn't control my thoughts: *Oh, what a silly movie! It's just not fair. I'm so mad that I came to watch this "comedy," and now I am here sobbing as if everything was so real!* Those thoughts bothered me so much that I repeatedly whispered them to Richard, and since he couldn't hear what I was saying, he angrily hushed me: "Shush, Fabi!" That shush drove me insane. Spoiler alert! The film was a tearjerker, not a laugh-out-loud comedy from the woman's diagnosis until her death at the end. (I hope you were not planning on watching this movie because I just gave it away.)

When the film ended, all I could hear was a crowd of women sniffling. I think it would have been fitting if a handsome man like Brad Pitt, dressed in a sleek black suit, had begun playing a violin to console our broken hearts, ripped apart from watching that movie. But no Brad Pitt appeared, and we were left in the theater with our own angry Pitts complaining about their loss of twenty dollars per ticket for a supposed comedy. The men left the theater cursing the loss of their money after watching that "dramatic Mexican soap opera."

By the time I left the theater, I had cried so much my eyes were bloodshot and swollen. I couldn't believe the screenwriter hadn't found a better ending for that woman than death. Richard, impatient to leave that theater, was dismayed as well, not because the woman had died, but like his fellows, he was frustrated by the fact that he had paid to watch a comedy and had instead wasted three hours watching a B- melodrama.

I was not as concerned about this monetary loss. What bothered me was the film's ending; it just seemed unacceptable and unreasonable. Little did I know that in two weeks, I would be the protagonist of a similar film, and it was up to God and me to change a tragic ending into one of hope.

$\mathcal{C}$hapter 7

PET Scan? What the Heck?

$\mathbf{A}$ll these memories raced through my mind as If I were watching a movie. It was as if the memories were trying to give me clues about what was really going on with me. That's when I came back to reality and those gloomy thoughts started to haunt me: *Did the doctor say I have to do a PET scan?* In my naivety, I thought, *I don't know what a PET scan is, but it's looking very serious for a simple headache.* Well, if you don't have any idea of what a PET scan involves, as was the case for me before this moment, the simplest way to explain it is to say that it is a super-powerful x-ray machine. It has a hole in the middle that you pass through on a matching, pristine white conveyer belt. As it scans you, this machine is able to show how your organs, cells, and body tissues are functioning.

While I was reliving all the memories previously mentioned, I started carefully running my hand over the lump, trying to decipher what my body was telling me. My thoughts were interrupted when I was called in for the scary examination. I couldn't help but wonder how much time this PET scan would take; time management was still a precious thing to me. Now I don't take it so seriously anymore. It's just not worth it.

I observed my surroundings as soon as I stepped into the room. It was as dark as a cave, and all I could see was a huge white shark ready to devour my body. This great white mechanical monster would determine how my coming days, months, and years would unfold.

A friendly nurse asked me if I had ever had this exam before. I replied that I hadn't, so he calmly explained that it wouldn't hurt at all. The most impressive thing about this is that he wasn't lying. He went over all the steps: I would have a radioactive glucose solution injected for contrast into my veins. I would feel a warm sensation in my belly, and I would feel as if I had peed, but it would only be a sensation. (I was glad about this; I had left home without an extra pair of cute undies.) He also informed me that I would have a bitter taste on my tongue. I would pass through the white monster, and he stressed that I would have to do everything that "the powerful master" ordered. I was a little frightened, but I was also intrigued to see what this machine would instruct me to do! Such a futuristic thing! To my disappointment, I wouldn't have an elaborate conversation with the white monster; all she could say was, "Breathe in! Breathe out! Breathe in! Breathe out!" From that exam, I realized that even though I loved jokes, whatever was happening to me was no joke. Unfortunately, there was a possibility that things could be a little more serious than I had expected.

Chapter 8

The Shocking Yet Obvious Verdict

Suddenly, the doctor who resembled an odd mix of Michael Jackson and Bill Clinton came into my room, pulled out a chair, and looked at me with a lost look. I would even say he had the look of a dead fish. However, his glazed, fishy stare wasn't important. For me, the long-awaited moment had finally arrived; he was going to announce my release and apologize for having held me in that hospital for so long. Unfortunately, the scene did not go quite like that, and I heard nothing of the sort. First, he looked straight in my eyes and said with tears, "I don't know how to tell you this in an easy way, but unfortunately, we detected cancer cells on the PET scan, which means that there is no chance that you are going home today or even traveling to Brazil on Sunday."

Me: What did you say? Did you just say I have cancer?

Doctor: Yeah. It's a difficult disease to treat, but from what I saw on your results, it looks like a "good" cancer. Unfortunately,

I can't give you an exact diagnosis, but I think it's a kind of lymphoma that is easier to treat.

My dear readers, those words echoed in my mind. I just could not understand where that man had gotten this absurd idea. I repeated it unceasingly to myself: *Cancer? Good cancer? Is there any such thing such as good cancer?* I have never heard of anything good about this disease. Why me? Did he just say I have cancer? I recently got married. I am so happy teaching. I'm just thirty. How can I accept that I have a disease that could kill me at any moment? What was it that this young man just told me? Through hot, burning tears, I tried to digest what was happening, but nothing he said made any sense. Since he wasn't saying anything I considered to be logical, I decided to offer my own solution and make things simpler for the both of us, as if I could still control the situation.

"Doctor, let's do this way: I will travel to Brazil in four days. I have been waiting for this trip for an entire year, and I just can't call it off. I know it may sound silly to you, but I haven't seen my family and friends in months, and I am just going there for one month to spend Christmas and the New Year's with them. It is a tradition in my family; we spend the holidays together. How about I go to Brazil, and I come back in a month, and then we'll start the treatment with full force—fancy machines, medications, and the works."

Seeing his perplexed and disoriented look, I understood that this proposal was the most absurd thing I could have suggested. Shaking his head several times in disapproval, he said, "You must not have understood what I just said. You've just been diagnosed with cancer. We can't waste a minute, let alone an entire month! I can't stop you from traveling; it's your choice, but if you get on a plane for ten hours, the change in air pressure may cause you to be unable to breathe, and there will be no one to help you."

My dear friends, the worst feeling in the world is when you hear from a doctor that you need to run for your life! It did not take me long to make the right decision. Can you picture it? "All right, Ms. Da Silva, would you like to travel to Brazil and perhaps die in the airplane or stay here in New York and try to survive treatment? It's up to you!" I knew I wanted to go to paradise—but in Brazil, not heaven. So, I quickly decided that my trip, family, and friends could wait.

After the doctor was gone, a flurry of questions started swirling around in my brain: *How am I going to turn to Richard and say, "Hi, I am so sorry I married you just seven months ago because now I have cancer."* What would I say to my parents? Someone should write a list of suggestions to show us cancer patients and survivors how to gently inform our parents of our unfortunate diagnosis without giving them a heart attack. I wondered which of the options below I would use to let my parents know what was happening:

Option 1 (incidentally): "Hi, Dad. How's the weather in Brazil? Oh, good, good! Enjoy it! It is still very cold here. By the way, I have cancer!"

Option 2 (abruptly): "Hi, Mom. How are you, beautiful? So, were you able to stop smoking? Girl, you have to be careful. Remember that I always warned you to stop because it's dangerous and causes cancer. I guess I didn't know what I was talking about; I don't smoke, but I'm the one who's been diagnosed with cancer."

Option 3 (jokingly): "Hi, how are you, *meus amores*? I have a joke. Who wants to hear it? No takers? I'll tell it anyway. Once upon a time, there was a girl who was born, grew up, and moved to another country. She got married and had cancer. Get it?"

Their response: "No, we didn't! Gee, Bi, what a bad joke! It is not even good to name these awful diseases out loud."

Mine: "Yeah, you guys are right. Oops, my bad! I really shouldn't have said the C word, but now that I've said it, I have to say, sorry, I have cancer."

In that blizzard of gloomy thoughts, a nurse came into my

room to let me know I would be taken to my new room. This made me even sadder: it was the first night away from my hubby. Things were starting to change quickly; from that day on, I would have to be escorted everywhere in a wheelchair. Can you imagine that? I had driven myself to the hospital thinking I would be out in half an hour. Then I started to realize that simple things like walking on my own two legs any time I wanted to would no longer be possible. Not that I wasn't able to walk right now; I felt great, but the doctors wanted me to save all of my energy for the treatment. However, before the wheelchair came the gurney. I was taken to my new room on a stretcher. For the first time, I started seeing things from a different angle. Instead of patients, equipment, and doctors' scrubs, all I could see was the white hospital ceiling.

I considered what kind of joke somebody was playing on me. I was asking myself if all this was real or if someone would come in and say, "You got punked! Put your clothes back on and get the hell out of here!" Or, "Smile! You're on *Candid Camera*!" I was sure it could not be real.

$\mathscr{C}$hapter 9

Wow! Water, Where?

My mother knew I had gone to the doctor for a quick checkup. She was actually the one who had insisted I go, even though I no longer had any pain. So, of course my mom was very interested to hear the doctor's diagnosis. My first impulse was to invent a good lie to tell her, at least until I could find a gentler way to speak of the feared disease that wasn't actually confirmed yet. I hesitated to call her, but I finally took a deep breath, closed my eyes, and dialed her number.

Me: Hi, Mom. How's everything going?

Mom: I'm so glad you called, I was already pulling my hair out with worry. Are you going home yet? What did the doctors say?

Me (with a firm tone so she did not suspect anything): Well, it seems I have some fluid in my lungs. I know it's nothing serious, but I'll have to spend the night here just for observation.

Mom: Fluid in your lungs? How did you get it? But you're still coming to Brazil on Sunday, aren't you?

Me: Yeah, I think so. No need to worry about that now.

After hanging up, I confess I felt a little bad about lying to her, but at the same time, I felt relieved that my white lie could postpone her suffering. I didn't know what her reaction would be when she found out I had something far more serious than anyone had suspected. I called Richard and very briefly explained what was going on. He offered to come to the hospital, but I told him it would be better for him to stay home. I only asked him to contact the head of the school, my principal, and Kate. I just wanted them to know that unfortunately I would miss the last two days of school.

Now I urgently needed to get onto my social network to warn my friends about the gifts they had paid me to buy for their children. The list of gifts I had purchased to take to Brazil was huge. It included dolls that could poop, shirts, lipstick, women's perfumes, stuffed animals, and of course a video game. How would my friends get these gifts now? How was I going to give them to my friends and family without going to Brazil? I had spent so much of my own money, and at that moment, the only solution that came to mind was to have Richard return every little thing, one by one. That night, I logged onto Facebook and apologized to my friends, explaining that I wouldn't be going to Brazil after all. I explained that I had been hospitalized that very night and had been advised not to travel.

I kept thinking about the sad faces of the children who would not receive their presents all because "Ms. Fabi" decided to spend her vacation in a hospital! It was my fault, and they didn't deserve that! But my friends were great; everyone was understanding. My biggest fear had been that people would think I was deceiving them, that I was making it all up to keep everything they had so carefully chosen. But everyone was very calm, and nobody worried about the material stuff.

It was night, but who could sleep with such an uncertain diagnosis? It was better to use this time to organize what I could from the hospital. I tried to get things done, but I noticed that once I was in my room, I couldn't use my phone for anything: my calls wouldn't go through, no messages could be sent, and there was no internet access. Just what I needed! To be stuck in a hospital, unable to communicate with the world. When I asked a nurse about the cell phone signal, she taught me a little trick: "If you need to use your phone, go to the hallway and stay very close to the window. Then you'll be able to talk."

I was grateful to her for teaching me a crucial hospital survival trick, but in the back of my mind, I couldn't help thinking, *Why didn't you tell me this when you brought me to my new cell—I mean, my new room?* I would have spent all my precious time in front of the window calling all my friends and family members all over the world. With the secret to communication in my hands, I jumped out of my bed and went to the closest window I could find. Since my hospital gown was too big for me, it hung a little open in the back (I don't know why they don't make it by sizes instead of one size fits all). While struggling to hold my gown closed with one hand, I held up my phone with the other, searching for a measly signal so I could call someone to ask for some sort of rescue from this antiseptic-infused prison.

As soon as I got a signal, I called one of my best friends in Brazil, Kablan. He would know how to help me. We had a pure friendship; it was so genuine that neither the years I had lived abroad nor the distance had deteriorated our friendship in the slightest. We had such a good connection that when we were together, no words were necessary; I knew what he was feeling just by looking at him. Unfortunately, Kablan had just lost a cousin to cancer, and I had no words to express how much I feared what the future might hold for me. We talked for hours, and I cried a lot. I didn't think I was telling my friend, who is like a brother to me, that the doctors thought I could die. With his loving words, he helped me realize that this was not the end; there was still hope, and any strength had to come from within me.

After I had opened up my heart and soul to Kablan for hours in the middle of the night, I knew I had to call my dad. It was only five in the morning, but I just couldn't think about doing anything else. I knew I had to let my dad know what was happening to me, but frankly, I just didn't know how to begin. I don't know if it was the right way, but I needed to let him know. I began with a serious tone and then dropped the bomb:

Me: Hi, Dad. How are you?

Dad: I am fine, and you? Your mother said you went to the doctor last night. Are you home yet?

Me: Not yet, Dad. Mmm … I don't know how to say this, but unfortunately, I won't be able to travel this Sunday.

Dad: Don't even joke about it, Fabiana! Your mom and your grandma have been preparing everything for you for months. Why can't you travel on Sunday?

Me: Yesterday, I had an examination, and my lungs are full of fluid. The doctors suspect cancer.

Dad: What, Fabiana? What did you say? I am so sorry, sweetie, but it doesn't make any sense! There must be something wrong with this exam!

Me (already bursting into tears): Yeah, Dad … I can't believe it either. We don't have the final results yet, but that's what the doctor told me last night.

Dad: Calm down, Bi. Everything is going to be all right.

I knew he was saying that just to comfort me, but the truth was that even though we all wanted everything to be okay, nobody was sure what the future held for us.

Me: Dad, please do not say anything to Mom yet. I don't want her to worry without being sure.

He (with a sorrowful tone): Sure, I'll do it, whatever you ask. I just want you to know that whatever it is, we're together, and you can always count on us for anything.

Me: That's all I wanted to hear. Thank you, Dad.

After that call, my dad was not able to go to work anymore, and I could not sleep for a second. Who would want to sleep knowing you can simply close your eyes and sleep for the rest of your life? And lying in that bed where so many people had laid before, I wondered what was happening to me. From the stony look on the doctors' faces, I could see that I didn't have simple pneumonia, let alone a cold. They looked at me with concern, even fear, despite being medical professionals who deal with cancer patients on a daily basis. Maybe that's why they felt sorry for me. Their reactions confirmed to me that whatever was to come was very serious.

From the bottom of my heart, all I wanted was to wake up in the morning and find that all this was just a nightmare and everything would be back to normal. I would wake up overjoyed because I knew I would be able to do what I love the most: have a normal day. Simple routines mattered so much to me: have a quick nutritious breakfast, wear a professional-casual dress, put on a splash of fresh perfume and a bit of light makeup so as to not scare the students away, wake my husband up with a kiss, drive to school, and teach. I was convinced this was all a horrific nightmare; I would wake up at any moment, ready to have my life back to normal. Maybe I just needed to pray with more fervor and ask God with great faith so this nightmare would end and all of my dreams and goals would come true.

Chapter 10

An Unexpected Visitor

The first night in the hospital was long and full of turmoil. I turned to one side, then to the other, but couldn't quite find a comfortable sleeping position. Everything seemed alarmingly white and deathly, and there was so much respiratory equipment that for a moment I thought I was at NASA.

We should try to find something positive in every situation, so I would say that having a bathroom right by my side was a definite plus at that moment. There was also a fancy TV, but after hearing the diagnosis from a doctor who looked at me as if I was a tiny squirrel that was about to be run over by a train, who cared about the current issues in the world? How could I turn on the TV and pretend nothing was going on in my own life? I don't even like to watch TV anyway, and I wasn't about to fall in love with it that night.

The room was somewhat large, and it became quickly evident I wasn't the only occupant. To make matters worse, not only did I have a roommate, but my roommate was a woman in a great deal of pain. She was about forty years old, very tall, with long, straight hair that was slightly messy but faithfully parted in the middle. My roommate was not a supernatural entity, but you wouldn't know that from her cries of pain. I heard her moaning and prayed that her clinical condition was very different from mine. As a patient, I have to confess we never want to be worse than our roomy. We might all be in the same boat, but we would like our boat to be less wrecked.

On the wall in front of me was a white board where I saw my name and my neighbor's. This board contained basic patient information, such as our nutritional restrictions. Since I have always had a curious nature, I glanced at my name. I could eat anything. My roommate, however, had to fast until the next day. I realized that in addition to being in a lot of pain, she was also connected to a small pole with wheels, like an oxygen cart, which she used every time she had to leave the room.

After a long day of work and the devastating revelation of possible cancer, I finally fell asleep. In the middle of the night, I heard a loud and squeaky noise close to my bed. I opened my eyes, and there she was, the entity most feared by us all, the one that makes any Christian bend their knees and pray, increases one's faith, and makes any atheist believe in God, the Grim Reaper. There she was, in her long black dress with her sickle, slowly approaching me. I knew Lady MacDeath was the one responsible for going after those whose time had come.

But it was too early for me, so before she could hit my head, I shouted, "No! Please go away! I'm only thirty years old, and I just came today." Bargaining for my life, I insisted, "How about getting someone who has been here longer?"

Suddenly, the Grim Reaper asked me in a raspy voice, "What did you say?"

It was then that the Grim Reaper turned on the bathroom lights, and I realized that horrible image was only my roommate on her way to the bathroom, which was on my side of the room. The sharp sickle that I had seen was only her oxygen cart, and the black gown the clothes she had worn during the day because she had refused to wear a hospital gown. Phew! Everyone deserves a second chance. I would not give in so easily! This is the price we pay for having an overly fertile imagination.

Death approaching

$\mathscr{C}$hapter 11

"Let It Go. Let It Go."

I woke up, but unfortunately, the nightmare wasn't over. It turned out to be my real life. I was woken up by a random text message from a close friend, Crislaine, asking if I would be at Priscilla's baby shower on Saturday. Priscilla is a really good friend; she was eight months pregnant, and I had been delighted to cohost her baby shower. Crislaine's message came at the right moment because I realized that I probably would not be at the baby shower that Priscilla's mother-in-law and I had been carefully organizing for months. I immediately answered the message, saying that unfortunately I would not be able to attend the baby shower because I was stuck in the hospital and didn't know when I was leaving. I stressed that I really needed her help as well as that of our other friends so that everything would go flawlessly, which is what Priscilla deserved. "Pink perfection!" I wanted everything to go smoothly, in dazzling pink, as beautiful as I had dreamed it would be.

Life can be so extremely unpredictable! I had spent days exchanging emails with Priscilla's mother-in-law to ensure that the baby shower would be a worthy welcome into the world for our little princess, Hope. I had spent days making phone calls to confirm who would be joining us, choosing the party's theme, and ordering Brazilian pastries, *brigadeiros* (a must-have Brazilian treat; it is a scrumptious bite-size Brazilian chocolate sweet that is so delicious it can make you forget any problem you may be facing. Don't even dare to call it a bonbon or a truffle; it's a piece of heaven!).

Everything had been carefully planned out; I had even bought my ticket to Brazil for Sunday, the fourth, so that I could host the baby shower on the third. But life was teaching me another lesson: I could meticulously make all of my plans, but it didn't mean they would turn out the way I had orchestrated them. I learned that we do not have control over our future. I never considered I wouldn't be able to travel or attend the baby shower that I was supposed to host. What kind of joke was life playing on me?

As for the baby shower, I knew I had nothing to worry about because I had another friend, Eliane, who would be able to take the lead. Eliane was ready to take it on. She was my copilot; she had followed all the planning. She had accompanied me to do research on cute invitations, banners, and games. The baby shower decorations and party favors were in my car, so it would not be impossible to complete that mission. Eliane to the rescue! All she had to do was work with Priscilla's mother-in-law to decorate the room. Priscilla would be happy, and that's what mattered to me.

I sent a message to Aunt Carminha, who also lives in the United States. I told her about the possibility of having cancer. I asked her to keep it a secret because I knew if my mom even dreamed of the C word, World War III would begin, and she would do anything to be here. If she couldn't find a flight to New York, she would do the impossible—hop on any big bird she found or flap her arms until she learned how to fly so fast that she would be here in no time. I just knew that as soon as my mom suspected what was going on, she would do anything to protect her baby bird from any evil hawk trying to harm me.

Right after Crislaine's message, I also received a text message from another great friend of mine, Ms. Kathy, one of the best ESL teachers I've ever known. Ms. Kathy is very elegant, tall like a supermodel, with stylish silver hair and vivid black eyes that always shine with her faith. We worked together in the summer school of 2013 and became close friends. I have so much love and respect for her, and we have a mother-daughter relationship. That morning, she had sent me a lovely message wishing me a great trip. Reading her text, I couldn't believe I was still in that hospital. I quickly sent her a message to let her know what was happening. She called me as soon as she received it, and I tried to explain the craziness that my life had turned into in those few hours. She promised me that she would be there with me soon, and I knew I could count on her. At seven in the morning, she was already making adjustments to the hospital rules:

Ms. Kathy: Hi, I'm here to visit Fabiana Da Silva.

Receptionist: Hmm, she's in the emergency room, but I'm sorry, you can't see her now. Our visiting hours start at 10 a.m.

Ms. Kathy (with a determined tone): Excuse me? Are you out of your mind? I'm Fabiana's aunt! She needs me, and I'm going to see her right now. I am really sorry, but I can't leave her alone for one more second. I have to go to her. Have a nice day!

She marched right past the receptionists and their gaping mouths and straight into my room.

It was so wonderful to see a familiar face that was not dressed in white and telling me I might have cancer. It was a gift from heaven to have such a friendly hug while the turmoil inside me was still raging on. The warmth of that sincere hug made me feel that I didn't need to struggle to hold back my tears. I was so frightened, like a child trying to escape a monster trying to get me from under the bed. I don't even know how to explain it, but her presence and spirit made me understand that I was not alone.

As the hours passed, I got more and more visitors. My room

looked like the flowery garden filled with beautiful flowers and women. Ms. Kathy was there with me. Soon, Crislaine arrived wearing a funny blue mask. Next, my pregnant friends, Priscilla and Caroline, with their beautiful big bellies. Then Ollie, the nurse who had invited me to the cancer walk, was there to support me. Sweet Lia, the school principal, and my boss and good friend, Kate, also showed up. They were all there, giving me strength and trying to make sense of what was going on with me. Even I didn't believe I was in a hospital because I felt so comforted.

Crislaine brought a super fortifying breakfast for all of us. I don't know when she found time to buy us so many goodies. I was glad my room didn't have that hospital smell anymore. It smelled like a five-star hotel restaurant that was getting ready to serve breakfast. We had everything you could imagine: coffee, milk, orange juice, cakes, cookies, brownies, Christmas treats, and lots of fruit. The party was on! I also got a beautiful fruit basket from the school where I worked. Boy, did I feel special!

Some hours later, I had a much unexpected visitor; thank God it wasn't Grim Reaper. It was our school headmaster, Brendan. When the headmaster takes time from his busy schedule to visit you, it is another sign your condition is even more serious than expected. It was the last day of the school year, and I wouldn't be able to celebrate it with my colleagues, but I was glad that some had dropped by to see me. Brendan was ready to go to the end-of-the-year party. He was wearing a festive suit, with a red tie that matched his red pants, which made us all feel cheerful. Together we laughed and cried. These were my first days in the hospital. I experienced such an abundance of joy once my many friends were with me, friends who wouldn't let me entertain the idea that something so bad could be happening to me. But whenever I recalled the doctor's somber look, I knew deep in my soul that the diagnosis wasn't a simple cold anymore.

Chapter 12

The Forbidden Word

Aside from all the madness of being hospitalized for two days, it was good to spend that quality time with my friends. At noon, my friends went to the cafeteria to grab some lunch, and as soon as they left, a cheerful lady approached me:

SW: Hi, sweetie. How are you? I am a social worker here in the hospital. How are you feeling?

Me: I'm fine, thanks, except for the fact that the doctors suspect I may have cancer; they're going to take some fluid from my neck to find out what it is. Well, I really trust God, so whatever it is, I will face it. I know that a lot of people give up when they face some obstacles, but we have to fight with all our strength no matter what the battle is, right?

SW (with a great deal of admiration and a knowing look in her eyes): Well, I am glad you have accepted it so well. So, I think you're already prepared for what I came here to tell you. Here at the hospital, we have a program called Beautiful and Healthy. It's a wonderful program! We teach you how to put on makeup, you get some wonderful products for free, and you get to meet people who are in the same situation as you.

I wondered what "situation" that lady was talking about since the doctors hadn't confirmed my diagnosis.

SW (she continued): You'll be beautiful. We'll teach you how to redo your eyebrows. There are cases where patients lose hair over their entire body, so I want you to know that we are here for you. Also, you qualify for two hundred dollars for ...

She hesitated when she saw that I, the strong woman she had approached only minutes ago, had turned into a five-year-old girl with tears in her eyes, terrified of losing her braids. In order to make her feel better, I quickly wiped my tears with the back of my hand and continued her sentence: "Two hundred dollars for wigs, you mean?"

She seemed a bit ashamed of having mentioned the wigs when there was no confirmation of the diagnosis yet, but her words served as a reality check for me. She said she was sorry that I was going through this. She hugged me and handed me a pamphlet with the two-hundred-dollar coupon for wigs.

My dear reader, let me check if we are on the same page. If I had been in the hospital for only one and a half days, how could I be ready to turn into a sausage woman with no eyebrows or body hair and accept that I would go bald on that same day? I know many of you may be thinking, *Hair is not a big deal. What really matters is to be alive.* I sort of agree with you. If you are a man, I believe you really mean it. However, if you are a female and you still think that hair doesn't matter, please do this exercise right now: Find a big mirror. Be silent for a while and imagine yourself first without an eyebrow. Then imagine that the other one has slowly disappeared. Keep staring at the mirror until your imagination becomes so vivid that you can visualize yourself totally bald. How did you like this exercise? Imagine if this was happening in real life! There are some who might say, "Don't worry about your hair; soon it will grow back!" Really? Hair grows? Shocking! I know that! However, I've seen women crying or even depressed because they got a haircut they did not like. So, I think it is okay for us to be sad about losing our hair. If no one cared, beauty salons would never be sued. I try to picture the scene: You go to the hairdresser and ask the hairdresser to trim the ends of your hair. Once he is done, you look in the mirror and realize that you are as bald as Michael Jordan. You turn to him and say, "Oh my God! What did you do to my hair? I'm going to sue you!" He responds, "Don't be silly. Your hair will grow in soon." You then say, "Oh, you're right. Thank you then." And everything is resolved. We all know that is not the way the scenario would go in real life. That's not the way it goes at all. We all know that hair does matter, but if the price of staying alive was to lose some hair, who wouldn't be willing to pay it?

When the girls returned from lunch, there I was, lying in bed thinking about everything that the social worker had told me. I didn't look cheerful anymore, and they wondered what had happened in that half hour they had been out for lunch. The truth was that when they left for lunch, I was hopeful, and when they came back, I was devastated. That's when I decided to talk about the pamphlet I had in my hands:

Me: Oh, girls, the social worker just came here and gave me this pamphlet explaining that if I present this flyer, I will get some fancy products and two hundred dollars for wigs.

Caroline (one of my friends): What? What are you talking about? Is this woman insane? Let me see this pamphlet now! Oh, pleeeee-ase! (And in a flash, she turned that paper into a thousand pieces.) What the heck is going on? This can't be true! Does she have the results of your exams? She doesn't even know anything. How does she dare come here to talk to you about wigs? Oh, for goodness sake!

Me (I started crying about the hair I would lose and the discount I had just lost): Calm down, Caroline. Maybe this pamphlet can help me somehow.

Caroline: I am sorry, but I ripped it up already. If you want, I will get you another one, but I just think she was too pushy. She can't come in here and talk about wigs without the test results.

At that point, talking about wigs seemed absurd. But slowly, the forbidden word began to resurface, and becoming hairless became less of a concern. Losing my life was what I feared the most.

A valuable wig

Chapter 13

Splish-Splash—My Lungs Would Be Slashed

The doctors had already told me that in the evening I would have a small surgical procedure to remove some of the fluid from my lungs. After this examination, they would be able to make an accurate diagnosis. The procedure was explained in great detail. The risks were minimal, and the procedure would be quick. Still, it didn't matter how well they explained it; the only thought that came to mind was, *They're going to cut you, and it's going to hurt like hell!*

By the time my nurse arrived, I was mentally prepared for my trip to surgery. But then I became aware of something lying in wait for me, something that reminded me I wasn't myself anymore: a wheelchair. I sighed in exasperation. *Oh, please, not again! Last night, I drove myself to this hospital, and now I'm no longer allowed to walk on my own.* Life changes quickly.

I felt sorry for the lady who would be wheeling me to surgery. She was about seventy years old, extremely overweight, and looked

53

as if she was about to pass out from fatigue. While she was push-
ing me, I could hear her panting, and as much as I was enjoying
the ride, I kept thinking, *Beauty is only skin deep.* How bizarre
was that? How could I be thirty years old, young, and energetic
and pushed around in a wheelchair by a woman who could be
my grandma and who looked so worn? I felt like I was taking
advantage of her. I wished I could sit her in my wheelchair and
push her to the room where I would be examined and thank her
for accompanying me.

My thoughts could not distract me from my destination. I was
like a curious newborn peering out at the world, eagerly trying
to absorb everything. I studied every detail carefully, especially
the bright paintings hanging on the white, mute walls. I longed to
be teleported into them, to escape into their depths as far as they
would allow.

I was introduced to an excellent medical team, who did their
best to reassure me. They were patient and kind. They explained
the importance of doing the procedure when I wasn't experiencing shortness of breath in order to obtain an accurate diagnosis.
The procedure was simple: they would insert a needle into my
right lung and drain as much fluid as possible. When I heard
that a needle would be piercing my lung, I realized I had to act
fast. In my despair, I presented them with what I thought was a
reasonable option. Since I was already in that hospital, and incidentally, wasting my vacation, I would be very happy if they gave
me a strong anesthesia—or even a general anesthesia would be
just fine. I explained that I was no longer in any rush. They could
give me anything to make me fall asleep for two to three days,
and I would be totally fine with it. I had already decided I didn't
want to feel any pain (as if I had the power to decide how much
pain I would feel, right?) *Brwaaaaaawkk-wakAwk—bwaaaarawkk-
waAwk—bwaaaarawkk-waAwk.* Awkward! I never knew I was so
chicken!

I don't know why they found my proposal amusing, but they reassured me it wouldn't be worth giving a general anesthetic for such a minor procedure. It's easy to say "suck it up" when that needle is not piercing your own lung. I realized there was no negotiating, so I trusted that they would do whatever was best for me.

Before we started, I was given a form explaining there was a slight risk of infection. According to them, it was a rare occurrence. With trembling hands, I signed it. I was so nervous that cold sweat began to dampen my gown even before the procedure had begun. For the first time, I had the thought that death keeps no calendar, that I might never see my parents in Brazil or my husband whom I was still just getting to know.

First, they asked me to sit in a chair, then to lay my head down on the bed. They placed a pillow under my head, making sure I was able to breathe. Unfortunately, I hate needles, and the idea that one was going into my little lung freaked me out. I was given a local anesthesia, and the process of draining the fluid began. My vision started to get blurry until I couldn't see a thing.

I heard the machine screaming, "Beep, beep, beep." I knew something was up. Suddenly, the doctors said, "Her pressure is dropping."

Another said, "She's breaking into a cold sweat."

When I heard that, I screamed, "Guys, please help me! I can't see anything!" I grabbed the doctor's hand with all my strength and wouldn't let go.

"Fabiana," the doctor said, "you have to be strong and stay still so that we can remove enough fluid. Just a little longer."

That "a little longer" went on forever. Then a doctor shouted, "Her lips are purple!"

And I thought, *Oh, dear, you could have saved this information for yourself; I didn't need to know that. Oh my God, I'm really going to die. Even my lips are already departing this life.* I thought then the color change was not a good sign, but today I realize that it doesn't necessarily mean death.

They continued: "Hold on. We just need to get a little bit more. You're doing great! Take a deep breath!"

And, I thought, *How can I be doing great? I've vomited and smell like a stinky, sweaty pig.* The doctor's hand that I was firmly gripping was all scratched from my nails. I wonder what they considered a "bad" situation.

Once they had removed as much fluid as I could endure, I was placed on a stretcher and taken to my room. I couldn't believe that just minutes ago I had been punctured like a chicken. I began to think about how vulnerable we all are. I was sure of one thing: if an apple a day keeps the doctor away, I was going to start eating an apple tree a day.

Chapter 14

A Literal Pain in the Neck

I returned to my room, glad to have more visitors. I wanted to describe to them the most terrifying twenty minutes of my surgery in detail. Then a nice nurse asked me, "So, Mrs. Da Silva, how did the fluid removal go?"

Me: I'd like to say it was fun, but it was horrible! But at least the torture is over, right?

Nurse: Oh, yeah. There won't be any more procedures tonight, but tomorrow you're already scheduled to have a fluid suction from the growth in your neck. Do you mind if I take a look at it?

Me: Of course, you can look at it. What's the suction for?

Nurse: Hmmm. It's very important for them to send a biopsy to the lab. Tomorrow, the doctors will explain the procedure. I'm just here just to give you some important medication.

Me: Sure, sure. I love medicine, as long as it doesn't hurt. That's really all that matters, right?

Nurse: Well, you need to take this medication to prevent coagulation; it is a blood thinner called Lovenox. You'll have a shot twice a day.

Me: What? Twice a day? An injection with "love" in the beginning shouldn't be so painful. (Ah, dear reader, I didn't have a clue what I was talking about.)

Nurse: Actually, it hurts a little when the needle is inserted; it'll burn a little.

One thing I've learned is that nurses and doctors don't like to talk about the pain you'll feel during a procedure. So if a nurse says that it'll hurt a little, you'd better start praying. If she's honest enough to say it will not only hurt but it will also burn, then you can expect the pain to be out of this world.

Nurse: We can give it to you either in your arms, legs, or belly. Most patients prefer to have it injected in their belly; they say it hurts less because we tend to have more fat there. Enough talking. Where would you like yours?

After all that propaganda about the painless shot in the belly, I was convinced. I lifted my gown and displayed it proudly. For the first time ever, I prayed to have a lot of fat. I just hoped there would be enough flab so that I would feel no pain. Dear reader, we all know that no woman wishes for a flabby belly. If that was my dream at that moment, you'll understand how desperate I was. I wouldn't even mind if people called me Flabby instead of Fabi. That night, I wanted to be Flabilous, not fabulous. The nurse filled the needle, then examined my belly with some disappointment. "Sheeish, you don't have a lot of fat, do you?" she remarked.

I understood immediately what that meant; it would hurt more than I could imagine. I replied sadly, "I guess dancing Zumba worked; I do it almost every day."

She felt sorry for the pain I was about to feel and whispered, "It'll only burn a little. On the count of three, I'll give it to you, okay? Ready? One, two, and three."

"Ouchhhhhh! Oh, my God! What was that? How long will I have to do this?"

"As long as you are in treatment."

Vague answer. I thought I might need it for a couple of days; little did I know I would have to get used to living with those syringes for eleven months, almost a year. Some people are afraid of snakes, rats, the dark, heights, and ghosts. But all my life, what I have feared the most is shots. As much as this went against my strongest instincts, I had to learn that shots were somehow good for me.

When I was little, I did everything in my power to avoid getting shots. For example, when I was four years old, I got bronchitis. To my despair, the doctor prescribed sixty injections, twice a day, in the morning and at night. I used all my tricks to escape those hated shots, like running away from my parents in the hospital at shot time, or even farting in the nurses' faces, all just to avoid getting them. That was low, I admit! I also remember my desperate father negotiating with me: "Listen, if you behave yourself when the nurses come and don't kick or scream at them, I'll get you a big present. Anything you want."

Without hesitation, I said, "I want a blackboard and some chalk." You may think that I am making it up, but my parents have my blackboard to this day. Since I was little, I knew I wanted to be a teacher, and I couldn't miss the opportunity to acquire this vital teaching tool.

But the sad reality was I was no longer that little girl. I couldn't kick or scream my way out anymore; tantrums at thirty would be ridiculous, and the nurses wouldn't think it cute if I tried the fart strategy. I was an adult and had to overcome all the barriers that life was putting my way. It was time to show my parents they had raised a strong woman who was ready for life; however, I'm not going to lie to you: even after eleven months of shots, I still hate them!

Time for shots

Chapter 15

Boom! Dropping the Diagnosis Bomb on My Hubby

It was getting dark, and I couldn't wait to see my husband. I was eager to tell him about all the fights I had won in a single day. But the truth was I also feared the reaction of the man I had chosen to spend the rest of my life with. I kept thinking, *How can I tell the man I married just seven months ago that I might die?*

I considered the gentlest way to let him know that the God he already didn't have a lot of faith in had allowed this heavy burden, a burden I wasn't sure I could bear. And it wouldn't be mine alone; this was not going to be easy for him either. While I waited anxiously for his visit, all our wedding-day memories kept flooding back. In our photo shoot, two hours before the wedding in a Bronxville park, I gazed deeply into his eyes, swearing that I would do anything to be a great wife to him. How could I break that promise so fast? Why didn't destiny allow us to be happy in our first year at least? Was this a fair start? People say that a newly-wed's first year is so great, which is why it's called the honeymoon phase. Really? If this is true, I will change ours to honey*boom*. Seriously, I felt as if I was a walking bomb, and nobody knew when I would explode.

I also thought about how happy we were, how we enjoyed each other's company and how we loved joking with each other. I thought about my creativity in the kitchen and how much pleasure I got from cooking up my crazy inventions. To encourage him to eat my questionable creations, I would quickly add that he should try it just because it was a special Brazilian dish. (I guess after he reads this chapter, I won't be able to use that trick anymore.)

How could I look him in the eye and tell him doctors were checking to see if I had cancer? My only thought was how unfair this was for him. Every newlywed should come with an instruction manual and an expiration date. Something to warn the spouse: "Be careful! This woman will become obese in three years, and she may also lose her front teeth," or "Warning: this man will go bald very soon; he will turn into a cranky old man and will not shower frequently when he gets old." I felt guilty for being sick and for having unintentionally trapped him in such an awful situation.

Night brought my worn-looking hubby. The dark circles under his eyes revealed he hadn't slept well either. He looked like a tired Kung Fu Panda that had lost a couple of fights. I was worried about him. He kissed me, ran his hands through my hair, and gazed at me.

R: Any good news?

Me: Well … I had a biopsy today. We'll get the results tomorrow, I think.

R: But what do the doctors think it is?

Me: It seems it is a type of … (I wish I could have said anything else—allergy, cold—but I couldn't lie to him, so I dropped the bomb) cancer, but they still do not know for sure.

R: Cancer? What do you mean cancer? There must be something wrong, Fabiana. It doesn't make any sense!

Me: Yeah, I know. I can't believe it either! What's it going to be like without hair? (I know it sounds silly that I thought of my hair. It's strange I didn't think about how harsh the treatment would be, how my body would react to treatment, or even if there *was* a treatment.)

R: This is so surreal! This can't be happening. Is this a nightmare, a movie, or what? Well, don't worry! It can't be anything too bad. Everything will be back to normal soon, and we'll be home.

It was my second night in the hospital, and I had asked him to bring me some things that would make me feel more comfortable: our wedding album, pictures from our dates, and some Spanish material that I was determined to master. He brought all that I had asked for, as well as a stuffed animal, an old brown lion that I disliked at first, believing it was a gift from an ex-girlfriend. I found out later from his mother that Richard had had that lion since he was a child. Maybe he wanted his lion to protect me when he couldn't be by my side. I thought it was cute! I began to feel more at ease in my hospital room as comforting objects from home began to fill it, but Richard's presence made me happiest of all. Still, I just wanted to get back to our nest. That night, he refused to leave. He slept in an uncomfortably hard chair by my side; before falling asleep, he kissed me on the forehead and then held my hand the entire night.

He couldn't know how much his presence strengthened me. I knew that I had a soul mate I could count on. His gestures of affection gave me the assurance that I was gifted with a goodhearted man who would always be at my side. He would never abandon me, especially when I was feeling more fragile than crystal.

Chapter 16

What Is Your Religion?

Those nights at the hospital were much longer than any I had ever spent at home. I felt imprisoned in that hospital bed, and time crawled turtle-slowly. With eyes closed, I felt the passing of every second, every ticktock of the clock. The uncertainty kept me awake, restless, and petrified. No sleeping tactic could help me—not even counting all the sheep on earth. When my mind finally surrendered, I was only able to get an hour of sleep before morning. I woke from my meager hour of unconsciousness when I heard Richard getting ready to go to work. Then I was able to sleep for another hour before being awakened by a nurse preparing the cursed shot I would have to get every morning and night for a year.

I realized that my roommate was still there, and I started to chat. After all, we were separated by only a curtain. And since we might be living in the same room for a while, why not take this chance to make a new friend? This was not my sole motive for starting up a conversation. There was something that intrigued me about my roommate. She received constant visits from priests and nuns. They prayed with her, comforted and laughed with her, and gave her the Body of Christ and a delicate pearl rosary. For me, nothing! Nada!

I thought it was odd that they didn't even greet me, especially since they had to pass through my side of the room to get to her. I decided to do a little investigating to find out why she was getting such special religious treatment. What could she have told them to receive all those blessings? There I was, so close and yet feeling so far from divine grace. Time for action!

Me: Good morning, friend. Did you sleep well?

Her: I didn't sleep at all, girl. These machines kept beeping the entire night, right? Not to mention that the nurses come to measure our pressure all the time. There is no way we can get a good night of sleep.

Me: I know it's not easy! (Sly as a fox, I turned to the subject I wanted to delve into.) Yesterday I heard you praying with the sister. It's so good to practice our faith, right?

Her: Yeah. When I was admitted, they asked me if I would like a priest or a nun to come and pray with me, and I said yes. All help is welcome!

Me: You're definitely right! I'd like that too. I don't know why they're not stopping at my side.

Her: Don't worry. I'll help you out. When the nun comes here today, I'll let her know that you'd like her to see you too. They're great! They even gave me this rosary. Look how beautiful it is!

Me: Oh, wow! It's lovely! I can't wait for her to come and bless me too. We all need some emotional support; otherwise, we can go nuts in here.

That afternoon, the nun came to our room. She was a very tall lady, her life experiences etched in her face with deep wrinkles. She had a moustache that didn't match her habit, but I was still looking forward to being blessed.

When she showed up at our door, I quickly sat up, fixed my messy hair, and even waved to her to catch her attention. Maybe she would realize that I too was eager to hear some friendly, comforting words.

However, she didn't even glance in my direction. Instead, carefully holding the golden bowl that contained the Body of Christ, she quickly passed me by. On the other side of the room, Sister Mustache spoke to my lucky roommate again. I listened patiently to everything. I was only waiting for the closing prayer, the amen, when my friend would mention to the hairy sister that I also needed a blessing. When they were saying the final prayers, my roommate quickly interrupted.

Roomie: By the way, my friend on the other side of the room said that she also would like to have someone praying with her.

Nun (with puzzled expression I suspected, judging from her tone): What's your name?

Me: Fabiana Da Silva.

Nun (looking at her clipboard): That's odd. They didn't tell me you wanted to receive prayers. I am sorry, but your name's not on the list.

Me: Oh, Reverend Mother, please, just write it down! I really need some prayers. I don't know what's going to happen next, but I want to be sure that I am in full communion with God so that I can overcome whatever this battle brings.

Nun (somewhat curt and not very cheerful): All right, daughter, what is your religion?

Me: Well, I'm Evangelical.

Nun: Hmm?

I realized I had given the wrong answer. Her furrowed brows and grimace said it all. Her look of indignation became worse when I tried to fix my answer.

Me: Sister, I'm really sorry. It's a complicated story, but I'll explain. I'm Catholic. I sang in a Catholic church for ten years, and I have a very strong connection with God. When I moved to New York, I searched for a similar church with happy people clapping, singing, and even dancing. I tried going to a Catholic church here, but the Mass was so sad it would me make me feel depressed too. I started looking for a church where I would feel uplifted during and after the service. Somewhere that I could feel joy again. A very good friend of mine from Guatemala, Lolita, took me to an evangelical church that I loved from the first moment. I felt very welcome, peaceful, and happy there.

Nun (already appearing to be losing the little patience she had): All right, but what is your religion?

Me (afraid of losing out on a blessing): I'm from the Religion of Love. I'm Catholic, Evangelical, Christian, Buddhist … The label doesn't really matter; what matters is what I have in my heart. That is real. I come from a religion that speaks about God as a good father, not as a scary Santa that may not give me a toy if I do something wrong. My religion teaches that we must love each other as brothers and sisters.

This answer seemed to be even worse than the previous one. The nun could not believe what she had just heard. Her mustache seemed to twitch from shock. Her cheeks turned red with rage, giving her the appearance of possessing supernatural powers, as if she could make me burn in the flames of hell in seconds. She gave me a stern look and said, "Unfortunately, I cannot give you the Body of Christ. You seem very confused and need to confess to a priest before receiving the blessed sacrament."

Dear friends, I do not mean to judge anyone or anyone's religion, but please—who in their right mind would deny blessings to a person who could die at any second? How could she know whether I even had time enough to confess my sins? My deepest desire at that moment was to knock her down and run with the Holy Communion to a quiet place where I could briefly explain to Him how I felt. I wanted to flee to a place where I wouldn't be judged and where I could feel His true love without having to fit into a particular or correct religious category.

I had so much going on in my life at that moment that I barely knew who I was. For example, I totally forgot that my last name had changed, and every time a doctor asked for my last name, I instantly answered, "Da Silva," forgetting I had changed it to "Da Silva-Boyce." Asking me to define my faith was not an easy task, especially at this time. I am glad Kate, Lia, and Ollie were in the room with me; otherwise, I would have thought I was hallucinating or having another nightmare.

A distasteful look was the last thing I needed that day; unfortunately, this was the only thing the nun offered me. In the end, everything turned out fine because her attitude made me realize that my friendship with and love of God extended far beyond denominations and that even if I didn't have my name written down on her oh-so sacred board, I knew I would be blessed all the more because I had people all around the world praying for and supporting me so that I could get out of that hospital as soon as soon as possible.

A mad nun

Chapter 17

Who Will Decide for You?

After that "holy morning," a nurse came to talk to me about my health care proxy. I had no idea what this was, but I began to understand that when you are asked for your signature in a hospital, don't expect anything good to come of it. You are either signing a document that certifies you understand that you might get an infection or that ensures you are aware you will have to pay the bill, whatever the outcome. And sometimes it's a form that is literally a life or death matter, or rather a matter about who will have the power to decide your fate.

Oh how I wished that just once a nurse would come in with a form and say, "Mrs. Da Silva, I am sorry to interrupt you and your visitors, but it is with great honor that I would like you to sign this paper; you just won a million dollars! Congratulations, sweetie!"

I knew that this proxy document couldn't be something miraculous because as soon as the nurse said health care proxy, all my friends looked at me in fright, as if they had just seen a ghost. At that point, I was so scared by all that was happening, I needed to know every minute detail.

Nurse: Hello. Mrs. Da Silva, I'm sorry to bother you, but I am wondering if you have already signed your health care proxy form?

Me: No, I haven't. And honestly, I don't even know what that means; it's Greek to me.

Nurse: The New York Health Proxy Law allows you to appoint someone who you trust—for example, a family member or a close friend—to make health care decisions on your behalf in case you lose the ability to make decisions on your own.

Every word that came out of her mouth felt like Mike Tyson punching me in the head. Several questions came to my mind: *Okay. Let me see if I got this right. I have to choose someone to make decisions for me? Why is that? I am only thirty years old, for crying out loud. Has my time come already? No way! Is there any chance I could lose the ability to make decisions on my own? Guys, what's really going on? I came here because I had a headache; two days later, I have to sign a paper that states others may decide for me?*

The nurse carried on as if she were giving a persuasive speech on a broken CSPAN radio. Maybe she didn't realize that what she was telling me was shocking, and I wasn't prepared to deal with this kind of information. Like a cashier who wants you to apply for the store's credit card, she continued.

Nurse: It's good to name a health care agent so you can be sure that health care providers follow your wishes. There's another advantage. Your agent can also decide on your wishes for changes that apply to your medical conditions. Physicians and other health care providers must follow the decisions of your agent as if they were your own. You can give the person you choose as your health care proxy as little or as much authority as you want. Another advantage of completing this document is that it can be used to document your wishes or instructions regarding organ or body tissue donations.

By the end of her health care proxy sales pitch, I was alarmed, to say the least! How could I sign that document, acknowledging that I was aware I could die at any moment and someone else would make decisions for me? The truth was I didn't want to accept the possibility that even though death is inevitable for all of us, I was the one closer to the Grim Reaper. Once this document had been handed to me, and the chatty nurse was gone, my friends and I started talking about what would be done if I lost consciousness.

It seemed as if another terrible nightmare had just begun. Possibly being diagnosed with cancer meant that I might have to forfeit life decisions. Was I in a mental state to make any wise decisions? Who could I choose to be my health agent? My parents were still in Brazil. I could not sign them up for that awful task. First, they were in another country, and second, how would they know what the doctors were talking about? I kept imagining the scene: "All right, Mr. and Mrs. Da Silva, Fabiana has been asleep for two days. Should we donate her heart?" My parents, in despair, without understanding a thing, would answer: "Yes, yes, yes!" I know that hospitals provide translators, but I don't believe my parents would be happy to make such serious decisions over the phone.

I knew that my husband would be my agent. But how could I approach a man I had just married and say, "Well, love, we've already been married seven months, so I'm thinking to designate you as my health care agent. No need to talk about our future, kids, or buying a house today. Since there is a big chance you will be a widower soon, let's talk about my death and what I'd like you to do if I become unconscious! Happy seven-month anniversary!" I know that some of my readers may find that I am overreacting, but c'mon! Isn't it scary to have this type of conversation with the spouse you've been married to for less than a year? Even if you've been married for thirty years, death is never something you want to talk about.

So, like a frightened child on the first day of school tentatively doing classwork, I started to fill in that document. I appealed to my friends and decided that Crislaine and Ms. Kathy would be my proxies if I became unconscious, but I got stuck when I got to the donation part. I was frozen; my pen would not budge. I couldn't write anything more. I looked at the paper and desperately looked at my friends. I simply didn't know what to donate, so I opened up the discussion.

Me: Well, I have to be honest with you guys. I have no idea what I'm doing.

Kate: Do you need any help, Fabi?

Me: I am done with the agent part, but it's the donation section that's bothering me. It's one thing is to say I want to be an organ donor when I'm getting my ID at a DMV; however, it's a completely different decision when you are sitting on a hospital bed.

Ms. Kathy: I know it is hard, Fabi, but we're here with you. There's nothing to be afraid of. It's just a procedure they need to do every time someone is admitted to a hospital. I also had to sign one when I was admitted the last time. Let's see what you've put down so far.

Me: I want to be a donor. I think it is super important, so I chose to donate my heart.

One of my friends: Only your heart? Oh, I think if you're willing to donate your heart, it's better to give everything.

Kate: Well, if you're willing to give your heart, you might as well donate something else as well.

Caroline: I don't know, guys. Oh, Fabi, please think before you sign anything. Well, you have to do whatever you feel is right, but there are so many people who could benefit from your organs. How about the cornea or kidneys?"

Priscilla: Oh, I'm not really enjoying this chat, folks.

There in that hospital room, my friends and I were discussing what parts of my body would be worthy of donation. Honestly, after I had fervently insisted they help me, it didn't even sound like we were talking about my body anymore. It seemed as if we were arguing about jewelry, clothing, or shoes that I stubbornly refused to donate. I knew they were right; I am all for donation. The only problem was that I was still very much alive, and I had to decide what to do with the organs of my body when I was dead. After much yada-yada-yada, I decided to put the document in a bag and fill it out another time when I was ready to give what I could of my body.

The months passed, and I never turned that document in, but to be sure, if something happened to me today, I would love to continue living in other ways, knowing that parts of me would keep others alive. I would love to know that my heart could beat strong in the body of a younger or older person, that my corneas could serve to brighten someone else's vision, a miracle tool for someone no longer able to see the vibrant beauty of colors, or that my lungs—well, I'd rather leave them off this life-giving list. I just remembered that they were not in their best condition. But I still had a lot of good organs inside me, and if I had to make my last wish, I would say that I still wanted to live longer so that I wouldn't have to donate anything quite so soon.

$\mathcal{C}$hapter 18

An Unusual Transfer

As I underwent another x-ray, my loyal friends waited for me in my room. They were not just regular friends; they were soldiers fighting my yet unknown battle with me. I will always be grateful to all of them, so essential in those two hellish first days. Their optimism gave me strength and the conviction that regardless of the diagnosis, I would somehow overcome it.

On the way back to my room, I had the impression that there was either an Italian party or an Italian fight happening on the floor. Everyone was talking so loudly I knew it could only be my gang. But when I was finally wheeled in, everybody looked overwhelmed. The pregnant ones, Priscilla and Caroline, didn't have that motherly peace that pregnant women usually have. They looked disturbed and had their fists up like they were protesting against whatever that doctor had told them. Ms. Kathy and Kate kept interrogating a short female doctor who also seemed to be nervous about explaining my diagnosis to them.

Meanwhile, my mom was calling every five minutes. Moms just sense everything. As much as I continued lying to her, saying that maybe I had pneumonia, she knew that something was up.

Some sweet nurses helped me into bed. Suddenly, I noticed that my friends were looking at me with disbelief; their abrupt silence seemed to indicate that they were asking themselves, "How are we going to tell her?" I kept looking at Kate. I don't know why, but I could see in her beautiful blue irises that something was up. Kate slowly started to tell me that the doctors had found a certain mass—which is when the doctor came to speak to me:

Doctor: Listen, I know that everybody is very worried about you, but all I have to say is that you'll be fine.

Me: Did you find out what's wrong with me? Why wouldn't I be fine?

Doctor: We still don't have the PET scan results, but the fluid we collected from your neck shows us that you have a rare type of blood cancer; it can be either lymphoma or leukemia. I really want you to go to one of the best hospitals in the United States, which is in New York City. They are experts in this disease and are better equipped to take care of you there.

I felt dizzy with all the information I had just heard. I couldn't think straight. It was confirmed. I had been diagnosed with one of the most feared diseases in the world, and somehow I would have to prepare for the battle that was just beginning.

Doctor: I don't know if I should send you in an ambulance. I just checked, and the hospital is at 108 percent capacity. If we transfer you from one hospital to another, they aren't obligated to take you, but if you go to their emergency room and check in, they can't deny you care. The best thing to do is just go straight there. You have no time to lose. Do you have someone to take you?

Me: My car is here in the parking lot. I feel great. I'll just drive myself.

Doctor: You can't do that! You can't just drive yourself to the hospital. Leave your car here, and ask someone to come pick it up. Don't worry about that now.

Mrs. Kathy, Ollie and Kate said that they could take me to the city—no problem. It was a relief to know I had friends I could count on, but I also learned that I would no longer be independent for some time to come. I realized that the woman I was—strong, determined, and independent—had become a child that, thank God, was being well cared for by many wonderful angels. I dressed quickly and was ready to go in minutes. We waited only for the test results to be discharged from the hospital.

While waiting, we were surprised by the hospital with a mini-buffet meant especially for us. They sent us a beautiful table, covered with an ivory cloth and fresh flowers in a beautiful vase. It had everything we deserved: all types of teas, sweets, crackers, nuts, fruit, and a variety of sandwiches. For a few minutes, this treat helped us disconnect from the news of that terrible diagnosis. We delighted ourselves, eating everything we could, laughing all the while; we might lose everything, even hope, but I knew we would never lose our sense of humor. These are small things that make a big difference. Those minutes of laughter and relaxation made us forget the madness the diagnosis had brought to our lives. And as soon as we got the envelope and the CD that contained all of the recorded procedures, we left with all the gifts I had already received: books and balloons with get-well wishes.

At the elevator, a girl came out carrying a large bunch of balloons and a beautiful orchid, my favorite flower. We could barely see her face because the balloons and the delicate pink wrappers of the orchid blocked it from view. I realized that that girl was my friend Eliane, who most certainly had come to see me. I shouted, "Elianeee! Come right back here!"

Eliane: Hey, wait for me. Where are you guys going?

Me: I have to go to a hospital in the city! I'm so scared, you can't even imagine.

Eliane: Don't worry. Everything will be fine. I brought these flowers and balloons for you.

Me: Thank you so much, friend. You guys are all amazing!

She had intuited exactly what would make me feel good—my favorite flowers, orchids! The flowers were dazzling white with a sprinkling of tiny pink and purple dots. In the vase, there was also a cute snowman that later turned into a Christmas decoration for my oxygen pole.

In the parking lot, it was decided that Ollie would drive me with Ms. Kathy. Kate would be in charge of making all the phone calls to let Richard and all of my other friends know where I was going. Saying that my friends were all sent by God did not quite explain their organization and efficiency. They were like a large, well-organized, and unified team, an orchestra. It was amazing how each knew how to play their instruments so well. Together, we performed a dramatic yet humorous and harmonious concert!

It was so cold out. The icy rain ran down our warm faces. It was coming down more and more heavily, and even some flurries fell on us as we hugged and kissed each other goodbye. It was an unforgettable Friday for all of us. At that point, I didn't care that I wasn't in charge anymore. I hardly knew where I was going, but I felt safe and sound, and I was already aware that I had to sit back and allow my friends to take care of me. Thousands of thoughts kept crowding my mind, and again, I just wanted to wake up and know that it had been a terrible nightmare, that everything would snap back to normal. Instead, we continued our journey through the nightmare, toward my next medical destination.

It was raining cats and dogs. Ollie drove us, and Mrs. Kathy punched the address in her GPS. We got stuck in traffic, so what would normally take an hour took two. Through the rain-swept windshield, I observed everything carefully; we passed places and bridges I had driven by before but without the scary ghost of a fatal disease. In that car, I kept thinking, *What did I do to deserve such a sad fate as this?*

It seemed impossible to find the hospital. The more Ollie drove, the farther away we seemed from our destination. The GPS took us to Queens, and we got so nervous that we even drove on the wrong side of the road just to get back to New York. However, this detour didn't deter my "Olliembulance"; she was determined to get me to that hospital.

Suddenly, Ollie's phone started ringing. Since she was driving, I quickly answered it. A voice said, "Excuse me, who am I speaking to?"

Me: Hi, this is Fabiana speaking. Ollie can't speak right now. She is driving. And who would like to speak with her?

Doctor: Fabiana! I'm so glad to hear your voice and know that you are well! Where are you? We're very concerned about you. You should have arrived at least an hour ago. I've been calling your cell phone but got no answer. I've also been calling the hospital every five minutes to see if you guys got there safely. Anyway, I am just glad that you are well.

Me: Thank you, Doctor. We are arriving at the hospital right now. The GPS took us to Queens; it's a long story.

Doctor: No problem. They're already waiting for you. I wish you the best of luck in your treatment.

Me: Thank you, Doctor.

When we finally arrived, the rain was pouring down in buckets, and we couldn't see anything in front of us. We all knew we were very close but had no idea where the entrance was. We ended up entering a college in front of the hospital, and a rude young man shouted, "Hey, you crazy ladies! Can't you see the 'Stop' sign here?"

Ms. Kathy, without losing her class, put her head out of the window, turned so that he could see her icy glare, and said in a polite tone, "Excuse me? Is that how your mom taught you to treat nice ladies? You don't even know what we have been through to-day. Before I forget, please, go screw yourself!"

Ollie made a turn, and we finally came to my second home—I mean the hospital.

*C*hapter 19

Did My Mom Deserve
Such a Cruel Truth?

While we were driving to the hospital, I thought it would be a good time to tell my mom that the "pneumonia" was something else. I thought about the best (if it exists) way to break the news. I wanted to be strong and let her know everything, but at the same time, I didn't want her to imagine my case was serious. I knew that for her, the diagnosis would be as painful as it was for me. After being advised by Ollie and Mrs. Kathy to tell my mother the truth, I mustered up the courage to give her a call.

Me: Hi, Mom. How are you?

Mom: We are so worried about you. How is everything going, hon?

Me: Everything is well, Mom, but the doctors thought it was better to transfer me to another hospital because they suspect it's … (the conversation became surreal; I couldn't believe what I was about to tell my mom) … they suspect it is cancer.

Mom (already crying): How is that possible? Cancer? It can't be! Those tests must be wrong!

Me (her tears were contagious; my eyes also filled up, but I tried to sound as positive as I could): Everything's going to be all right, Mom. Don't worry. I am being transferred to one of the best hospitals in the US for cancer treatment. I know they'll take good care of me. Many people would give anything to go there. Looking at the positive side, at least I was diagnosed just four days before my trip. Can you imagine if I hadn't listened to you and hadn't gone to the doctor two days ago?

Little by little, and even though my news was shocking, I could tell she was calming down. Knowing that my mom was less worried made me feel calmer. It gave me the strength to dodge all the bombs that were being thrown at me. I didn't tell her, but I felt I was being sent into war against a fearful enemy. No one had given me any ammunition, so I had to fight with everything I had within: faith, optimism, and a good sense of humor.

Me: I need you to help me. Please, try not to cry because I need a lot of strength to overcome this! Knowing that you are strong gives me the strength to fight here. Unfortunately, I can't be in Brazil for Christmas or New Year's as we had planned, but at least I know I'll be receiving the best treatment possible here.

Mom: I'm thinking … to myself … your father and I are going to New York!

Me: No, Mom, I'm fine. I know you weren't planning to travel to New York again this year, and last-minute airfare is so expensive. Please just pray for me and send me your prayers and positive thoughts. You will be helping me immensely this way. Be in peace and trust God. I know that I'm going to a great hospital; they're experts in cancer treatment, and everyone that I've spoken to here has told me wonderful things about this hospital. Also, Richard and my friends have really helped me. I don't want to cause you guys any more stress. I already called the airline to call off my trip.

I also spoke with my dad, who already knew of my diagnosis and had given me so much strength. I knew that he would have to be stronger still to help my mom as well. I have no doubt that this was the longest night of my parents' life. After that call, they got on their knees and prayed together, weeping. They asked God to give them the wisdom to make the best decision, and that we would all have the strength to carry the cross we had to bear.

Mother Teresa's words came to mind: "I know God will not give me anything I can't handle. I just wish that He didn't trust me so much."

Whatever cross you have, carry it with love and grace.

*C*hapter 20

Arriving at the Second Hospital

When I went to the emergency room, my vision seemed all blurry, but I quickly recognized the familiar face of Lia, my school principal. For a moment, I felt totally confused; it seemed we were both in the wrong place, and in a fraction of second, questions crowded my brain. *Aren't we supposed to be at school? Did I forget an important meeting? What are we doing here? Are the students okay?* But this was real. There we were, in a somber waiting room, in the midst of other persons who all looked extremely worried.

What kind of joke was life playing on me? Unfortunately, this wasn't a joke or a prank or anything that could bring a smile to my face. I had so many questions, and this mysterious place brought even more uncertainty to my life, my future. Would I still have one? I kept asking myself. Lia gave me a strong hug that helped me forget for a moment that I was the main reason why all of us were there. She comforted me, saying that I could count on her if I needed anything. Her words warmed my heart and filled it with peace. I felt that everything would be okay. I looked around, searching for Richard; I knew that my friends had told him which hospital I was going to. I wondered where he was and, more importantly, how he was dealing with my diagnosis.

Minutes later, I saw him; even though he was present physically, he wasn't there mentally. He didn't even seem to be in the same room with us. He stood stock-still as he gazed at me. If I believed in ghosts, I would say he had just seen one. Maybe I was the ghost. He had a strange blank look, as if he were hypnotized. Then he hugged me as if his arms could protect me from anything life would throw at me. Ironically, I felt that he was the one who needed comforting, because the diagnosis was obviously devastating for him too.

I knew that his body was there, but it felt like his mind and soul were in a distant, faraway place, where, even if I forced my way in, I wouldn't be able to find his exact location. My hubby's stricken face worried me, and I kept trying to guess what he was thinking. On that day, as a newlywed, I would have given a thousand dollars for one of his thoughts. Now that we have been together for five years, I would save the thousand bucks and simply ask him.

Soon, the nurses called me in to do more blood work. With the naivety of a beginner patient, I replied that I didn't need to do any more blood work that day because I had already had some done earlier at the first hospital. The nurses probably realized that I was clueless about what I was getting into; they smiled and told me that from now on, pricks would be inevitable. The torture sessions started; I call it torture not because the nurses were mean or anything like that—they were actually extremely kind—but the search for the juicy vein, as some nurses like saying, was not a joke. Although the nurses said it was just a tiny needle, from my perspective, their innocuous needle loomed like an enormous, sharp knife about to lacerate my innocent, defenseless hand. I quickly learned that getting stuck in the hand is worse than in the arm. I'm sure that even the pro patients loathe these shots.

After this torture session, I was to be taken to yet another room to be hooked up to an EKG (electrocardiogram) and have my blood pressure and temperature checked. I thought this was going to be easier: no needles, no pain. However, even though no needles were inserted into my hand, I experienced an even worse pain. The revelation of what my life was becoming became clearer when I entered this room. My journey would be far scarier than anything I could have ever imagined. It was as if I had been suddenly teleported into a horror movie; the patients waiting in the hallway were coughing and sneezing. They looked weak, and they were all bald. They were all dressed alike, in pajamas with white polka dots that reminded me of the book that I had just read with my students—*The Boy in The Striped Pajamas,* a powerful book about a forbidden friendship between Bruno, a German boy, and Schmuel, a Jewish boy.

Entering the assigned room number 8, oddly my favorite number, I thought about the grayish skin tone of the Jewish kids. The majority of patients in that sad hall had the same grayish hue; some were the yellowish shade of a sun blanketed by snow clouds, while others were as white as the chalk I used on the old blackboards when I first started teaching in Brazil. What I saw on the opposite side of the front desk must have been something like what Bruno uncomprehendingly witnessed on the other side of the fence.

Maybe I was hallucinating, but I was struck by similarities between the book and my situation. The first and most shocking similarity, as previously noted, was that both the patients waiting to see the doctor and the Jewish prisoners in the book were bald. In the novel, the Jews had to wear the same white and blue striped pajamas. In the hospital, everyone also wore identical gowns, only our pajamas had blue and white polka dots; I realized that by wearing this gown, we lost our identity. From a distance, you couldn't distinguish the identity of a patient, let alone the gender. But at this moment, gender didn't really matter, did it? What really mattered was to survive. Isn't that what Schmuel had also wanted? Even if you looked like Yoda, you would still be happy as long as you were alive.

In the book, the characters were in a concentration camp, imprisoned by Hitler's tyrannical insanity and senseless prejudice. In that hospital, we were trapped by a tyrannical, senseless disease: cancer. In that corridor, I had the impression of walking to a death sentence. Then I saw the similarity that scared me the most; the majority of patients had the same look as the characters in the book, a look without any spark, a terrifying gaze devoid of hope.

However, unlike the Jews in the book, the patients seemed to be sure that sooner or later they would end up in their personal gas chamber. In the story, the prisoners were told only that they were going to shower, when in fact they were being taken to gas chambers. I had the impression that most of the patients before me were certain that death was very close. Now, I wonder if ignorance isn't bliss for us all. We all know that one day we must die, but, folks, you have to admit it: there is nothing more disturbing than being told with certainty by a doctor that you can die at any moment. You may be thinking, *But I don't have cancer, and I'm also going to die!* Of course, you are! But you wouldn't like to have a doctor asserting that reality in your face, would you? We usually say that when we die, we are going to a better place, but the problem is nobody who has passed away has ever returned to let us know of the wonders of this so-called better place.

For most of us, the unknown is scary. Now, you might be wondering, *But don't you have faith?* Hell yeah! Of course I wanted to be close to our Father, but since I was only thirty years old, I was hoping to meet him much later. At ninety or 120 would be fine with me. For now, I was completely satisfied hugging my Father from earth. I hope God isn't upset that I don't want to go now, but I'm sure we'll find another opportunity to catch up on our hugs.

Chapter 21

Going up ... Ready or Not, Here I Come!

I couldn't stop crying, and Ms. Kathy, Ollie, and Lia hugged me tightly to give me strength to endure what lay ahead. Not really understanding what was happening, I felt bad about being ill, and I felt bad for questioning God. It all seemed so senseless. Could it be possible that this was the end of my life? I wondered. *What a strange and meaningless life, God. What was the point of getting married and seven months later leaving my husband whom I hadn't even gotten to know?* A world of thoughts invaded my mind: religion, karma, and so much more. Was it my fault? Was I guilty of something awful? Was I to blame for having this disease? What had I done to deserve such misfortune in my life? People say that God does not abandon His children, so why then was I being abandoned now?

It was starting to bother me that no one would explain what was happening. I felt it was okay to question God when facing a bad situation. He is strong; He can definitely handle my critical questions. In fact, there is nothing wrong with being mad about a bad situation; it is cathartic to be able to get it off your chest, to vent when you feel something is unjust. The only thing you mustn't do is give up or resign yourself to a hopeless future; despite the horrifying verdict, having hope—no matter how fantastic it may appear—is what helps you strive for a new beginning.

Leaving me with their support, my friends had to say goodbye. Richard and I were alone now, not knowing what to do next. He was awkwardly looking for something to say but found himself tongue-tied. He seemed anesthetized by everything. I had begun to understand the seriousness of my case from the somber attitudes of the doctors as they dealt with my medical situation. While all the other patients still waited in the hallway, we were quickly sent to the upper floors of the hospital where I would begin receiving treatment.

The doors of the elevator opened to the seventeenth floor. Here, patients with emaciated faces could barely stand or walk. Their exuberance for life was gone. It was as if they had never learned to smile or as if they feared an invisible sign threatening them with electric shock therapy if they so much as even considered a smile. They had been made to understand this was no joke. It was as if they were just living out their extra time here on earth but had long been ready to leave for another world, wherever that might be. *Will we go anywhere when we leave earth?* I thought. I started wondering if all those beautiful conversations about going to a better place were merely delusions for us cancer patients.

The nurses took us to my new room. I placed my fancy bag, my old HP laptop, and my students' homework assignments on the nightstand. I sat on my comfortable bed with soft, warm white sheets. Even in this comfort, I kept looking out my window, dreaming I would leave any minute. From my room, I could see the beautiful NYC skyline, the prominent skyscrapers and rooftops I had frequented with friends. Right then, I would have given anything to be in a favela in Brazil, living a simple life.

Now that we were finally alone, my husband gazed at me, not knowing what to say. He had always seen me as a strong, cheerful, smiling woman, almost a lioness. But at that moment, all he could see was a frightened little girl afraid of the one certainty in life, death. In a few seconds, cancer had transformed that strong lioness into a fearful, little kitten. I had gone from a strong roar to a weak *meow*. I let out a sigh. Now was a good opportunity for us to take charge of the situation. I asked Richard to do a search on his phone to find out my chances of surviving this type of cancer. That was a big mistake. He was sitting in the blue leather armchair for caregivers. With the eagerness of a child opening a Christmas gift, he began researching the different types of cancers that had been mentioned by my doctors: lymphoma, acute lymphoblastic leukemia (ALL), or acute myeloid leukemia (AML). I could barely pronounce these names, and just from trying to pronounce them correctly, I knew they didn't sound like any present a kid would like for Christmas, Hanukkah, Lunar New Year, or any celebration.

Once he started his Google search, an act I thought would provide us with hope, a pained, sorrowful look crossed his face. Again I realized I might not have much time left. It seemed as if he had read my looming death sentence. He tried to keep his eyes from revealing what he had seen. He was extremely hesitant to share what he had read. And brave mouse that I had become, I thought it was best not to dig too deep just yet. I decided it was better to receive the actual diagnosis from the oncologist rather than from the internet.

After Richard's research, we started discussing the "injustice" that we were living. Futilely, I considered the corrupt politicians, thieves, and rapists who were well while destroying other people's lives, and I, who had done nothing bad to anyone, was stuck there in a bed. I knew I was no angel—we all have our failures and regrets—but I knew I didn't deserve to die for my wrongdoings.

My husband, who had little faith in God, continued questioning everything I insisted I knew about God and my belief that what goes around comes around. I used to tell him that we can only reap what we sow. I wondered what I had sown to get such an awful harvest. Geez! Whatever I had done, I wouldn't hesitate to say sorry and promise to never do it again. After asking Richard several unanswerable questions, it became apparent he was frightened. I thought it would be better for him to go home and leave me to face that first night alone with my questions in that impersonal but deceptively comfortable room, so different from our warm, cozy apartment.

Once he was gone, a kind nurse came in with a yellow notepad and pen. She suggested it would be good to write down all my questions for the doctors who would be stopping by my room the next morning. She hooked me up to a heart monitor and told me not to hesitate to call her if I needed anything. The remote control tied to my bed had a red button for ringing the nurse's station; she said I could push this magic button as much as I needed, and she would come. If she had known how much I would be pressing that button, she would have covered it with duct tape! About five minutes later, I thought I'd check to see if it worked. *Braynk, braynk!* The receptionist quickly answered.

"Can I help you?"

"Yes, thank you. Can I talk to my nurse, please?"

"Just a second. She's on her way."

The nurse came into my room. "Hi, Mrs. Da Silva. Do you have any questions?"

"Yes. Am I going to die?"

The poor nurse turned red; she didn't know where to hide her face. Perhaps, most patients on their first night ask about possible treatments or medications. In my case, not having an accurate diagnosis, I didn't want to beat around the bush. As if she had any superpowers to keep me alive, I started listing the many reasons why I couldn't die right then. Naively, I told her that I had just gotten married and how healthy and active I was. I wanted to convince her that I couldn't die so suddenly. I didn't want to die. Who did? Nobody! I was way too busy to die, and I couldn't simply disappear from the planet like a flash, gone in an instant. There were so many things that I hadn't seen, so much I still needed to accomplish. Today I realize that I wasn't trying to persuade the kind nurse; my intention was to convince myself that I would not die. If silence is worth its weight in gold, that night I would have been dirt-poor.

Chapter 22

An Incomprehensible Roommate

When the nurse had gone, I went over everything. The lady with whom I shared the room was also on my mind. Even though only a brown curtain separated us, I was certain of one thing: we shared the same fears, doubts, and anxieties. Were we going to survive? There was one difference between my roommate and me. She didn't speak a common language, English, Spanish, or even Esperanto.

In her raspy voice, she blurted unintelligible words, but they were too hard for anyone to decipher. The amazing nurses tried really hard, but they couldn't understand the dialect. I'm not sure why, but I was scared of my new neighbor, maybe because the other side of the curtain symbolized what I would see in the mirror in days or months. I would have liked to avoid her altogether, but to get to the bathroom, I had to cross her side of the room. I walked softly, trying not to look at her. Before crossing her side, I had peeked through the curtain and could see that her face was a little scary. She had sunken eyes, as if she hadn't slept for two hundred years, her hair was a dull gray, and her bony cheeks were starkly pronounced, as if to alert everyone that she was, in fact, not long for this world. *How could God have let those cheeks be so pointy and without flesh?* The impression I had was that if she turned around very fast, she would cut her face with the sharp bones that either God or the disease had given her. I promised myself that I would go to the bathroom without looking directly at her. I had to be brave and not hesitate. I needed to come up with a plan: I would tiptoe as fast as I could so that she wouldn't notice my presence; however, my plan was a failure because as soon as I started tiptoeing, I glanced over at her.

Her eyes were wide open, as if in wait for me so she could speak to me. I couldn't resist those watering eyes begging for help. And so began our friendship. I was determined to take care of her.

Lying on my bed, I heard my new friend cough. I pressed the red button. When my nurse came, I explained. "Look, I am really sorry for bothering you, but my roommate can't speak. I'm trying to help her out as much as I can. She can't speak or push the button, so every time she needs you, I'll press it for her. I'm free and have nothing else to do. It's always good to try to help someone, right?"

The nurse, with a somewhat dull smile, explained to me in a very soft voice, "Well, Mrs. Da Silva, I can see you have a very kind heart, but you don't have to worry about your neighbor. That's what her nurse is for."

I believed my nurse was already tired of being called so many times in one night, but of course she wouldn't let it show. We started playing a little game of pretense: she pretended that she wasn't fed up when I called her for every fart, belch, or grunt that my noncommunicative friend gave, and I pretended not to know I was being a pain in the ass when I did so. That's how we survived the first night. I am sure that it was an unforgettable night for my nurse as well because she had no time to sit down. Nurses are angels.

$\mathcal{C}$hapter 23

What Is the Condition of My Bone Marrow?

The doctors came to my room the next morning around seven. My room was drenched in sunlight, which illuminated the seven doctors standing in my room. They greeted me and began to explain the severity of my disease. They seemed tense but sure of what they were saying: I had a rare form of blood cancer for adults—leukemia.

I heard the feared disease escape their lips—cancer. I don't know why, but I've always associated this horrific word with breast cancer, perhaps because this is the most recognized form of the disease, or because it's the one that affects more adults and therefore the one I have heard about the most. I also knew of lung cancer. But leukemia? The doctors asked me if there were any cases in the family, but nobody that I could recall had had any type of leukemia.

"Good morning, Ms. Da Silva."

Those voices were not like those of my students, and I would have given anything to hear my students' voices instead.

"How are you feeling?"

"I guess I am okay. Do you guys have any news about my medical condition?"

"We got the results from the first hospital, and unfortunately, you've been diagnosed with leukemia."

"Leukemia? Leukemiaaaaaaaa? But how? Where did I get it?"

"Unfortunately, the cause is unknown. Some researchers believe it's due to radiation exposure. Do you work with anything that transmits radiation?"

"No! I'm a high school teacher!"

"Hum, I see."

"With all due respect, couldn't it be anemia? I remember a cousin of mine who had a very rare type of anemia, and her doctors misdiagnosed it. They said she wouldn't live to be twenty-five or have kids either. Today, she's thirty and has a handsome son. Maybe I have the same disease."

I always ate so healthy. How could it be? I kept trying to convince myself that it was only anemia. It sounded less terrifying.

"In fact, leukemia can give you anemia, but in your case, it's not only anemia."

The doctors quickly killed my hopes of being a regular anemia patient. That was it; I had the cancer label, and nothing was going to erase it from my life.

"Um, I thought it was the other way around." I knew they had already answered it before, but I insisted again. "Why did I get it?"

"We don't know. We know it's very common in children, and the cure rate in such cases is very high."

As I heard those words, my thoughts spun fast. *Why are they telling me this? I'm not a child. That means I'm going to die.* But then I turned my doubts into something less scary for the doctors.

"I see. And what is the survival rate for adults?"

"Well, every case is different."

What kind of answer was that? I felt like a teacher again!

"Complete answers, kids, please!" Didn't they have something more exciting or comforting to say? I felt it was a response from someone who was hiding something. You know when we tell a child that the injection won't hurt at all, and the child looks straight at the needle and just *knows* that the thin, piercing steel needle about to enter their body will not tickle? That was exactly how I felt; they were lying—or rather being purposefully evasive so that I wouldn't be more scared than I was already. I guess my face looked as if I had seen the devil right in front of me, but that didn't stop them from explaining what the next steps would be.

"But don't worry. You're in good hands; we'll take good care of you. Our first step is to find out if the disease is in your bone marrow. If so, we'll have to rely on a donor, who may be someone in your family, usually brothers. How many brothers and sisters do you have?"

"Then I am screwed! I don't have brothers or sisters; I'm an only child. To make matters worse, most of my family members are in Brazil."

"Um … I see. Anyway, let's not worry about that now. We need to look at the results from the first exam. Then we'll be able to tell if you really need one; we can put your name on a donor-matching website and hope someone who is compatible can make a donation."

That's what I call a perfect match.com!

"But what if I can't find a compatible donor?"

"Don't worry. You need to have the exam first. We'll take it from there."

Don't worry! How can I not worry when my life might depend on someone I've never met?

"When am I going to have these exams?"

"Tomorrow. First, we need some x-rays to see if the fluid in your lungs has stopped accumulating. If it hasn't, we will need to do another drainage. We'll find out the results from your bone marrow biopsy this week. It's a very quick exam; it only takes between twenty to thirty minutes. We'll inject a little anesthesia into your back, which will go into your spine, and then we'll remove some fluid. We'll be able to see if there are any leukemia cells there. If nothing is found, you won't need a transplant, but if we find something, we'll have to find a donor and do the transplant as soon as possible."

"Could I please have general anesthetic? I hate pain. I really can't take it, you know? I really don't mind sleeping for a few days; it would actually be great to be away for a few days."

"No, we don't give general anesthesia for bone marrow exams. There's no need because it's minor surgery. It's considered a bearable pain, and so a local anesthetic is best."

I kept thinking, *Bearable pain? But it's still pain, right?* However, I had no choice; I had to do whatever the doctors thought best. The truth was that they flooded me with so much information in such a short amount of time that I couldn't digest everything that they patiently tried to explain. All I knew was that one day I had a severe headache, and the next, I had this rare disease. I had to have tests that would hurt like hell, and I still might need a bone marrow donation from a brother I did not have. If I needed a transplant, I would have to rely on a Good Samaritan who had the same genetic characteristics that I do so that I could stay alive. Really? How could I comprehend all of this and convey it with a positive spin to my parents, husband, and friends in a different country?

$\mathcal{C}$hapter 24

Do I Get to Pick? No!
It's PICC Line Time!

$\mathbf{I}$ was told that before we started any other treatment, the doctors would have to insert a catheter in my vein called a PICC line (peripherally inserted central catheter) so that I didn't suffer too much while receiving all the medication I would be needing. I didn't know what a PICC line was, but from the nurse's explanation about the insertion procedure, I knew it wouldn't be like any fun roller-coaster ride or comedy I had ever watched in my life. The chubby nurse tried not to be too descriptive about the process, perhaps because she didn't want me to be too scared. To sum up the experience, it would hurt a lot! Basically, a PICC line would be inserted into my arm to serve as access for serum, blood, and medication, eliminating the need to stick me as often. At least there was a positive side to this! But the idea of having my arm opened was not to my liking at all; I knew it was for my own good, but I wondered if it would hurt and if it would be done without anesthesia.

I had been fortunate to have had so many visitors, but that

afternoon, for the first time, I was alone in my room, and so life had become darker than usual. That's when the nurse who does the PICC lines came in.

"Hello, Ms. Da Silva. I'm from the access team; we'd like to do the procedure in a few minutes. Okay?"

On a tray, she began to lay out her torture instruments, mostly needles and scissors. It was so natural to her, as if she were laying out her dinner utensils.

I answered in the affirmative, but in my heart, I was thinking, *Dear Lord, how am I going to allow someone to rip my arm open without anesthesia? To make things worse, I am here by myself without anyone to support me and tell me that I'll be fine!*

In that instant, I felt another presence; there was a shadow by the door of my gloomy room, and to my surprise, I saw Lia, my school principal.

"Hi, Fabiana! Am I interrupting something?"

I stared at her in disbelief. *How does my school principal appear just at the very moment when I desperately need someone?* Any familiar face would have made me believe in myself again. My room was dark, as the shades from my windows were all drawn, but the light from the hallway was lit, illuminating that petite, kind woman with a sweet, calming, and familiar voice that made me believe in the impossible. Perhaps I would be okay after all. If I didn't survive, at least somebody would be there to say, "She tried really hard." I didn't want to die like a coward. I had no doubt that she was an instrument of God sent to calm my fears. We started talking.

"Wow, I am so happy you are here today. I didn't know you were coming today! Thank you for stopping by, just in time!"

"I just dropped off my daughter at her ballet class here in the city. I'll have to pick her up soon, so I won't be able to stay very long, but I really wanted to see you today. I brought you some magazines."

"The nurse is going to put a catheter in my arm right now. You can't imagine how happy I am to have you here in this room with me. I can't thank you enough."

"Please, don't thank me!"

Our conversation was interrupted by the nurse who was ready to start the cruel yet necessary procedure: "Okay, Ms. Da Silva, are you ready?"

"I guess so."

My voice couldn't have sounded more meek and frightened. When would I ever be ready to have anything inserted into my body?

"If your friend wants to stay, she can. I would only ask her to stay at the end of the bed, where she can hold your hand."

I knew that Lia was always busy, so I didn't think she would be able to stay, but she did. I had no doubt that Lia was sent by heaven; she stayed with me from the beginning to the end of the procedure. At that moment, there were no formalities between Lia and me. She held my hand tightly and rubbed my feet. When the tubes started travelling inside my arm, I heard Lia's sweet voice: "You are so strong, Fabiana! You are so brave! It is almost over. Just keep strong!" Her calming voice sounded like a lullaby while my poor little arm was going through a hard rock concert.

I felt like a child being sliced up by Freddy Krueger. At that moment, I was just a small, defenseless, weeping girl. I decided to use the soft white pillow to absorb all of my fears. The poor pillow was definitely not the same after that procedure. I bit into it so that nobody would hear all the screams I wanted to let out. In a fraction of a second, that unfamiliar hospital pillow turned into my security blanket as it quietly soaked up the tears that poured like a waterfall from my eyes. I really don't know how Lia saw the brave woman she kept saying that I was, but I truly believed every word that came from her lips. I bit down on the pillow with all my might so that I could endure the pain.

After minutes that seemed like hours, surprise! I was a woman with a brand-new catheter! I wish I could have ended that sentence with a different word: brand-new bag, brand-new shoes … but no, no, no, it was not a fancy object that I adored. My new accessory was that plastic thingy. That little catheter symbolized that I was not Bi, Fabiana, or Ms. Da Silva anymore; it was confirmation that I was a new cancer patient, a label that couldn't be erased.

By having the catheter in my arm, things would change a bit. For example, my baths or showers would be different. From now on, every time I showered, I would have to cover it with plastic to prevent the catheter from getting wet. That's when I learned not to take anything for granted; little things became huge to me. The simple action of taking a refreshing shower was now a task that required help and patience. Before cancer, a shower was just a shower. I never thought that at the age of thirty, I would need my mom's help to shower. To make matters worse, I always loved water, but now I had to get used to the idea that with my new little "Cathy friend" I couldn't even think about going into a pool or hitting the beach. Ah, everything in this life has a price, and I was paying an expensive price to get my health back.

I thanked my principal for the surprise visit and for all the support she had given me during that twenty-minute procedure that seemed like infinity. She made me believe that I was strong, that this was just another obstacle to get through. I felt extremely blessed by such genuine friends who stopped whatever they were doing to help me.

*C*hapter 25

A Full Schedule: The Second Fluid Removal and Bone Marrow Biopsy

I knew that my new schedule would not be as fun as my old routine: Portuguese classes, English, English as a second language, online TESOL class for teachers from Vienna, and of course my Zumba workout that I loved from the bottom of my heart.

The day's activities were different from any of the tasks I'd ever done before. My morning would be "easier" compared to the afternoon schedule. The doctors had scheduled fluid drainage from my lungs. Unfortunately, the liquid that had been removed the week before was building back up again, and according to the doctors, I would have to do an urgent drainage so that I wouldn't get short of breath.

Clasping the hand of my friend Kathy as tightly as I could, I once again felt the sting of the needle sliding into my right lung so the doctor could begin sucking out the mysterious poisonous liquid that insisted on flowing into my lungs. Ms. Kathy bravely put up with all my strong squeezes, and I confess that, as unpleasant as the procedure was, it wasn't as horrifying as the first time. Perhaps I was just getting used to the pain that life had decided to put me through. I just laid my head quietly on the pillow and held still as a statue so the doctors could prolong—or who knows, even save—my life.

That afternoon, I was more sought after by doctors than Apple or Google stocks. Since the fluid removal had not been painful enough, I was scheduled for a bone marrow biopsy. Gotta do what you gotta do to stay alive, right? I had no clue what this test involved or what I would feel, but one thing was certain, I wanted Richard with me. The doctors had explained the procedure, but the only information I retained was that they would give me a local anesthetic, make an opening in my back, and extract fluid to determine if I would need a bone marrow donor or not. Richard held one hand firmly, and my other hand clutched the teddy bear he had brought me the week before. I never liked seeing that teddy bear at home because I suspected it was a present from an ex-girlfriend. Despite my attempts to ask him why he had that teddy bear, he never revealed it. After the bone marrow biopsy, I learned from his mother that this bear was the stuffed animal he had slept with as a child. That meant a lot to me! It was thoughtful of him to give me his childhood stuffed animal. Besides that, I loved that he had let his guard down. Knowing that he is a reserved person, it was great to see that he did not worry that others would get to know something that was private. We had been married for seven months, and there was still so much we didn't know about each other.

The torturous procedure lasted about twenty minutes; Richard stood by my side, keeping me calm. He bravely watched the doctors shake and press my back so that they could collect the liquid they needed. I felt a strong pressure on my back, like they were trying to cut my bones with a saw. The doctors said that even though I was skinny, my bones were very strong, which was great for me! Phew, at least one good thing—but no. On the one hand, the hard bones showed that my skeletal structure was strong; on the other, this meant it would be more difficult for them to reach my marrow and collect the fluid they needed, and that meant more pain for me.

Those examination results could change everything in my life. Had the cancer reached my bone marrow? And if the tests came back positive, who could, or would, help me if I didn't have brothers? My parents were only 50 percent compatible considering I was made of 50 percent of my father and 50 percent of my mother. I confess that in my desperation to live, for the first time, I thought it would have been okay if my father had fooled around and could give us the saving news that, in fact, I had a bunch of brothers and sisters in Taubaté, where he was born, and some more children in Campinas, where he worked, and a couple more children spread out in São Paulo. I would have so many choices!

Unfortunately for my marrow, but fortunately for my parents' marriage, my father had been faithful to my mother. Unlike me, my mother had a less absurd idea than fictional infidelity: she was ready to have a child to save my life! My father found the idea a bit strange and jokingly said that at their age (I don't consider them old at all, but my mom is closer to menopausal years than childbirth years), the baby would be old and would have a wrinkled face, like a Benjamin Button baby. According to my funny father, my future brother (or sister) would be too traumatized because the poor child would have parents old enough to be his/her grandparents.

There would be no need for any of these fantastic solutions, from finding someone on a bone marrow donor site, to my father having illegitimate children around the world, or to my parents making a child to save my life, because in a few days, we had the results—negative. In other words, I didn't need bone marrow from anyone because cancer cells had not been found in my bone marrow.

All the friends who were following my story on the internet celebrated this wonderful news. I thanked God for the blessing of not having to burden anyone with the task of locating a bone marrow donor so I could live, and I prayed and will always pray for my cancer friends who need to find a donor. Dear reader, if you are in good health, you should consider being a bone marrow donor; it doesn't hurt, and you can save somebody's life. But then I wondered, if not in my blood, and not in my bone marrow, where were these cancer cells? I didn't have to wonder long. I soon learned the answer I did not want to know.

Chapter 26

My Parents' Arrival

Fortunately for me, my parents always had their passports and visas ready to go; they came to see me at least once a year. As soon as they learned of my diagnosis, they bought tickets for the earliest possible flight. They would be with me in two days. This really gave me peace of mind. They couldn't begin to imagine how happy I was that they were coming to stay with me. When I was first diagnosed, I thought my husband and I would be able to handle everything on our own, but then I realized that I didn't need to be so independent anymore, and I decided to welcome the support of all of those who loved me. All I wanted was to have my loved ones since birth by my side.

I longed to hug my parents tightly, to feel their warm embrace. I would trade everything I had to spend time with them. The independent woman in high heels was gone. I longed to sit in their cozy laps, be nursed, and listen to their assurances that I was still their little girl, that all this nonsense was just a nightmare from which I would wake to discover that all was well. Since I couldn't be a child anymore, I at least wanted their reassurance that this was just a bad phase in my life that would soon go away. When I was a crazy, naughty little girl, I would run and fall, scratch my knees and elbows, and come back home bleeding; each and every time, they cleaned my wounds and took care of me. I wanted to believe that my mother would simply put that antiseptic that burned on my soul, that my father would hold me so tightly that I would never flee. My mom would put the Band-Aid on the awful bruise, and soon I could go back to the streets to play again. Of course, I knew they couldn't really do any of this; the cancer treatment was no simple bruise. It was hard, intense, and arduous. No antiseptic or Band-Aid would cure it; my bruise was tattooed in my body and soul.

On this day, all that mattered was the arrival of my heroes. I imagined the scene as they arrived in my room. They had always seen me upbeat, happy, smiling, and determined. For the first time, they would find me in a hospital bed like a frightened kitten, helpless and uncertain about the future.

When I opened my eyes in the morning, my vision was slightly blurry. I saw the image of a dark-skinned man of medium height, with a beautiful smile. It had to be my father! Immediately I began crying and exclaimed, "Dad, I am so glad you came! I'm so glad you're here with me!"

The poor man looked at me in wide-eyed astonishment and replied, "I am sorry I woke you up. I am just here to take out the garbage."

I guess I was so anxious to see my parents that I couldn't even distinguish my dad from the nice cleaning staff member who politely took the garbage out of my room.

For the first time, my parents would be coming to New York and I would not be there to pick them up at the airport. But God was kind enough to provide me with many friends willing to pick up the "caring bears" as I call them. Crislaine had offered first; she would pick them up from the airport and bring them to me. Almost anyone who is sick would want to have their parents around, but my relationship with them went far beyond the typical parent-child relationship. Our connection is so strong; I consider them to be my best friends. God couldn't have given me a better combination. My mother is an angel in the flesh: calm, affectionate, gentle with words, the embodiment of nurturing. My father is a wise, friendly jokester. I think it's from him that I inherited the ability to make jokes even in the most desperate circumstances.

They arrived around eight in the morning. I was energized by their warm and sincere hugs. We were all so happy to see each other again and cried at our joyful reunion. I only wished they could see me in better health. There was something about their familiar, smiling faces and fresh unique scents that made me feel home again in spite of being in the hospital. Looking at the bright side, at least the family was reunited, as we had planned for a year—not in Brazil but in the US, not at home but in a hospital. What mattered was that we were together. With their magical parental touch, they made me believe that I would be fine and that I would be strong enough for the battle that was just beginning. They insisted that I always focus on the positive: I was young, and my body would respond well to the treatment; I had friends from all over the world supporting me in every way possible; and I also had a family and a husband who loved me and would be with me from the beginning until the end of my recovery. Looking at it this way, even though the situation was still serious, I could see the hope. That's what my family is for me, my hope.

Chapter 27

We Never Forget Our First Shower in the Hospital

As soon as my mom arrived, I made my first request: I wanted her to help me take a shower. I gazed at her fondly, grateful for her kindness, but I could not believe the situation I now found myself in. How could I imagine my mother bathing me, a thirty-year-old woman? I was always so independent; it would have been comical if it were not so tragic. Sometimes I felt like I had entered into a time machine and had turned into an old baby. I could see too many similarities between me and an infant. For example, babies didn't have control of where they wanted to go because they were pushed in a stroller; I was pushed in my wheelchair. New restrictions came with the new phase of my life. From now on, only healthy food was allowed in that room. Playing or going outside was totally out of question! At least I could still express myself with more than a simple gu-gu-dá-dá. Even though I felt like I wasn't in charge of my life anymore, I knew that having my mom with me 24/7 was essential to regaining the strength to escape this imposed second childhood and return to my former independent self.

Everything had changed. Not even my baths were the same. It's amazing how small things become so precious when we no longer have them. A bath that only took minutes before had become more complicated than the instruction manual for building a jeep from scratch. First of all, before starting the bath, my catheter had to be covered with sticky plastic to keep it from getting wet. The importance of preventing water from ever entering the catheter could not be stressed enough. I am not really sure why, but I figure it was to prevent infections. It would have become a bigger problem, rather than the solution to the needles that I hated. Forgive me for my negativity, but the truth is that despite my natural optimism, a shot will always remind me of pain. Besides my mother, I had another partner with me in the bathroom, my medication pump. As I frequently had to take intravenous medication, I was "blessed" with Mr. Pump's constant presence and the beeping it made at my slightest movement.

So, I learned that from that day on the need to constantly adapt to my new, not so fancy lifestyle. This was not the first, nor would it be the last bath where I would be attached to a medicine pole connected to my catheter. Acceptance and adaptability were two essential lessons I needed to learn. I had to be humble enough to relearn everything I had once been able to do easily for myself. From now on, the simplest activities required much patience. With much gratitude and respect for those around me, I was willing to learn everything I could from my mother and from all the amazing nurses who patiently taught me how to do things the new way. And, like a baby, I gradually learned how to take my first steps.

As I was showering, I reflected on how we take life for granted when we are healthy. We don't do this because we are evil, mean, or ungrateful but because our smallness doesn't allow us to see what is happening beyond our own little world. Who would think that bathing without being tied to a pole would make a big difference in someone's day? I never even considered that this could be anybody's problem before it happened to me. But I decided to do my best to focus on the good things. The days that I didn't have anything good to think about, I would think about the days I had been through that were not as bad as others. So I let the warm water fall on my head and wished that every little drop could wash and purify my body and soul. For the first time, I felt every drop that fell on my scalp and shoulders, and I was grateful to be able to feel each one of them.

In those moments, I thanked God for giving me the grace to at least be standing and showering "alone" because I knew that some of my neighbors on the same floor no longer had this privilege. Since this awful disease had disabled some of the patients, they could no longer walk or even stand. In order to be clean, they had to rely on the nurses who would gently rub a moist, warm towel over their bodies. Even this could be looked at from a different perspective. Perhaps for some patients, this type of cleaning could also bring mixed feelings: while some might feel humiliated (as if that kind of a bath was a setback), others could be thankful and feel relieved. Being cleaned with a towel was certainly better than having to stay dirty or wear soiled diapers, especially while being fully aware that everything can change in the blink of an eye. Within seconds, we can go from being an independent, successful person to a totally dependent one, relying on the kindness or goodwill of others.

With that first bath and all the realizations that came with it, I learned that I was part of another world. I understood that with cancer came unknown obstacles, some of which are unpredictable. Now I belonged to a world in which everything was more difficult, but I had many reasons to fight, and I had no time to waste complaining about how fast my life had turned around or how unfair I thought life was.

Chapter 28

What Is the Subtlest Way to Drop the Bomb on My Friends?

My friends in Brazil knew that I was coming, and they were all eagerly expecting me. I figured a safe, practical way to let them know that I wasn't coming was through a social network; I would just post a detailed update about what was happening. Not that I wanted to grab people's attention. After all, who would want to draw attention to something so negative? It wasn't as if I was announcing I had won the lottery or showing off my vacation pictures. I just felt that my real friends deserved to be part of the good and the bad moments, just like in marriage—right? Also, I was not naive enough to think that everyone who was on my Facebook really cared about me, but I knew I had many real friends there, not just numbers on my page. Once I posted my news, I began receiving many messages. Everybody was devastated when they read the sad news. Those who really knew me were aware of how active I had always been and how I liked to take care of my health by eating healthy food. They were shocked by the explosive nature of the news. Some expressed disbelief, saying they had read through the entire message hoping for me to say it was just a prank.

Others expressed their admiration for my dignified reaction to such a scary diagnosis. One thing was certain; I didn't want anyone's pity. What I did want and need were prayers from everyone! To this day, I am thankful to everyone who followed me on the internet during my treatment. The chain of people sending me good vibes and prayers grew and grew. I felt I had to share all my victories in my battle against cancer, as well as losses with all my friends who were following and supporting me. So, this is how I decided to break the sad news to them:

December 12, 2013

My beloved friends,

For those of you who have called me this week, you already know … For those who do not have a clue what I am talking about, today marks the one-week anniversary of me going to the doctor because of a headache and leaving diagnosed with cancer. I know, I know! It is quite shocking; I still do not believe it myself!

It is weird to think that we spent so much time making so many plans, thinking that we would meet each other, and now we simply can't. I spent the entire month asking my mom to cook delicious Brazilian food, asking my dad to make some yummy barbeque, but now I'm stuck here! I guess no meat for me! I also bought so many Christmas presents that I don't even know when, or if, I will be able to hand them out. Anyway, only God knows what kind of lesson I need to take from this. Those of you who know me well know how much I hate sadness, especially on Facebook, but as I have an enormous amount of affection for my friends and always share my moments of joy, I thought I should share this moment of great pain with you as well. Guys, I am not going to lie; it's not something easy to accept because everything happened so fast. It started off with a pain here and there; I went to the doctor several times until I was tired of complaining about the same pain, and the doctor decided to do an x-ray of my lungs. It was the beginning of the terror!

On Wednesday, I was admitted to a hospital and was later transferred to an amazing hospital in Manhattan, where I will dwell for weeks, unfortunately! But looking on the brighter side, I'm being very well looked after; if I let out a *pffffttt,* the nurses rush in to find out if it's a stinky and smelly fart, and of course it's always stinky lol! I could not miss out on a joke; this whole speech was already getting way too dramatic, right? Lol. But now, on a more serious note, I am very happy that I am able to be in such a renowned hospital. People from all over the world come to this hospital and are treated here, and I am glad to say that many of them come out alive. Lol. I guess it is a good thing, right?

In a tragic moment like this, we tend to ask God, "Why? Why me? I am not a judge, but just from common sense, I know a handful of awful people who deserve this to pay for all the bad things they have done to others." Frankly, these thoughts did not help me out. So, I decided to tell my parents (I was trying to save them from this worrisome event, but I couldn't do it for that long). To keep my own sanity, I decided that the hospital is not really a hospital. It is just a nice, fancy spa. It is just a calm place where I was designated to be so that I could catch up on my phone calls and see many dear friends all the time. I have to say that I am being very spoiled by them all. I have beautiful, colorful flowers all over the room, Christmas lamps, pictures, wedding pictures spread everywhere, beautiful letters, get-well cards, some nice slippers, beautiful socks, and I have received so many beauty products that you can't even imagine. I even got an iPad from the teachers from my school. I have had so much affection that I will never be able to thank them all enough. From all of this, I can say that a person who has a family and true friends has it all!

I strongly believe in God. I have wonderful parents, an extraordinary husband, and people from all over the world praying for me, so I will fight and do everything possible to win this painful battle. I know I can and I will do my best to win it. I am already thankful for the prayers that I know I will have from all of you. Please, do not waste your time feeling sorry for me. This feeling will not help me at all; if you really want to help me, just pray and ask with all your heart that I have the daily strength to endure the pain that this stupid disease brings. Lots of love to you all! Enjoy every second with the ones you love and who love you. Remember: our time here is short, and the journey here is not ours. No matter how much we plan, the plans may come out very different from what we wanted, but the main point is that we understand the purpose of our lives. More love, less hate … I think that's it.

P.S. I am very happy that my parents arrived today. I love being cared for by those who are and always will be my greatest loves.

$\mathscr{C}$hapter 29

Accommodation for My Parents?

$\mathbf{A}$ practical question came to mind once we had exchanged those first hugs. After caring for me during the day, where would my parents stay? Of course, our apartment in Westchester was a possibility, but how would they visit me in Manhattan? Luckily, our apartment is close to the hospital. By car, it only took about thirty minutes to get there, but my parents didn't have international driver's permits, they had never driven an automatic, and they didn't know how to drive in hectic New York City traffic. I could picture my dad annoyed, cursing the yellow taxi drivers in Portuguese. So, this option was out of question. Another option would be to stay at home and take the subway into the city. This seemed like a good solution, but once again, questions popped into my mind: How would they get around without knowing the city or the language? How would they buy tickets? How would they know what station to get off at? Subway routes change often, but the changes are only announced once we are already inside. Since they didn't speak any English, how would they understand these announcements? The truth was they would be more lost than the boy in *Home Alone*. The huge difference was that English was Macaulay Culkin's native language, and my parents only knew the ABCs. I could trust my mother with the usual greetings, "Hi" or "How are you?" but my father only communicated through his smile, lots of mimicking, and his sympathy.

We started looking at hotels and even hostels meant for students and teenagers, which were much cheaper, but the choices were not good. Even though we found some affordable options, they were all too far away. We even talked to the hospital social worker, who gave us a list of hotels and accommodation, but the daily rates for these made us want to pull out our hair. No need to bother with chemo. (My dad, the top of his head proudly naked, was already ahead of the game.) We finally came up with the following solution:

My parents would stay in the hospital with me until someone said they couldn't. If no one said anything, they would just continue to stay by my side throughout my treatment. And so they did; my mother slept in a somewhat comfortable blue leather armchair, and my father slept on the floor, on a duvet that Richard had brought from home. Some nights, he switched places with my mom because sleeping on the cold floor gave him a backache. In the middle of the night, I would hear them whispering to each other, "Oh, I think today it's my turn to sleep in the armchair, isn't it?" They survived this way, between a hard chair and a duvet on an even harder floor, for nearly a month.

How could I not be grateful for these two blessings in my life? Marta and Deroci Da Silva, my first two loves. Thank you for crossing oceans to be by my side to hold my hand in the darkest moment of my life. Thank you for teaching me, even as a child, that when a storm happens, I can be and have to be strong until it passes. I am forever grateful for everything they have done, and continue to do for me! What I found exceptionally beautiful about them was that despite all the discomforts they endured during this ordeal, they never complained: the many nights spent sleeping on a cold, hard floor, the hospital food, the huge expense of traveling from Brazil to New York, the days when they simply could not take a shower, the freezing temperature, the gray skies, a Christmas without supper and a New Year's without champagne. They simply loved me without limits; that unconditional love showered over me.

May God repay you double, triple, and quadruple for what you have done for me. Even if I live a hundred years, I will never be able to repay you, simply because love is priceless. On second thought, I am glad that love is not repaid with money, because if it were, I would have to give up every strand of hair on my head, and I've already lost it all—my hair, I mean—never my love.

$\mathcal{C}$hapter 30

Books Change, Life Changes

Writing on my social network was a way to unburden myself, and I felt it was necessary to keep posting, to be engaged with the world, even if it meant engaging through a computer screen:

Adaptations

All of a sudden, life hits you by surprise, and you don't have a choice but to learn to adapt to the new changes: my IB, IGCSE, and Spanish books changed into books about fighting cancer, my frenetic teaching schedule at four different schools into slow walks and breathing respiration exercises in the hospital halls with my mother. My energetic, noisy, happy Zumba lessons have been replaced by board games, peaceful movies, deep, meaningful conversations, and fond memories with my loving parents, caring friends, and supportive hubby. That's how we slowly get used to what God offers us, without whining about what we don't have but being thankful for having the blessing of one more day of life, regardless of our challenges.

Once more, I'd like to thank everyone for all the love and care I received from you during my time in my new "home." I feel really blessed for being surrounded by so much love and such great demonstrations of affection. My hospital room was the epitome of all the love I received. Every corner that I would lay eyes on let me feel the closeness of my friends' presence. In one week, my room was fully decorated with saints from so many different countries, healing, shiny crystals, Bibles in different languages, silver and wooden crosses, stuffed animals, postcards, colorful get-well balloons, the intangible but palpable care of my family, the love of my husband, and an enormous will to beat leukemia with all the strength I have.

Chapter 31

Pee in the Hat? Write Everything Down!

One beautiful morning, the nurses woke me up, gave me the lovely painful morning shot, and gave me unusual news. They told me that I would need to change the way I peed. *Huh? Did I hear that right?* They said that from that day on, I would have to pee in a hat. Those words had a shocking impact on me; I wondered if I had gone completely nuts or if my hearing was suddenly getting worse due to all the medication I had been taking. All I knew was that that conversation did not make any sense to me. For a moment, I asked myself if this was a new expression I had never heard of. Like Amelia Bedelia, I imagined myself peeing on one of those fancy hats that the beautiful and fancy ladies from Saratoga wear while they watch the horse races. I felt embarrassed to tell them that that sounded like science fiction to me, but I needed to confirm what I had heard, and I sputtered to the nurse, "Pee in the hat?" To my surprise, the nurse confirmed that I had heard her correctly: I would have a hat to urinate into.

The good thing about it is that it wasn't a fancy hat adorned with pink plumage; it was just a container, a transparent cup with millimeter measurements. My main job from that day on was to pay close attention to the amount of pee I had made and write the amount on a piece of tape so that the nurses could verify whether or not I was releasing most of the chemo from my body. In those tapes, we exchanged smiley faces, and they left words of encouragement. Love them!

One lesson I learned was that if the pee was clear, it was a good sign. It meant my body was not retaining all the toxins brought in by the chemo and some other medications I had taken. So, every time I looked at a hat full of crystal-clear pee, I felt like giving myself a high five for drinking enough water. That transparent pee was proof that I was hydrating myself well and that I was trying to do my best to help my body heal itself. I know it sounds silly, but that pure pee really made me feel like I deserved a pat on the back and a "Great job, Fabi!" A teacher at heart, I was reminded of how we compliment our students who have diligently turned in all of their homework assignments on time.

At the time, the new peeing process sounded ultra-complex to me. After some time, I understood that all the nurse was saying was that I would have to pee into a bucket and write the exact amount I had made so that the doctors knew if my body was being able to release the chemo. Needless to say, I religiously followed everything they said and started writing down every single drop I left in that hat. The desire to be healed was bigger than anything else I have ever wished for. All I wanted was to strictly follow everything the nurses and doctors told me to do so that I could get out of that hospital as fast as I could. As I was on an IV (intravenous therapy) 24/7, I needed to go to the bathroom every half an hour. The simple act of peeing was no longer as simple as it had been for any healthy person. I couldn't freely stand up and walk to the restroom. I had to keep reminding myself that I was not "wireless"; I was literally wired to a pump machine from which I received the lifesaving drips night and day. During the first weeks of treatment, I had taken so much serum that I gained twenty-seven pounds in one week. Therefore, it was also in my interest to expel all the liquid that I could. Every simple thing that I used to do before was now far more complicated, and every time I needed to pee, I had to follow the steps below:

Step 1: Carefully turn off the machine without yanking it from the outlet. If I was careless, the catheter on my arm would tear from my body.

Step 2: Silently maneuver the serum pump machine to the bathroom without hitting any furniture to avoid making any slight noise that could wake up my next-door roomy.

Step 3: Open up the heavy bathroom door with a single hand while holding the machine with the other hand, so that I wasn't run over by my own cart. Then, take a deep breath and push the machine so that it could slide over the floor's bump that some smart architects decided to add to some bathrooms. He or she may have thought that a baseboard in a cancer patient's bathroom would give a nice touch to the architecture, but that baseboard actually made our path to the restroom a bit harder.

Step 4: Place my special hat on the toilet and finally pee! This last step seems pretty obvious, but it was important to add to the instruction manual. I am pretty sure that if I had used my room-mate's hat, she wouldn't be happy.

After spending some time in the hospital, I noticed that I started to become a germaphobe. If a headache turned out to be leukemia, I wouldn't want to know what else I could get from sitting on the wrong hat. Virus? Infection? Anyway, I had to be attentive about the hat I was "wearing."

Step 5: The last step was to write down, on the masking tape, the hour and the amount of urine expelled.

Step 6: The return to my bed was quite similar but less stressful because at least my bladder was empty, and I didn't have the added pressure of potentially having an accident. My main goal was to walk back in the dark without hitting any furniture or my parents, who were lying on the floor. Once this task was complete, my next mission was to turn the machine on, or it would start beeping because its battery would be low. Some nights, it would start beeping for no reason; if I turned in bed, it started. It sounded like a crazy parrot and would wake up the entire floor. If it was not mine, my roommate's pump would beep, and that's how we, cancer patients and caregivers, spent our nights, with those ear-splitting chirps that kept reminding us where we were, even in our dreams or nightmares. It sounded like a crazy orchestra in which a string of inept musicians could not decide what song they were playing—a real madhouse! The noise of those machines reverberated in our heads even when we returned home.

That's when I started realizing how things that any healthy person can do become way more complicated for those who are ill. In my case, thank God, I had nothing to complain about because I knew I had the help I needed. My father turned into a kind of bathroom nurse. I would just sit down in my bed, and he would rush to turn off the machine, push the wheel with extreme care all the way to the bathroom, and then open up the bathroom door without making any noise to avoid waking up my roommate. After doing this procedure so many times, he got so good at it that he even started to help me record my urine levels. He gently whispered, "How much did you pee? Let me write it down for you." Basically, he became an expert in conducting me to the bathroom. When I lived in Brazil, I was always worried about his insomnia, but during those moments, for the first time, I was very thankful that he slept lightly. I am not going to lie; it was great to know he was there for anything I needed.

It was as if I had my own Superman who was by my side 24/7. I was so lucky! He seemed to have extraordinary night vision and was able to hear any little noise from any distance. He also had superpowers where he was able to make me smile even when I felt like crying, in addition to catering to my bladder's demands. He did all he could to make my life easier without any complaints! You are my hero, Dad!

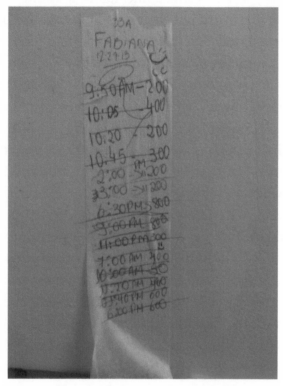

Documenting everything!

*C*hapter 32

Every Princess Has Her Own Throne. Was I Part of the *Game of Thrones?*

After taking the first doses of the darn chemo, it didn't take that long for my body procedures to become foreign and out of sorts. I woke up in the middle of the night feeling, uh, how can I put it in a beautiful way … feeling a very strong stomach ache. The term "stomach ache" was used only to beautify and soften what was really going on with me. But I guess at this point of the book, we have already built some bonding, so I do not need to be so formal, and there is no need to beat around the bush or fluff about anything anymore. I am not going to waste any lines or rumble about it, so to make a long story short, the diarrhea had started. Dear reader, you have been with me since chapter 1, and you followed all my ups and downs, so I feel that it is my obligation to warn you about the content. Unfortunately, this chapter will be one of my down, gross, and stinky moments.

Warning: feel free to skip this chapter if you want to. No hurt feelings. I totally understand that some people may feel grossed out reading about things that people usually do not write about. But since it is part of the story, I felt I had to warn you that in this chapter, I need to let it out, literally … let it out!

Well, the truth of the matter is that all the steps that I described in the previous chapter about the peeing process had to be done at a snap of a finger, or something really disastrous would happen in that room. I had no doubt that a volcano was about to erupt in my stomach; I no longer had time to even think about all the steps that I planned for my bathroom trips. With any slight movement I made or any breath I took, I could clearly hear my stomach groaning and making weird noises. I didn't know what was going on, but from those powerful, bombastic sounds coming from my stomach, I could feel the lava brewing in my intestines, and it was ready to burst at any second. I quickly realized that the power and the damage that a naïve fart could make in that room would make me look like a thirty-year-old baby who had had the messiest diaper ever.

I spent the whole night going through a marathon that I was not prepared for: sit up, stand up, run to the outlet, unplug the chemo machine, take the hat—meant to be used for the pee—out, put the poop hat in, and to my relief or optimum embarrassment, the stinky mud was out. I have to say that at first I was embarrassed to have my father help me run to the bathroom. Even though he just helped me with the running game and waited for me outside the bathroom, I felt bad that a grown-ass woman needed help to use the restroom. I felt bad that even if I tried to make no noise, he woke up every time I sat up in bed, and I knew that every time I sat on that throne, he knew exactly what was going on inside the bathroom, and he stood there like a British soldier, except he had the added challenge of sustaining a stone visage as he inhaled the ubiquitous bodily odor that came with the excrement lava. However, my father, who has a great sense of humor, always made me feel at ease with his silly jokes: "Oh, gee! What did you eat to-day, girl?" or "Sheesh, this one was so powerful!" "Wow, I am glad you came out of the bathroom. If you stayed there, I feared that you wouldn't come out of there alive. This one was really stinky!" And of course, with my Superman making fun of our sad situation, I realized that there was no need to be ashamed of anything. The second time I went to the bathroom, I was not embarrassed anymore and loved that my dad was the one who helped me in that bathroom marathon.

The following day, I was dead tired from the most grueling marathon of my life. The morning nurse arrived, and looking at the dark circles under my eyes, she asked me how my night had been. I told her about my tiring night. Feeling sorry for all the sordid details I described to her, she said in a calm voice, "I'm going to order a commode for you." I have to confess, I had no idea what she was talking about, but at that point, I would take any medicine that would prevent me from going to the bathroom every second. Five minutes after the nurse left, another nurse came in my room carrying a portable toilet. Then I understood what the fancy word "commode" was: a potty for grown-ups, which I thought was totally unnecessary. I knew I was not feeling well, but it was not so bad that I couldn't get up to go to the restroom. Unplugging the machine and running without making any noise, so as not to wake up my roommate or my mom, was undoubtedly a hassle, a pain in the ass, but having to use a bedpan was humiliating. I had to keep my poop pride! I ignored it the entire day and raced to the restroom as fast as I could every time my stomach started growling.

Well, friends, that pride did not last long. With evening came the diarrhea. I ran to the bathroom a couple of times, with my dad maneuvering my inseparable serum machine. Then I thought, *What am I doing? Why would I be embarrassed about using a bed-pan? If the nurse brought it, it is because I really need it. I am here running like a crazy chicken without a head when I am about to have an accident in my pants, and I have the solution to my problem right here.* I looked at that simple plastic commode, and in my mind, it suddenly transformed into the shiniest golden throne ever. *When am I going to have an opportunity to sit on a private throne ever again? What else could I want? I'm a princess, and if the nurse placed this throne right here, it is because I really deserve this regal honor.*

I surrendered to my throne. Like a princess, I practically glided to the bedpan, sat calmly on it, and the royal chocolate cakes were out! Oh what a relief to me! Everything was so quiet and so peaceful! It is only with experience, dear readers, that you realize that every little thing, even the "shitty ones" that are taken for granted by a healthy person, become such a huge accomplishment to a cancer patient. I no longer had to turn off the machine and run to the bathroom as if I was participating in the Olympic Games' obstacle race. Now I felt like real royalty; I certainly did not have the monetary wealth of one, but at least I had the throne! The nurses already treated me and family like royalty, so that day, I decided that I was one. The only annoyance was the smell, but as we say, you can't have it all!

Having my mom and my dad by my side overcoming all these obstacles reminded me of when a priest, or anybody who officiates a wedding, asks us to say our vows to our spouses. I thought that the same vows could be said in a maternity ward when the new parents are about to leave with a newborn. This is how I imagined the conversation would go:

Nurse: Do you, Marta Da Silva and Deroci Da Silva, promise to take care of little Fabiana Da Silva?

Da Silvas (full of excitement): Yes, we do!

Nurse: Do you promise that you will stay with her in health and in sickness, in happiness or in sorrow?

Parents: Yes!

Nurse: Are you sure? I don't mean to let you down, but one day she will decide that she needs to be more adventurous, and she will move to another country.

Parents: Well, we will raise her for the world, so whatever makes her happy! Can we take her now?

Nurse: Let me just take a look at her future health profile. Oh boy! It is not good! It's really bad!

Parents: What can you possibly forecast in this health chart?

Nurse: Unfortunately, she will have cancer, and since she is in another country, you will have to travel there and sleep on the floor of a foreign country's hospital for a while. In order to get better, she will have to take medicine that will, ironically, make her feel worse before she gets better.

Parents: Oh, wow! I guess we will still take her.

Nurse: Wait! I am not done yet! While she is in the hospital, the chemo will mess up her intestines, and you will have to put up with the most odoriferous farts ever.

Parents: That's too much! Can we return this baby and get a new one?

Just kidding! There was no need to make any vows because while I was in the hospital, I understood that once you become a parent, most understand that these are unspoken vows. I certainly learned about unconditional and truthful love during those nights that my parents stayed with me. They could be anywhere else, yet they had decided to be with me.

Needless to say, my family stayed together despite the circumstance. They realized that with the new commode, our strategies had to change a little bit. From that day on, there was no more running to the bathroom. The steps were as follows: The moment I heard the first groan from my stomach, I would jump from my bed and hop onto the commode. Once the product was made, my father—the court jester—very gently woke up my mom—the sleepy queen—so that she could get rid of those smelly cakes as quickly as possible. I remember she often had one eye open and the other closed (and I think she was holding her breath as well). The royal perfume could defeat any amount of caffeine or smelling salts needed to awaken anyone. She quickly went to the bathroom, dumped everything in the toilet, flushed it, and boom, that was it! She patiently washed the throne with a little shower designed only for it, and right after, she put my little throne together in anticipation for the future—and inevitable—deposits. Production was never low there!

That was exactly how we spent several days and nights, in which everyone participated.

From that night on, I just used the bathroom when I had visitors during the day; otherwise, I used my throne, looking at the Brooklyn Bridge, reflecting on how life can turn upside down in the blink of an eye. One day I had a headache and was about to travel to Brazil, and then a week later, I was in Manhattan, not in a fancy rooftop dancing with my husband but in a hospital room watching the beautiful view that God and the hospital provided me with while I ejected everything I had eaten. I would say that the end of this chapter was sort of shitty, but at least you were warned.

New throne!

Chapter 33

My Room: A Magical Place

One lesson I learned is that when you are going through deep pain in your life, friends are the best doctors that can heal your wounded soul. They naturally bring with them a magical potion that you need so that you can get through any phase in your life. They have that powerful, optimistic shot that you need, and they will do whatever it takes to make you feel better.

All demonstrations of love were needed and appreciated. It was certainly the first time that I felt surrounded by so much love coming from all different directions and from a vast array of people. I was a newly excavated gem that needed to be cut and polished, and even though it was a harsh process, my angels-lapidaries were there to help me through the rough layers so that at the end, I could enjoy the true brilliance: life.

These angels transformed my hospital room into a cozy place. I got so many gifts that I can't thank my friends enough for the genuine love they surrounded me with. The gifts were the most diverse you can imagine. My colleagues chipped in for a brand-new iPad so that I would not get too bored in the hospital. I had a supportive team with me, and they thought about every detail to ensure that I would be fine.

I got so many flowers that my room turned into a makeshift botanical garden. We had all types of flowers; they were exquisitely vivid with a pleasant, sweet fragrance that almost masked the "royal brownies." Every time I thought about being blue because of the dark situation I was going through, I looked around, and the bright colors of the roses and orchids reminded me that life could be colorful again; it was just a matter of time.

I also got so much body lotion and perfume in a variety of smells, flavors, and types that I probably could have opened up my own Fabiana's Body Works. If Bath & Body Works served as a competition for me, I could have at least opened my own fragrance booth in Union Square. I also received several saints' medallions from countries that I had never visited, as well as shiny crystals, incense, pictures, healing rocks, crosses, and rosaries. They were all part of my hospital room's interior design, and I also received a Bible that I used to read and ask for guidance every night.

My team did everything they could to make me smile. I even got some unusual and sexy presents with suggestions, hinting that Richard and I would have to use the daring gifts as soon I left the hospital: leopard panties, nightgowns, and leopard slippers. "Roar-roar." I got a pink, furry, soft robe that made me look FFF: fabulous, fancy, and funny! Most importantly, they kept me warm in those hospital halls. Vivid red lipsticks and nail polishes were given in mass. Chocolates, a set of red drinking cups, M&M's, and bowls and spatulas to bake cookies were all part of this endless gift list. I quickly realized that the gifts represented how much everyone wanted to cheer me up and how they cheered for my recovery. I saw it in their hopeful eyes, how much they wanted me to be out of there.

I also received several magazines, books, and Brazilian comic books. Although neither my friends nor I realized this at the time, the abundant reading material was an indication that my stay would not be as short as we wanted it to be; with the gifts came the understanding that normalcy had exited. I would have time to read all of the literature from cover to cover, especially knowing that cancer was that constant ghost on my back, reminding me that life was shorter than I thought.

I got hundreds of caring get-well and Christmas cards, newspaper articles about a possible cure for leukemia, cheerful text messages, and funny videos that made me smile. All that love and affection gave me a great deal of strength, so I would not surrender. I thought, *God, this cannot be the end of my journey! If You can't make this miracle for me, I beg You, make the impossible happen for these golden-hearted people who are in this fight with me and have been praying for me.*

My presents accumulated into a mountain, making my husband's primary job turn into driving our car to the hospital once a week and loading it with as much as he could so that we could all fit in the car the day that I would be discharged. Believe it or not, the day I left the hospital, we still had no space for ourselves, so we shoveled what we could in the trunk. When I looked at the back seats, I could barely see my parents because they were covered in a blanket of presents.

The presents were just a simple representation of how much I was loved, but the present that I loved the most was my family and friends' presence and support.

My magical place

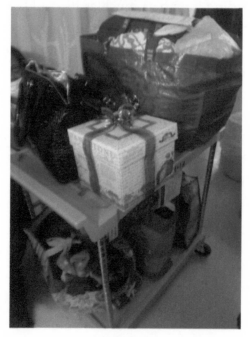

Presents

$\mathscr{C}$hapter 34

A Nurse Sent by a Friend

An unknown nurse from another floor came into my room desperately looking for me. She seemed to be in her fifties, a woman of short stature with a friendly smile. She said that a friend of mine had asked her to come over and give me some support. As I was about to bathe, she gave me her card and said that I could reach out to her in case I needed anything. I found it great to have this extra help, and I really wished I could have spent more time with her, but once you are in the hospital and are getting ready to bathe, you have to do it fast because you never know if your roommate will need to use the bathroom for an emergency. I just wanted to avoid any inconvenience, so my mother and I went on our mission, and my father, who barely speaks any English, stayed to talk or mime whatever he could to say to the nurse. From the bathroom, I could hear that she was doing her best to start up a conversation with him.

"Do you speak Ingles?" she asked my dad in Spanglish.

"Sorry, no English." (He learned this phrase quickly; it became his custom response to those who began to ask him questions in English.)

"Okay, no problem. Come to the computer screen. I want to show you all the treatments that Fabiana will have." She slowly kept pointing to the computer screen and explaining to my dad all the chemo I would take and the side effects of each one.

Confused by the unfamiliar English and added medical lingo displayed on the computer, my father said, "Eu acho que deve ser super interessante o que a Sra. está falando, mas eu não estou entendendo NADA." (Translation: "I know you are probably saying something that is very interesting, but I really don't understand a word you are saying, sweetie!" My dad kept saying it in Portuguese. "Sorry, no English!")

Meanwhile, my mother and I cracked up inside the bathroom. And the nurse kept trying:

"Hablas Español?" (Do you speak Spanish?)

"No, no. Só Portuguese."

"Sí, sí. Zapato, entiendes?" ("Do you understand it?" she frantically asked, pointing to my father's shoe.

"Sim, sapato, sí. Que que tem meu sapato?" ("Yes, shoe, yes. What about my shoe?")

She repeated herself with increasing desperation, and my exasperated father called out to my mom in Portuguese, "Oh, Marta, please help me out! The nurse is pointing to my shoe, and I do not know what she wants."

They had communicated by pointing to things using gestures and body language. My dad repeated whatever she said, just trying to be polite; they spent about five long minutes talking about nothing and everything at the same time. She was so interested in showing my father the treatment that I would undergo, and my father was very much interested in knowing what she was trying to say, but from the moment they started the shoe conversation, the communication was lost, and no one understood anything. To this day, when we remember this moment, we wonder what my father's shoe had to do with my treatment. Perhaps she moonlighted as a show saleswoman. At least it served as a distraction from my cancer journey.

Chapter 35

Tumor, Where?

With time, I began to understand more and more about the severity of my condition. Each patient had a medical team that was aware of each patient's case, and every morning, my team of doctors came to see how I was doing. In this team, there is always a primary doctor. My primary doctor was a tall, snowy-haired man who reminded me of a slim Santa Claus. He had calming emerald eyes. There was something special about him; he was so caring and kind to me. Every time he came to see me, I felt that I was not just one of the many to him. He also had a great sense of humor, expressed with a soothing German accent, followed by a slew of medical jargon. With only this to go by, I somehow decided that he had a lot of experience in oncology—that, and he was the primary doctor, so I was pretty sure he had the credentials and experience to help heal me.

When he brought in the results of my examination, he hugged me tightly and said that he was very happy to let me know that my cancer was curable. I cannot begin to effectively express how grateful I was for that assurance! I didn't know if it was like a time extension plan on earth, but I knew was that I was very happy to hear that sweet suffix, *able*: you *can* be cured. It was not a death sentence anymore.

"Good morning, Fabiana. I come to you with great news. I am very glad to inform you that we did not find any cancer cells in your bone marrow!"

"Oh, wow! This is the best thing I could hear! I'm very happy that my bone marrow is clear! But, Dr. D.D., if this cancer is in the blood that begins in the bone marrow and you have not found anything in my bone marrow, where do you think the cancer cells are?"

He glared at me and then went straight to the point: "Unfortunately, you have a mediastinal tumor."

"Medi ... what?" To say that I was puzzled is an understatement. I didn't know if this was something that I should be happy or sad about. I quickly started thinking about the prefix "med." *Middle? It's in the middle of what?*

"Mediastinal. From the CT scan, it seems to be around your heart."

"The tumor is where, Doctor D.D.? What do you mean, the tumor is around my heart? I am sorry, but it makes no sense!"

"When you had the CT scan, we were able to see that you have a very large mass around your heart, and it will probably be dissolved as soon as you start with chemotherapy."

"Probably? Did I hear that right? Probably is certainly a negative uncertainty when the subject is your life!" So, slowly, I tried to digest the probability that I could die from this tumor, which two moments ago I had never heard of. "Around my heart?" I repeated in disbelief. "This is pretty darn serious! I don't want to die now," I kept repeating, as if he was the one who could give me a free pass for life, as we give students a tardy excuse when we find out that they were on a trip or were seeing the nurse. I tried to wrap my head around this information, but those new words, "tumor around my heart," it sounded sour to me, and I couldn't stop thinking that death seemed so close to me.

"Let's not think about it, Fabiana!" Dr. D.D. said firmly. "Nowadays, the survival rate for leukemia is much higher. Fifty to Seventy percent of patients can go into remission and have a normal life."

How could I not think about death as he gladly told me that only Fifty percent of patients survive? Was this information supposed to console anyone, or did it serve to encourage one to commit suicide by jumping out of the window? All I wanted to hear was that I was and would be fine, that I was (as always) exaggerating and being overdramatic and that the chance of dying for me was zero.

According to him, my leukemia had begun as a "wrong" cell, and my body did not eliminate it; instead, it began to multiply it. *What a stupid cell! What are you trying to do here, sweetie? Are you planning to commit suicide by cloning all these bad cells instead of killing them?* All I knew was that it was hard to be kind to a cell that was trying to kill all the good cells in my body. *How dumb can a cell be?* The best way I could understand it was that I have just been aware of a suicidal cell whose main goal was to kill herself, but why? *What have I done to you other than provide you with a cozy shelter to live in and great food? You are even surrounded by angelical cell friends that you are turning into little devils! What the hell do you want from me? Do you get that if I die, you also die, you dumb cell!* I felt betrayed by my own dumb body!

At that moment, my world stopped, and I remembered all the pain I had felt before being admitted: heart pains, headaches, thick veins, shortness of breath, red spots on my face when I ate meat, vomiting, a sty on my eyelid, as well as a lump on my neck. Dear readers, thank God I did not listen to my previous doctors who insisted that my body was only telling me that I was "stressed." Instead, I listened to a greater healer, my mom, who repeated the advice: "Sweetheart, please go get checked again!" Moms are always right, or at least they are most of the time!

A thousand thoughts ran through my head, and one of them was, *Am I still going to be strong or should I just give up from something that came from nowhere?* But it was not "from nowhere" anymore. Damn it! According to the doctors, I had a tumor around my heart. Fuck! Excuse me for the language; I usually don't curse at all. But if I were to die, I could curse in Portuguese, in English, even in Chinese if I knew how. It was no longer a cold or a headache. It was a *tumor*! This word played in a loop in my head. How could my body have fallen into this trap? Instead of killing the deadly cell, it decided to procreate and spread its malice, sculpting a tumor on my little innocent heart, which only tried to produce life and love? At that moment, I realized that what I had watched in those melodramatic cancer movies was now happening to me. It was the realization that disasters happen not only to others but unfortunately to all of us! It was not a soap opera anymore. In this movie, I was the protagonist facing with my antagonist, cancer, which rested inside, waiting to take both of us down! All I knew at that point was that I didn't want to be in a tragedy where the tragic hero dies; I wanted to have a happy and healthy ending—a new beginning!

Chapter 36

Your Choice: Your Life or the Life of a Bucket of Eggs?

The expression "when it rains, it pours" certainly applied to my life. In my case, when it rained, I knew I should get ready because Hurricane Katrina was about to come. Life decided that being diagnosed with cancer when I was just thirty, having been married for only seven months, having liquid build up in my lungs, and having a tumor around my heart was too easy for me to take. The following day, my doctor told me that there was one side effect of chemo that I should be very aware of because it could affect my entire life. With delicate yet direct words, he spilled the beans: "It is important that you are aware that after going through an intensive treatment like yours, there is a risk that you can become infertile." It felt like somebody was sticking a knife into my heart. Sometimes I thought I was participating in a prank where there were hidden cameras hidden everywhere. I felt that one of the producers would come out of one of the beds, laughing and saying: "Cut! I am sorry, Fabi. This prank was too inappropriate, and it is not even funny anymore! Everything is fine; forget about everything you heard. Actually, D.D. is not even a doctor, he is just one of our actors, but I guess he played you well, huh? Kind of a Jo Shmo prank." Unfortunately, I was not being punked.

The doctor had just confirmed that perhaps I would not be able to bear any children of my own, which was really painful. I felt that it was kind of an easier and "better" way to kill me; actually, I felt that it was a slower way to softly kill me.

Those words were more painful than taking any shots or any dosage of chemo. Nonetheless, after a lot of reflection, I remembered that I would have to learn how to live with it, and the doctor quickly reminded me that I was lucky enough to be able to have my own life back; bearing another life would be a miracle that I just did not know if I would be blessed with. I learned the hard way that after a cancer diagnosis, you must take baby steps, even when the disease may take your right to follow your own baby's steps. The irony of life!

I slowly started digesting that moldy bread that life had just fed me. That bombshell was worse than the crater left by the news of my tumor. How could a person get admitted into a hospital with a headache and then, the next week, have cancer, liquid that is constantly increasing in the lungs, a tumor in the heart, and have to undergo chemotherapy—which would make me lose all my hair. (If I was lucky enough, I could keep my eyebrows, and thank God they did not fall off; just so you know, in the cancer fight, every stray hair counts). But now I had a much bigger problem that I didn't know how to handle: the possibility of not being able to carry a baby in my own womb, feeling him or her move in my belly, breastfeeding—all gone! I was mortified. How could I tell my parents that I would never be able to give them a grandchild? How could I tell Richard that perhaps he would never be a biological dad to his own kid? How would his parents react when they found out that Richard may have married a dead uterus?

This news left me devastated. I always wanted to be a mother, always dreamed of having my little baby, holding his/her little hands, inhaling that pleasant newborn scent, giving him/her kisses on his/her belly, touching that soft skin that feels like the fuzz of a teddy bear or a soft peach. I wouldn't have the blessing of being able to watch her/him take those glorious first steps, seeing my little belly turn into a huge watermelon and everything else that comes with the package of being a mom. I knew that 50 percent of my dream was terminated, and there wasn't anything that I could do to stop Mrs. Life from killing my dreams.

Looking at the bright side—if there was any bright side to it—I did have some options, though not too many. However, when I asked the doctor about my alternatives, he once again was clear and direct: "You do not have many options to have kids now. The priority here is your life! You really need to think about that and make a careful decision. I will refer you to a fertility specialist who can give you more information to confirm if there is anything that should be done now."

In the afternoon, a doctor who specialized in fertilization for cancer patients came into my room. She was very kind and had grayish hair that had beautiful and tight curls. She had a motherly way about her and vivid black eyes that paid close attention to every word I said. With despair, I started telling her about my case:

"Well, Doctor, thank you so much for coming here. I talked to Dr. D.D. this morning, and I am very worried about my situation. I literally just got married, and I am sure that when this treatment is over, I would like to have some children."

"When was the last day of your menstrual cycle?"

"Two weeks ago."

"Well, Fabiana, I'll be quite honest with you. Unfortunately, you do not have time to do what we call the egg collection. I'm really sorry, but it would be very complicated for us to collect your eggs because you just had your period. If you go for it, we shall have

146

to induce another period, and it would take at least three weeks for it to happen, and from what I discussed with your doctor, you have been diagnosed with acute leukemia, which can spread through your body very quickly, so I would not recommend that you take three weeks off from your treatment so that we can retrieve your eggs. This is my recommendation, but of course you and your husband will be the ones who have the final say."

Richard always made it clear that he was not eager to have children right away. While we were dating, we had a silly little fight when he said that between having his own son and adopting one, he did not see any problem in adopting one instead. At that time, I thought his way of thinking was weird, especially knowing that I was always nuts about children, but now, adoption seemed like our sole option. I always thought it was beautiful to adopt children, but it never crossed my mind that one day this would be my only option if I wanted to be a mom.

When Richard came to visit me in the evening, I told him about the two appointments I had during the day, and I also told him that the fertilization specialist told us that we did have the choice of saving some eggs so that I could get pregnant after the treatment, but those weeks off from the cancer treatment could adversely impact my prognosis. What if, within those three weeks in which I had the chance to be saved, I lost my life because of my dream babies? I was not even sure if I would survive or if the babies would survive. And what would happen if the egg collection was a success and later on we found out that the cancer had spread because I had chosen to spend weeks to save some eggs to have some babies that I didn't even know if I would be healthy enough to carry? Wouldn't it be selfish of me to simply leave Richard with a bucket of eggs ready to be fertilized and give up on my life?

Some readers may find this to be a selfish act, but Richard and I decided to save my life instead of our potential biological children. The children would come in one way or another, naturally or by insemination or adoption. There was still a light at the end of the tunnel; I could not hold on to despair and let that take away my desire to live.

Chapter 37

The First Chemotherapy We Never Forgot

The day of the first chemotherapy arrived. To make matters worse, it was Friday the thirteenth, and I quickly found out that I was not afraid of seeing a black cat or breaking any mirrors; the only thing I feared was the red chemotherapy, Vincristine, that would be injected into my body in a few minutes. I knew that that liquid symbolized a change in my life.

My parents were in my room. Richard, his parents, and my friends were also with me. I wondered about a lot of things, I naively thought that when the chemotherapy was given, my hair would begin to fall out. I also thought that something weird could happen to me at that time, such as turning different shades of colors, or that the room would begin to spin and I would wake up with nothing—no hair, no eyebrows, and looking on the brighter side, without hair under my arms and on my legs. At least this chemotherapy came with effective, pain-free hair removal. Or at least that's what I innocently assumed.

There was dead silence in the room. None of us knew what to say or if we should say anything. As I had my catheter, a compassionate male nurse injected me with my first chemotherapy. It didn't last more than five minutes, but during those eternal five minutes, I watched moments of my entire life slide by. The second chemotherapy injection was also administered—on the same day, a big bag that was placed on my poll. Surprisingly, I did not feel pain. The third round of chemo was a pill that I took; the nurses warned me that I would feel more energized, which, for me, could become a problem, as I was already naturally hyper. If that medicine made me even more hyper than I already am, that meant I would have the energy to run a show of my own 24/7 to two hundred kids, without any stage assistant. Once the nurse finished injecting me with the chemo, I did not feel anything at all. Everything was normal, and I continued talking as if nothing had happened. I thought it was cute when my father-in-law asked the doctors if there was a way they could remove the tumor from my heart with surgery. They quickly took away our hope by replying that surgery was not an option because the tumor was nestled between my arteries, and they could not risk cutting any of them. Furthermore, the removal of the tumor would not guarantee that I would be in remission.

In other words, the cancer is like a mold that grew in my heart. For the first time in my life, I felt totally vulnerable, unable to control what was going on in my own body. I also felt guilty that I had brought so much worry for everyone around me. My parents had to fly from one country to another to stay with me. My husband had just married a bomb woman who could explode at any time. My in-laws had known me for a very short time, so who knew what they thought when they saw me in such a poor state, wearing that horrible hospital gown. Jokes aside, I did not want to be a burden to my friends, who were doing everything they could to visit me and send me love during the busiest time of the year. It was time for them to be thinking about their families, yet they did everything to ensure that my family was all right. What I also knew was that I could not blame myself; I had not caused that mold. It was simply growing inside of me. The only solution was to fight, fight, and fight not only for myself but for all the ones who sacrificed everything to be by my side!

The first treatment was quite different from what I had imagined. To my surprise, my hair and my eyebrows were still intact. Phew! However, I felt so nauseous that my hair and eyebrows were the last things I was concerned about. I woke up vomiting a green, blue, and yellow foam. Perhaps I expelled these particular colors because I wanted to go to Brazil so badly; after all, these are the colors of the Brazilian flag. I felt an emptiness in my stomach, as well as very strong pain, as if someone was stabbing me from the inside. I quickly lost control of my body, and all I could do was just hold my mom and the nurse's hands as I threw up everything, praying my stomach would disappear. It was strange to think that a medicine that had been made to help me live made me feel like I was really close to death.

On that day, I decided not to have any visitors except for my family; I did not want anyone to see me as fragile and broken as I was. I spent the day resting; in fact, I slept all day. It was much better to sleep than stay awake and throw up all the time. An unforgettable sleep took me away from the reality; it was new to me, scary to my soul, and painful for my moldy heart.

*C*hapter 38

We Need to Put a Little Bucket in You, Okay?

According to the doctors, although they had already removed the fluid from my lungs twice, the liquid was still building up. Even though I was not happy about having a contraption inserted into my body, the doctors strongly believed that by adding a drain that looked like a tiny bucket inserted in my belly, that would drain all the water that the leukemia cells insisted on proliferating in my lungs. I didn't know how exactly the leukemia cells worked, but I imagined them to be like those little lactobacillus that I used to add to some milk, and the following day I had some yummy yogurt to drink. The only difference was that with the yogurt, we knew that if milk was put therein, it increased; as for the cells, no one knew the reason why it was still building up, and nobody knew where they were coming from.

I prayed a lot and asked God to take the lead on that new mini-surgery, as the doctor called it. I woke up very early, had breakfast, and anxiously waited for the nurses who would take me to the room where they would place the new "bucket" in me. When one of the nurses came in, I realized my situation was complicated; even though I felt strong, the nurse said that I couldn't walk or even roll in wheelchair. Instead, I was taken as I lay in my own bed. When the nurses were wheeling me to my room, I saw the leukemia team that was in charge of me in front of my door. They were discussing my case when I heard Dr. D.D. ask, "Are they taking Da Silva for an x-ray?" A younger doctor replied, "No, today she is scheduled to have the drain inserted so that it will remove the fluid in her lungs." I nodded with a smile and was taken to the second floor where they would do the mini-surgery.

While the nurses were taking me to the second floor, I was paying close attention to the importance of each painting on the walls, hoping to teleport myself into them. I also carefully observed the beauty of the bright Christmas ornaments. For some reason, they seemed much more beautiful than any other decoration, any other year—perhaps because I did not know if I would ever see them again. It is amazing how the angle from which you observe objects changes how you perceive things around you; since I was lying down, I tried to admire corners of the walls that I hadn't noticed before when I was still able to walk the halls. I felt a sensation of weakness and incapability. I knew that I could walk; however, after a cancer diagnosis, you are no longer in charge of what you can or cannot do. You wisely let others take control, and I knew that if the doctors said that I had to be wheeled, wheeled I would be. I felt that they were doing the best they could do to help me survive. Slowly, I was learning that it was okay to not be in control; perhaps that was one lesson I had to learn on my cancer path.

Upon reaching the operation room, one of the doctors once again explained to me how "fun" the procedure would be. Between you and me, who would want to have a bucket attached to his/her belly? How does that equate to fun? The doctor kept emphasizing that I would have a small one, but for crying out loud, who cares about its size? I think we can all agree that nobody in their right mind would ask for it as their Christmas present.

The doctor said that in a few minutes they would begin the surgery. And there I was, alone, surrounded by a frightening silence. I squinted and started praying with all the faith I had, just asking God to not let me suffer a lot. Somehow my prayers were heard: a miracle happened!

After anxiously waiting for over one hour for the torture to begin, one of the doctors, who had spoken to me before, entered the room.

"Mrs. Da Silva?"

"Yeah! Can we start already?" (At this point in my life, I did not care about being polite anymore.)

"Actually, your doctor decided not to do the procedure."

"What do you mean? They will not do it anymore? Why? Not that I am dying to be sliced up, but this sounds very crazy! I have been anxiously lying down for one hour. I am sweating here, wondering how the surgery will be. Why did the doctors change their minds?"

"We sincerely apologize for the inconvenience. We had already received the okay to start your surgery when your doctor said that we could not go through with it. The team leader, Dr. D.D., after discussing the matter with the team, decided that the surgery would not be necessary, at least not for now."

"Then I'll have to undergo this surgery but at another time. Is that right?"

"No, the doctors believe that with the chemotherapy that you are taking, the liquid in your lungs will stop increasing, so they have decided that it is better to wait a little longer."

"Well, I'm thrilled with this news!"

It was an inexplicable feeling to know that I would not feel pain simply because someone had decided that it was the "right thing to do." I was wheeled back to my room, and the view of pictures on the walls and the Christmas decoration was outstanding; I paid close attention to every Christmas bell and bow on the wall. I felt that it was a sign that God was by my side and that the impossible could happen. I learned that I had to let things take their course, so I just left everything in God's hands and hoped that He would continue to amaze me with more good news.

$\mathcal{C}$hapter 39

Unforgettable Moments with my Parents

None of us were prepared to fight against this disease. But seriously, who would be ready for it? There are no directions to follow; we just do what we feel is right at the moment, and we hope we are making the right move. But I have to say I have some fond memories about the time we spent in the hospital. Cancer takes a lot of things away from our lives, but it does bring all the best people closer to you. Some of these memories are described below.

My father had brought his English translation book from Brazil, and from day one, he walked back and forth with a book from a school where I had taught English in Brazil many years ago. He was always "talking" to the nurses, or better yet, practicing speaking his few words with the nurses, and they somehow were always interested in helping him learn new words. To be honest, I still don't know how they communicated, but they became good friends. My father showed the first page of the book to them and said loudly and clearly, "'To drink' is *beber*, okay? To eat is *comer*. Repeat with me, amiga! Now, it's your turn. You teach me, okay?" The nurses read some words from the book, and my dad attentively repeated the new words. I believe my dad was trying to improve his pronunciation; the nurses carefully corrected his Brazilian accent, and in the end, we all laughed. After watching them so many times, I learned that they did not need to speak each other's language; they spoke a universal language of love, humor, and respect.

It was also funny to see my father facing his first winter in New York. He thought he could take it well. One day, we had a freezing temperature, and he cheerfully said, "Hey, guys, I'll go for a walk in Central Park, and I will be back soon, okay?"

"But, Dad, it's freezing outside! Today is below zero, and you are wearing these thin pants. I don't think you will be able to stand the cold! Just stay in!"

"Oh, stop it! It is totally fine! It is not even so cold out!"

He waved to us and confidently went to go on his expedition in Central Park. Five minutes later, my father entered the room, his nose red like Rudolph and his teeth chattering. We laughed our asses off with his comment: "Bbbbrrrrrrrr! Darn it! This is no joke, guys! I think I am in Alaska. I felt like I was completely naked out there. I wish I could be in the roasting-hot sun in Brazil right now."

On another occasion, he was walking by my room when he found a picture of one of the doctors on the ground. Desperately, he asked, "What is this picture of your doctor doing on the ground, Fabiana?"

"Oh, Dad, don't worry. He only gave it to me so I would not forget his name."

"For God's sake, Fabiana! The dedicated young doctor comes here to see you early in the morning every day, and suddenly, what do I see? What do I see? His picture laying on the dirty ground! This is not right, daughter! Ah, you have to treat this guy with more affection. Gee! This is the man who will save you with God's help! Let's put his picture here in this frame close to Richard and you! I will put him right there in the middle. It will look good, and he will be happy and look after you very well."

Every day, my father carefully adjusted the picture of the doctor, leaving it well centered in the frame, dusting it and sometimes even talking to the muted portrait—that is, until one morning, the team of the doctors came in to see how I was doing. One of the leading physicians looked at the big cork frame where all my photos were displayed and said, "Mrs. Da Silva, I only have one question for you."

"Sure, sure, Doc. What is it?"

"Why in the midst of so many beautiful photos have you decided to ruin your photo collage with a photo of our intern, right there in the middle?"

I explained my dad's reasoning for adorning the collage with a picture of the intern at its center. My dad mistakenly thought that the intern was my primary oncologist, Dr. D.D., and that Dr. D.D. was like an intern who was trying to learn about the new kinds of leukemia treatment. He may have been confused because Dr. D.D. always came to examine me with the intern. Dr. D.D. would always listen to me first, and then the intern would listen to my lungs as well. Before knowing that the younger doctor was an intern, my father would always grumble when Dr. D.D. examined me. Dad told me that every time my oncologist came to examine me, he thought, *Ah, come on, oldie, take your hands off my daughter! Let the doctor (intern), fresh from college, who knows all the new medicine, take a good listen to my daughter.* When I told the team that my dad thought that the intern was my primary doctor and that Dr. D.D. was an intern, learning on the job, we all burst out laughing, including the intern who had given me his picture. My father, who did not understand a word of what I had said, laughed right along with us. Dad just loves a good laugh!

I also have fond memories of my mom. I don't know how I would have fought this disease without her. Every day, we walked laps around the hospital halls, and one day, we decided that our "gym" would be stationed right in front of the elevator. We used to walk nine laps around the reception area, and when we stopped in front of the elevator, we started stretching and even jumping. She turned into my personal trainer and attentively wrote down all of the exercise sessions that we had done every day. I loved her commands: "Lower, daughter! Rise slowly! Try to straighten your back!" I religiously followed all the steps. I just wanted to be well and would have done anything to get out of the hospital. Relatives of other patients, who took the elevator, were looking at us, amazed at our determination. The nurses were also scared to death that I would inadvertently yank the catheter out of my arm.

My mom was also my intercessor. So many times, the nurses came into my room to give me the nightly shots, and they caught us kneeling, holding hands, holding the Bible, crying and asking God to not take my life away. We asked God incessantly to have mercy for our family that was already small; we did not want it to decrease. I felt bad for her, to see her daughter in such a sad situation, and I feared that if God's desire was to take me with Him, her life would be colorless and sad for a long time. We also used the TV as another tool for healing and meditation. There was a channel that played a pleasing sound of falling rain and calming water, and it reminded me of how badly I wanted to be on a beautiful blue beach in Brazil. That sound brought me peace and the assurance that God was there, looking after me through my prayers and my meditations, and I learned to let my soul sink in them.

Meditation time!

My mother also brought several bottles of holy oil from a church that she went to as soon as she learned that I was sick. Everything I had was enough to make me strong enough to take any pain I had to endure. I had my mom, her pure love, her beautiful faith, and her bottles of holy oil that she used to spread all over me—on my forehead, chest, and belly. Not even my legs escaped her oily blessings. Literally, she anointed me from head to toe until she knew I was slippery like an icy road. Before my mom left Brazil, she made sure she had a stock of the blessed oil in her bag. I am not sure how she was not stopped by the security board; if they had checked her, they would have thought she was trafficking oil. Moms are angels sent by God!

$\mathscr{C}$hapter 40

Unforgettable Visits

I started doing a process called visualization. My friend Tarah Welsh taught me how important it was for me to try to see myself well in the future, and she advised me to think of the wonderful things God had in store for me. It was not easy to do when I was tied to a post through which I received a liquid that destroyed the bad cells and, unfortunately, the good ones as well. I closed my eyes and prayed, and after a few seconds of meditating, I could see myself very healthy, beautiful, and happy, wearing a red woolen sweater in front of a fireplace, which I knew I did not have in my house. I realized that since it was just a visualization exercise, I could have everything I wanted. Even a glass of red wine could be added to that scene—something that would be impossible for me to have for at least three years.

I also loved to use my imagination to see Jesus working on my body. I closed my eyes and imagined myself wearing a long, white, silk nightgown. I was in a beautiful field full of green grass, with red fragrant roses around me. In this place I used to run freely, the sun shone on my face, and I knew I had a mission to find Him.

Every time I ran, I found him: Jesus. In these visualizations, he always hugged me like a father who embraces his child. After that, we would walk to a white operating room, where I would lay down on a hospital bed and just wait. I always thought that this part of the visualization was funny. Once we left the beautiful fields, Jesus would have a yellow construction helmet on his head, and he would wink at me and say, "Hey, girl, you are a troublemaker! Since you came in, I haven't had a break!" After that, he started working on my body. With a lot of care, he used a big set of tweezers to pluck out some cancer pebbles around my heart and lungs.

I remember saying, "Oh, dear Jesus, I am sure you are very tired and the job is not easy at all, but please work on my body from eleven p.m. to seven a.m., because at seven in the morning, the other doctors always arrive, so they can do the day shift."

Jesus

Our Lady of Salette

In these visualizations, I came to see Our Lady of Fatima, of Aparecida, and of Salette. I always thought she would intercede for her Son to help me. And suddenly, with my eyes closed, I could see a strong flash, and then her image started forming. At first, light lines outlined her frame, and then her shape grew stronger. She always used to visit me at night. She came with her white or blue dress and a crystal crown or pink flowers. Those images brought a lot of peace and a certainty that I would be okay no matter what was going to happen. I always felt comforted by her presence. I felt I was protected by her and her Son, Jesus. I was certain that I was doing my part, and the rest I would have to leave to the doctors' and God's hands so that they could hold me and not let me fall into dark, torturous corners.

Human visits were also very important to me. The teachers at the school where I work created a "Fabi Agenda" and made it available online, with access to everyone who wanted to visit me. With this agenda, they made sure that everyone knew if I was free to receive visitors or if I already had somebody visiting me in my room. How thoughtful and caring were they! The truth is that during the twenty-five days I was there, I had friends and colleagues coming in to visit me the entire day and night. It was so good to feel pure and genuine love! I have no doubt that the medication I took was important for my recovery, but getting all that positive energy and receiving prayers from across the globe made me believe that I could beat the unknown demon I was fighting against.

The visits brought a special touch to my heart. The majority of them made me very happy, but some visitors, without knowing it, made me realize that what I was facing was no joke; I could see in their scared, sad eyes that what I was going through was not something easy to face.

Some visitors were extremely excited; they were the ones who sang songs in languages that I could not comprehend, but so what? Music is universal, so I enjoyed the beautiful performance they put on. While they sang, my parents, Richard, and I tried desperately to understand what the song was about and the simultaneous translations that were done by one of the members of the family. My room turned into the city of Babylon, a real mix of languages: one person sang in Ukrainian, the other translated the lyrics to Richard and me in English, and then I tried my best to translate the song to my parents in Portuguese. I remember one song was about a lion in a beautiful field; I couldn't really understand how the lion and I were connected, but we all carried on, enjoying our private performance. When the singer reached the highest notes, I was grateful that I did not have any roommates that night; if I did, she would have probably complained about the revelry.

Some of my best friends who used to visit me were pregnant: Priscilla and Renata. They were both expecting girls. Carol and Fabibella were expecting boys. Even though Fabibella lives in Florida, she became so present through phone calls that it seemed like she was there by my side. One of these friends learned that it was not good for pregnant women to visit me because the staff on my floor or I could pass radiation to their babies. Oh, that news was devastating to me! I would never want my friends' babies to be born with health conditions because of me. It was difficult, but I made a strong decision: for the sake of all their babies and their own safety, none of my pregnant friends would be allowed to visit me.

One day, Kate, my boss, came to see me and asked me, "How are your friends doing? How are Olli, Priscilla, and Carol doing?"

"Olli and Cris are doing great, but I haven't seen Carol in a while. I thought it was best for Carol not to come over because I learned from another friend that it could be very dangerous for those who are pregnant to be in a place where there are cancer patients."

"What do you mean? I'm pregnant!"

"Oh, my God! Congratulations, sweetie! I'm so happy for you, but you have to leave this building right now."

"This cannot be true! I'll be back soon. I'll let you know."

Minutes later, she came back with her beautiful, smiling, and angelical face. "I just talked to the nurses, and they assured me that there are no objections to pregnant women coming to this building. They even said that there are nurses who are pregnant, and they work on this floor without a problem. I am sure that pregnant women should certainly not go inside the x-ray rooms, but it would just be crazy to do that too, right? And the other girls, are they still coming here?"

"Priscilla has already asked her doctor, and she said that her doctor said that there was no risk at all, and he said she could visit me as much as she wanted. She keeps coming to visit me every day; her belly is huge now, and it is so cute to be able to see her and her big tummy. Renata, from Connecticut, is almost five months pregnant. She came to visit me, and Fabibella is now six months pregnant, but since she has been living in Florida, they are both totally out of danger," I said with laughter.

Kate, who was four months pregnant, and Priscilla, who was eight months pregnant at the time, continued to visit me throughout my treatment. During snow, when it was not snowing, and even when it was freezing cold, they did their best to be with me. There they were almost every day, always with great joy, with fun lipstick, scarves, and anything else they thought would make me feel good. And most importantly, it is with great joy that I write today that both babies were beautiful and very healthy, and they are two huge blessings in our lives.

I had so much luck with the friends that God put in my life. My room was always crowded with formidable, smart friends from all over the world. Ollie is a good friend of mine from Brazil who worked as a nurse in Westchester, and I loved how she was always in the halls, talking to the nurses of the hospital, making sure that I was taking the right dosage of each medicine. Ms. Kathy, an English professor from Fordham University, always came to visit me. She always had a kind word for me and even brought pumpkin pie that had the beloved fragrance of home.

My colleagues were always present as well. Tania Kawabi, an economics teacher, and her son, Joseph Kawabi, the math teacher, were always around. Even though their subjects required logical and rational reasoning, we discussed the spiritual soothing. Every time they came to visit me, we made a circle, put our hands together, and prayed for my recovery. We always prayed in communion; everyone said whatever they had in their heart, and I felt that my little room was filled with the power of the Holy Spirit. Whenever they left my room, I had the full assurance that my room had been restored, and I felt a great peace.

To my luck, the visits were nonstop. The Maurillos sisters, the sweet Spanish and English teachers, always came to see me with words of hope and pink roses that made my moldy heart swell with happiness. They gave me one little angel that is now one of my Christmas ornaments. The newly married Miss Kanta, the Thai and English teacher, and Ms. Pang, the Chinese teacher, both looked at my wedding photos displayed on my table and somehow understood why I needed to have those pictures there; perhaps they understood that those pictures symbolized the happiness that I had and that I did not know if I would even be able to have it again. Ms. Johnsen, the Norwegian teacher, and Mrs. Hanh, the Vietnamese teacher, also made my days more peaceful. Ms. Jeannie, the drama teacher, and Mr. Lopo, the English teacher, with his lovely wife, Anne, also added to my days. With their constant visits, they allowed me to travel to several parts of the world that I didn't know much about, and most importantly, I was able to travel to their souls and find out who they really were. We were not together for professional development or for a lunch meeting; rather, we were together because they cared about me, and I needed to see them because I also cared about them. With every visit, I realized that love has no boundaries. I felt privileged to have them with me. They all sculpted time from their busy schedules to ensure they were there for me. I have to say that I still hate cancer, but it certainly showed me the beauty of feeling real love and having deep, meaningful conversations. Cancer showed me that I was loved in a way that I had never felt before.

The most philosophical subject teachers did not miss out: Mr. Britan, a theory of knowledge teacher, who is very funny and an expert on all topics came, as well as Mr. Jee, an SAT teacher, both came with books, cards, flowers, and fruit. My room had more knowledge inside it than any library in the world. I do not only speak of subject knowledge but also human knowledge. I realized how lucky I was to have all those amazing people close to me every day in the teachers' lounge, and I never knew how special they all were. Even though I saw them every day, we barely had time to sit and talk about deep topics, to know who we were, what we wanted in our lives, and to discover our dreams or frustrations. To me, it was clear that all of those who came to see me taught me more than any school in the world could teach: life lessons, love lessons, caring lessons. We always laughed a lot, and it was good to feel that they believed in my recovery and interceded for it. During these visits, I also received Havaianas slippers and Monica's Gang comic books from my super friend and coordinator, Will.

The literature teacher, Charlie, visited me too. Her classroom was adjacent to mine, and after a lot of meetings and lesson planning, our friendship grew stronger. I had a special affection for her. When I had hectic evenings where I had a bunch of homework to correct and lesson plans to do, I used to scream her name, "Charlieeeeeeeeeeeeeeeee!" and she would always come help me and listen to my crazy stories. She has a heart of gold. She is one of those rare people that if they are in your life, you can't let them go. When she came to visit me, she brought with her a beautiful purple crystal that her grandmother had given to her when she was little. That gesture of love made me speechless. I knew that the gift had a special sentimental value for her, and without thinking twice, she gave it to me. I was stunned by the abundance of genuine love that my friends poured out to me. I needed the energy of everyone and everything, so I accepted it, but I promised her that as soon as I got better, I would give it back to her.

A special necklace

The Ukrainian teacher, Roxanne, with her unique and exuberant way of being, always came with funny jokes, songs, laughter, her family, and a special Russian saint, which I promised to return as soon as the madness was over. The Russian economics teacher, Poliana, always appeared with presents, such as earphones with Russian dolls, a huge loaf cake, and many other items. Ah, my parents and I will never forget the scents of the fruits and the softness of the panettone.

My friend and literature teacher Ms. Tarah Welsh would always visit me. She taught me the importance of breathing correctly. We sat on my bed that moved up and down so that the patient did not have impaired circulation. It looked more like a toy, or a ride from Six Flags, and if not for the noise, I would even say it fit well into our Zen moment. Namaste! Ms. Tarah spoke softly with a calming voice but a firm tone. "Close one nostril, inhale everything you wish for, and then exhale what you do not want in your life. Let's do it again, Fabi." She always surprised me with presents that touched my heart: a frame about friendship, a crystal cross, a Christmas lampshade, and one of the most unforgettable presents—her son's visit! I always called him my little prince. He gave me a tiny stone that said, "Be Strong," and in times of great distress, it was this stone that I held on to. Tarah, in one of her visits, also brought one of our students, Luli, who assured me that I would be fine. She gave me a medal of a Brazilian saint that I was named after, Nossa Senhora Aparecida, and she said that she would certainly put me in her prayers. I was spoiled by it all. I was lucky to be part of a group of teachers, administrators, and students who were such kind, beautiful people inside and out.

The visits never stopped, and I am so grateful for each one of them. Crislaine and her mother did everything they could to see me at night. She left her son, only a few months old, with her husband and always made sure she was there at night. Eliane always appeared also; she caught a train and found a way to be there with me. I will always be grateful for everyone's effort.

My friend Cilene also taught me a lot. She is an elementary school teacher with whom I did my internship in a school in the Westchester area for six months. I learned so much from her, not only about ESL and methodologies but about life! We became friends because of my internship, and I am glad we kept contact after it ended. A few days after I was admitted, she came to visit me. This time, she didn't teach me about ESL methodologies or the best SIOP strategies; she came to teach me something that was crucial to my recovery: nutrition! She taught me a lot about the importance of helping my body heal itself. She kept explaining that I would need to help my body recover from all the nutrients I was losing every time I had chemo. On the same day, she also gave me a peculiar present: two buckets with a string attached. I have to confess, I had no idea what they were, but I thanked her and gave her a tight hug. I knew she was an expert on nutrition, so I knew they would help me somehow.

She said quietly, "I am so glad you accepted the enemas. Have you used them before?"

A little afraid of what these enemas entailed, I apologetically said, "No, excuse my ignorance, but I have never used it, and to be sincere, I do not know even what that is."

She came very close to me and whispered in a soft voice, "How do I explain it? It is actually a coffee to clear your intestines."

I noticed that she started getting red.

"Well, I'm not a huge coffee drinker, but if you think it will save me, I can certainly gulp it down without a problem."

By her facial expression, I noticed that she was a bit uneasy. She continued, "Did you see the one with the pipe, right?"

"Yes, I did. How does it work? Is it a special straw that I will need to drink it from?"

"So … this coffee has to be consumed from your behind."

Still confused with the new coffee-drinking system, I asked, "What do you mean by drinking coffee from behind?"

To my surprise, she stared at me and kept pointing to my behind, which made everything crystal clear! She did not need to explain herself anymore. I immediately started imagining a not-so-pleasant afternoon. After the cancer diagnosis, I knew things wouldn't be the same anymore, but I thought I would be able to drink coffee through my upper hole and not my lower one. I tried to digest everything I heard, but this procedure did not make sense to me. It felt like I had been abducted from earth and now participated in alien conversations and suggestions, but that was my new norm: eggs, buckets, drains, tubes, and buckets somewhere else. The need to adjust was surreal!

I knew that all the information I was given was for my own good. Other teacher friends, such as Melinda from Ecuador and Estrella from Mexico, were amazed with all the great information Cilene gave and believed that I should listen to her carefully in order to complete the treatment successfully. As for the enema, they had heard about it, but they had never done it. I was skeptical about using the enema; I kept thinking that if I drank from the lower hole, it would come out from the upper hole, and I was already tired of throwing up, so I decided to keep the buckets. I swore that if I got worse, I would use the pail and hoses every day if necessary—but not for the time being. The enema was one remedy that I decided not to follow.

Chapter 41

Canker Sores

After some chemotherapy, I learned the paradoxical feelings I had about a medicine that was supposed to heal my physical pain, but while it healed, it also caused hair loss and emotional upheaval—not to mention the frequent cramps, vomiting, and diarrhea. The doctors warned me that I would have to get ready for the canker sores that would soon part of my battle. When they mentioned it, I did not take them seriously. After all, what could be worse than two daily injections in the stomach? You guessed it—canker sores!

You must be wondering why canker sores would be a big deal when you are undergoing a cancer treatment; they don't hurt that much. You may be thinking this is nothing compared to everything else I described. I agreed, until one day I woke up and realized that I didn't have one—but thousands of canker sores in my mouth, and some were perhaps hidden in my throat. It became worse when I realized that even my saliva hurt. I could barely talk and probably sounded like a drunken old lady who had no idea what she was talking about. I learned that life was manageable with one canker sore, but with a whole world of canker sores in my mouth, I could barely move my lips, let alone smile.

I woke up, ready to order my favorite breakfast, "make your own omelet." I read it from the fancy hospital menu. The previous days, I read that sentence with pleasure, but on canker sore day, I gained no happiness in reading it. I was barely able to speak, but I decided to make an effort to call the kitchen to inform them how I would like my omelet prepared.

"Please, I would like to make my own omel ... omelet." By the time I finished saying the word, I was already drooling.

Patiently, the receptionist said, "I'm sorry, but I am having some trouble understanding your request, lady!"

"My mele, which minh omel ..." Drooling again, I could not pronounce the words.

"Ah yes. What would you like on your omelet?"

"On my mele, pease bacon, mozzarella cheese, and spin, like what Popeye eat, right? Okay? Oh, and two sausa ..." That's all I could say without drooling.

"The connection is getting cut. So, just to confirm, madam, you would like bacon, tomato,

mozzarella cheese, and spinach, right? And two sausages will accompany that. Would you like anything else, madam?"

"Yes, yes. A strawb iogur and a bisna and a co with shoe ..."

"All right, madam. A strawberry yogurt, a biscuit, and coffee with sugar, right?"

Once they brought in the tray, I felt like crying. The scent of my favorite omelet filled the entire room, but because of the chemotherapy, I was too nauseous to eat it. Not to mention that, because of its delicious smell, my mouth was watering, which made the canker sores burn even more. I became a part of a duel in which I struggled against myself: I wanted to eat, but I just could not do so. So, with great pleasure, I gave my breakfast to my parents. I was sad because I could not eat it, but I was very happy for them because they were able to eat my super breakfast. It was a pleasure to see them eat! I tried two bites, but the sting of the canker sores would not let me go on. For the first time in my life, I cried in pain for having food and not being able to eat.

I also began to better understand why oncologists always reminded cancer patients to do their best to not lose too much weight during the first phase of treatment. My doctors kept reminding me that even though I was in pain and nauseous, eating and hydrating were crucial so that I could successfully get to the end of the treatment. Before I had the canker sores or felt so nauseous, I wondered, *Why would a cancer patient not eat when we know it is such a crucial part of the treatment?* Life quickly answered: people did not stop eating because they simply didn't feel like it but because some days were so bad that they could not put anything in their mouths.

As for the canker sores, the nurses helped me a lot by teaching me the importance of rinsing out my mouth with salty water as often as I could. Something that also helped me a lot at this stage was a pink remedy, which I called "pink magic liquid." I took it fifteen minutes before eating, and like magic, my throat would be completely numb, so I was able to enjoy a meal without feeling any pain.

No eating for me!

$\mathcal{C}$hapter 42

The Pastor

With each passing day, I realized that my case was way more serious than I expected. Everyone who came to my room had to disinfect their hands with sanitizer when they came in and when they left, and they also had to wear masks while they were in my room. Back then, I thought they were doing it to protect themselves because I may have been contagious, but then I learned that I was the one they were trying to protect. After all, I was the one who had very low immunity due to all the chemo I was taking in.

I was always open to having visits from anyone who wanted to share some words of encouragement or support. I cannot stress enough that my friends and family members played an essential role in my recovery, but at that point, I was so desperate for any word that consoled me that any stranger who had anything positive to share was welcome in my room! One day, a very tall, well-dressed African American man who had vivid eyes stopped by my room; he said he was a pastor from a Christian church nearby and asked if he could come in. I immediately welcomed him in; after all, since he was a pastor, I felt I had so many things to ask him.

Since the doctors did not seem to have a lot of answers, maybe a man who probably had a closer relationship with God would be able to give me a better explanation as to why I was here, why I had to endure this mess.

While I stared at him, I felt that his eyes transmitted peace. I was not sure if he would be the person who would have all the answers to my questions; however, I knew he would listen to me without being judgmental. In a dulcet tone, he said that he was there to listen to me and to comfort my heart. He started off by saying, "I am all ears, my sister. What troubles your heart?"

"Well, Pastor, I have so many questions that I do not even know how to begin."

"Do not worry about anything. Feel free to ask anything you want. I am here to listen to you. Open your heart."

I took a very deep breath and began to speak about everything I had in my mind.

"Look, Pastor, I am here today in this hospital bed. I can barely speak because I started my chemotherapy, and my mouth is full of canker sores. The truth is that I am here today, and although I have already accepted my condition, I cannot understand why this is happening to me. And to be quite honest, I do not know if there is a reason. What I know is that two or three weeks ago, I was very happy. I had a normal life; I worked as a teacher, and I am a newlywed. In fact, I was only married for seven months when I was diagnosed with leukemia. So, if I may ask you, Pastor, why is it that I do not have the chance to live my life with my husband? Why would God want to see me separated from my husband, or why did He have to let us get married in the first place? Would it be fair, Pastor, if I am chosen to die from this surreptitious disease?"

Crying and begging for answers, I continued, "Pastor, why do I have to be the one wondering if it will be possible for me to have a child when there are so many mothers who never wanted to have their children, and even though some end up having them, they mistreat or abuse them? Some opt for aborting it just so they don't need to change their lifestyles. How come they are the ones who get to live a normal life? I don't mean to judge them for what they have chosen, but if they could make their choices, why can't I have the choice of being a mom? Being a mom was something that I always dreamed of, and I never felt that this would be something that I would have to question. However, I just spoke to my doctor, who was very clear about my chances of having kids while I am on this treatment; if I insisted on having a child, I would either have to freeze my eggs and not be able to complete my treatment, or I could decide to continue my treatment, but maybe I will become infertile. Is it something that God would want his daughter to go through?

"Why me? I always had a healthy lifestyle and watched what I ate. I never smoked, and now I am the one diagnosed with cancer. Meanwhile, some people who try to kill themselves every day with the use of tobacco, alcohol, and drugs are well. Does that make sense to you, Pastor? Why do I have to go through all this pain? Is it fair to my husband? How about my parents? They had to fly all the way from Brazil to help me; they will have to spend Christmas, the celebration of Jesus's birth, in this hospital, while the rest of the world celebrates it outside with friends, great food, and presents. All we are asking for is the gift of health. Is it too much to ask for?"

I thought about the contradiction of life. I was sentenced to death by a cancer diagnosis, which made me strive to live so much so that I fought for my life with all my strength. Others were living their lives without the slightest inkling of the fragility and beauty of life; they were the ones who tried to kill themselves with their addictions, such as smoking crack. Some other questions also invaded my thoughts: What had I done that incurred this death sentence as a "fair" punishment? I was not a saint—neither are you, dear reader, I am sorry to break it to you—but I wouldn't wish a disease like this on anyone, not even to some corrupt politicians who we know damage so many people's lives. The truth of the matter is that nobody deserves to have cancer!

The way in which I articulated all these questions and assertions seemed as if they were scripted, as if I had written a discourse and waited for someone who had the courage and audacity to try to answer them. The poor old pastor looked at me in dismay. He even apologized for … I don't even know what. He started looking at my wedding photos that I had hung on the wall, and when I thought he would answer everything with a magic word, he began to cry. It was hard to believe that he was also moved by my story. Perhaps he also thought about the atrocities that come with this disease, but how could we challenge the will of God? Never! And after wiping his tears, he composed himself and asked if he could pray for me. And there, the two of us, holding each other's hands and crying, called on God to have mercy on me and to come down with His power and take anything that did not belong to Him. With beautiful words, he calmed me down and left the room still crying, shaking his head, and wiping his tears with a tissue as if he did not believe what he had just heard.

As time went by, I learned that all my questions would be answered. One of the first lessons I learned was that no matter what happens, God would always be by my side; love would never leave me, and I would regain the strength that I never knew I had. I began to understand my story; unfortunately, I was not the only one impacted by this disease, but I had the power to turn it into something positive for me, my family, and my friends. I did not have a solution for the problem, but how I dealt with it was in my hands. I had always been a positive person, so I decided to be even more optimistic. At that moment, I made an important decision: the moments of sadness would be no greater than my days of joy! Perhaps my days were slim, and they were certainly very special to me, too special to be wasting them, weeping over what my life could have been. The only thing I knew for sure was that I was alive that day. I had no idea if I would be able to have one extra day on earth, so waiting it crying rivers would be a waste of my time.

Chapter 43

Unusual Patients

After spending several days in the hospital, I began to realize that some patients could be characters from my book or any other book. There were those who cried more, those who complained about everything, and the apathetic ones who were confined by their diagnosis and their prognosis. There were some who were very friendly and did not seem to be discouraged by the miserable situation we all found ourselves in. However, there was one particular patient who really caught my attention. I have named him the Sportsman. He was tall, black, and appeared to be strong. I would say he was about forty years old. What impressed me the most about his character was his insistence to live. He was the only one on our floor who did not wear the blue and white hospital gown. He was always wearing a cool pair of black Adidas shorts, a white tank top, and a headband. He also did not wear sandals or fleece slippers like the other patients and I used to wear; he had some super-cool running shoes.

Despite being tied to a post like me and every other hospital buddy, he ran the halls. I'm not saying that he walked, and the rest of us did not. He literally ran around and around. He ran like a businessman who was in a hurry to close a big deal on Wall Street's New York Stock Exchange. He ran with the determination of reaching the finish line; this finish line was invisible to us cancer patients, but he still aimed for it. We, the cancer patients, could only see the finish line of life, which was more ominous to us than to others. His goal was not to reach this finish line but to reach another, in defiance of this one. Perhaps this was the strategy that he used to keep so strong. He did not see himself as a sick person, despite being surrounded by patients depleted of energy from the chemotherapy; he used all his energy to enjoy every second granted to him because he had learned every moment of our lives was unique, so he had no other option than to do what made him happy—run.

Unconsciously, our marathon runner gave us the message that if we really wanted to do something, we should not worry about what others thought about it. And if his passion was running, why wouldn't he do it in a hospital? Perhaps some people would think he was crazy. Perhaps he would have to hide from the nurses or patients who followed the norm of walking in the corridor. This patient showed me that originality was everything and that I should not stop doing the things that I loved because I had cancer. I could do anything I wanted if I believed in myself, in my strength, and in God who strengthened me and blessed me with His continuous lessons. At that point, I felt that my mission was not to keep those lessons with me but to share what I was living with, with healthy people, so that they were not afraid of being who they were or doing what they liked to do because others may disapprove. I understood that some of the limitations we have are set in our minds due to the circumstances we are living in; however, our inner strength helps us break and over-come barriers that once seemed so insurmountable. So, I could cry and lament for myself, or I could fight every day for what I believed was right for me, to live as the person I wanted to be. Whatever you are going through, remember that how you deal with the circumstances—not the circumstances themselves—is what truly defines you.

*C*hapter 44

What a Headache!

Everything was going well until the moment my doctor came to see me.

"How are you, my dear?"

I was always very happy to see him. Every day, I received him warmly, with hugs and a lot of jokes.

"Dr. D.D., I was just talking about you. So far, so good. Actually, not that good. I've been having a lot of headaches lately. I had one last night and another this morning."

"Hmm, not a good sign. Could it have moved to your head already?"

"I am sorry, Dr. D.D., but what could have moved to my head?"

"Unfortunately, with this type of cancer, we have to be very careful to ensure that the cancer cells do not go to your head. We'll have to start with the chemotherapy injections in your spine as soon as possible. They are called IT, which stands for intrathecal methotrexate. We need to act quickly!

"Oh, Doctor, please, what are you talking about? Injections in my spine? I am really sorry, but I cannot take any more injections. I am already taking two in my belly every night and day."

"Yeah, I know, but we have to be proactive. This type of cancer spreads very fast. The IT injections do not hurt that much; it's just a little prick in the back. They place the chemotherapy in your spine, and then it goes straight to your brain."

Needless to say, I thought very little of this platitude that the doctors used to calm us down, "It does not hurt that much." With all due respect, and I understand he was trying to be kind, but the injection would not go into his back but in mine. I knew I would feel the bite of a snake. And, the worst thing was not the little prick but the idea of having somebody insert a needle in my spinal cord. I would rather have a massage; enough with the shots already! But I knew that I had to follow the doctor's orders for my own good. I would have to hold on because my will to live was stronger than my fear of becoming a pin cushion.

$\mathscr{C}$hapter 45

Christmas Eve! Ho-Ho-Ho! She Got the Wrong Hole!

$\mathbf{B}$ack in Brazil, our Christmas evenings were always very cheerful: lots of music, food, drinks, and of course, something we never lacked, lots of joy! But, for obvious reasons, our Christmas Eve of 2013 would be way different. I tried to keep positive, but at 5 a.m. on December 24, I was awakened by a nurse with a curt "Good morning. I need to draw your blood, Ms. Da Silva!" It was the same nurse who had given me a shot in the belly hours earlier, with so much force that the moment she finished giving me the shot, I told my parents that I had never felt so much pain from one shot. When I saw that she was the one who was tasked with drawing my blood, I was kind of scared, but I thought, *What could go wrong?* It was only blood drawn from my catheter, and I was so used to this daily procedure that I decided to just close my eyes and think about a pleasant future and reminisce about a festive past. I started to remember all the wonderful Christmases I had had with my family—until I heard the nurse saying, "Oh, no!"

Nurses are familiar with gruesome sights that would make most pass out from fright, so when they scream in fear, you know with certainty that the incident is truly horrifying. When I opened my eyes, what came into view was one of the most striking scenes I had ever lived through in the hospital. The once-pristine white wall adjacent to my bed was now adorned with a splattering of my blood. This inept nurse pulled the wrong syringe from my arm, so my room, which was once so beautiful, full of colorful balloons and decorated with Christmas lights and small pine trees, quickly turned into a canvas that would intrigue the great Sherlock Holmes. My pink robe and my stuffed animals, gifts from my friends, were dappled with red dots. It seemed like all of us had just witnessed a homicide.

The nurse, embarrassed, quickly apologized and within a few seconds asked for help. As soon as the other nurses came in, they stared at me and at the new Jackson Pollack wall decoration in disbelief. They started scrubbing the walls and changing the bloodstained sheets. With tears in my eyes, I stared at my father. I did not want to cry over spilled milk—or blood in this case— but I could not believe that our first Christmas in New York had begun in such a tragic way. My father, too incredulous, stared at the nurse. I know that if he spoke English, he would have had a serious conversation with her, but he simply glared at her and kept on giving her what I call the death look. She knew what his look meant; no translation was necessary. My dad and I both had the same questions in mind: Why is this happening today, my favorite holiday of the year? Haven't we suffered enough?

Besides this whole mess, what upset me the most was to see my three wedding pictures, which adorned the board next to me, marked with blood. I kept staring at them and could not hold back the tears anymore. The nurse, noticing my despair, tried cleaning the pictures with disinfectant, which left one of the photos opaque and lifeless. I feared that that picture was the representation of what my life would be from that diagnosis on. I was afraid that the damaged picture symbolized that my marriage and all my happy moments were slowly vanishing. In real life, what was slowly eating me alive was a disease that invaded my body. It was hard to believe that I was the one diagnosed with it; it was hard not only for my parents, my husband, and my friends to understand and accept it, but I could not comprehend it either.

$\mathcal{C}$hapter 46

Happy Moments and Unexpected Visits

The negative moments of that day did not overshadow the happiness. Santa Claus came to visit all the patients, and it is kind of weird to confess, but I was thrilled when old Saint Nick came into my room. It is incredible how we get so sentimental when we are ill. Seeing Santa Claus and his helpers brought me back to my childhood; I felt like an eager five-year-old girl who was about to see Santa for the first time ever! I knew that he was a fantastical figure, but inside my heart, I wanted to believe that perhaps he would give us our most desired gift, the cure for cancer. Maybe I was asking for too much from Santa Claus, but since everyone always asks for the impossible, why not ask for health?

Ding-dong, ding-dong! I heard the bells ringing in the hospital halls. A Christmas carol was coming close to my room. I quickly sat on the bed so that Santa could see that I was ready to welcome him. I don't know if it was the emotion due to the uncertainty of having other Christmases, but I felt a tremendous happiness to be in a hospital where we could celebrate the birth of Jesus with great joy and enthusiasm. When the music got closer to my door, I was surprised by a group of teenagers wearing red and green striped elf clothes, singing "Feliz Navidad" in my room. I broke down and started crying and laughing. It was so great to see them singing cheerful songs, flooding the halls with hope. I enjoyed the whole song and loved their encore performance.

My father also enjoyed their music and excitedly sang "Feliz Navidad" with his crazy few Spanish words that he either knew or had just invented. Suddenly, we heard, "Ho-ho-ho!" It was him! My father excitedly said, "Hurry up, hurry up! Get off your bed and sit in the armchair. Santa is coming!" I guess the Christmas carol made me so excited that I simply jumped off my bed and sat on the armchair. As soon as I sat down, Santa stepped into my room. Santa Claus gave me the warmest hug that he could have given me. He had a beautiful red bag full of presents, including a baby blue scarf made of silk, which perfectly matched one of my dresses. Santa also gave me a lot of lipstick in various colors, a fancy dress, a summer hat, and many brands of overpriced creams, fragrant perfumes, candies, and even toys.

I felt much loved by my new visitors. I was very happy, not because they gave me presents but because it was so good to feel their joy and see that they were not afraid of being in my room. While my disease was not contagious, their love was. These volunteers of love had one goal that day, to put a smile on each patient's face, and they certainly succeeded. They managed not only to put smiles on our faces but also to facilitate the springing of happy tears from our eyes. It happened not only to me but also to my roommate, who, despite being older than me, happily showed her parents the gifts she had received from Santa. Perhaps those toys brought forth fond memories, but I listened to her and shared in her tears and waves of laughter.

Another visit broke my routine that week as well, two dogs with peculiar names, iPhone and Samsung. IPhone was a fancy chihuahua with a diamond collar and matching shoes. Samsung, a funny and docile Yorkshire, paraded around in a pink dress that matched the little bow between her perky ears. They were pleasant, and their happiness cheered me up. Even though my roomy had made it quite clear that she did not want the dogs on her side of the room, I welcomed them to my side of our shared dwelling.

I had never imagined seeing dogs in a hospital, but I knew that any visit, especially from those loyal, doe-eyed creatures, was a treat. It was, of course, a healing therapy that made me forget that I was a dreaded sick patient, at least for a few moments. I didn't know who their owners were, but the fact that they had made them available to spend time with cancer patients was really kind. It was so good to feel their warmth on my lap, looking at me mercilessly and without fear, reminding me that I did not have that much time to live.

I had the impression that I was living in a dream, or more accurately a nightmare, but whatever it may be, I wanted to live every moment. I had only one certainty: I had a great desire to live, and all the programs offered by the hospital that could help me in any way, I accepted without any hesitation. I did not know how much time I had left, so I wanted to enjoy every single second: massages, arts and crafts, music therapy, bingo, card games, dominoes, glass painting, wood painting, musical concerts, dog visits, therapists' visits, priests, pastors, rabbis. People of all religions were more than welcome to comfort me in all possible ways, and I welcomed all of them with love and respect, because it was the best thing I could do for them and for me.

I did not deny any type of help from anyone or anything. I knew all their help was beneficial, and I tried to turn each situation, whenever it was possible, into something positive. With time, I also learned that the diagnosis was not my fault or anyone else's, and what I feared the most was to become a bitter person, complaining about my fate and inadvertently ending up making everyone's lives miserable too. I could not do that to my parents, Richard, and my friends. The truth was that it was not easy to stay optimistic when I knew that not even the doctors were quite sure if I would recover from one of the most feared diseases in the world, but with the love of everyone and my inner strength, I knew I would be better off living one day at a time without worrying about my future, because I clearly did not have any control over it; complaining about it would not make my life or anybody else's life easier. Unfortunately, we were all stuck in this nightmare together, and I wanted to do everything I could so that it was less painful for all of us.

Of course, this diagnosis was devastating, but I knew that being negative about it wouldn't make the disease disappear, and staying positive gave me enough strength to face the treatment. My doctors could not grant me a future. I also did not know what was going to happen; therefore, I just had to enjoy those moments, to enjoy every second in the best way I could, and if I could choose how I would take on this battle, smiling through it was more favorable than wallowing. This experience certainly taught me a lot of lessons, one of them being how to let time exist without worrying about every second passing. Through my pain, I learned that it was better to leave the past where it belonged, in the past. The present was a gift to be lived now, and it should be lived intensely because it was the only certainty I had. I was not sure that I would be granted with the best present in the world, having a future. However, this uncertainty was a worry I had to learn to push aside so that I could enjoy the certain—here and now.

Chapter 47

Lucky or Unlucky Thirteen

Christmas of 2013 was not the best one I had, but I could not whine about it because the ones I loved were by my side, and that is the true essence of Christmas: love. However, I have to admit that that holiday was unlike anything I had ever experienced. It was the first time I spent Christmas in a hospital bed. Even though my room was decorated with Christmas trees given to me by loved friends, and Christmas lights given to me by my in-laws, my parents, Richard, and I felt that something was missing.

As the hours passed, the emptiness was palpable. We missed the joy of Jesus's birth, the delicious dinner my mother made, my father having some drinks to "refresh" in the hot weather of the wonderful Brazilian summer in December. We also missed the countdown to midnight and all the merry Christmas greetings from cousins, uncles, aunts, and my grandmas whom I love so much.

Through the hospital windows, I viewed the Manhattan sky-scrapers and thought of all those people who enjoying Christmas without thinking about its real meaning. Unfortunately, some people were still celebrating this date as a mere day off in which they got to stay home and exchange lots of unnecessary gifts and eat some good food. The following day, they would have to deal with the "hassle" of returning the presents they didn't like, and everything would be the same: some would complain that they had to go back to work or that they were unemployed; others would complain about the weather being too cold or too hot for the season. Perhaps some would have forgotten about the meaning of the previous evening. It is when we should reflect on the important aspects of our lives, the meaning of spending time together, and forgive and be empathetic and compassionate with one another.

Looking out the hospital building, I thought about how many people were right there in that hospital experiencing a shared ache: how could the world be in celebration, when all of us were there in so much pain? It saddened me to think that on the floors below me, there were children who wanted to play, yet they were tied to a hospital bed; there were teenagers full of dreams, but they couldn't go after them. I couldn't forget the elderly people either; even though they had had a life, they did not deserve to be brought down by this disease. Some of us had pain, and others didn't. Some were unconscious, but we were all alive, and knowing that our time was limited was painful for all of us. The truth is that among the many reasons we had to cry, it was difficult to find a good reason to smile.

It was at that point that I began to think that whoever was out there had no idea what we were going through inside that hospital. So I decided that the best thing to do was to stop thinking about how my life was before the diagnosis in the outside world, and I began to appreciate the positive things that I had inside the hospital. There were not many, but I could hold on to what I had. The most important one was that I was still alive; so many did not have the chance to celebrate this Christmas. I was being treated in one of the best cancer centers in the world, and I had caring doctors and nurses by my side. If I had been in another place, perhaps I would not have had all the attention I had. I had been blessed with the opportunity of having my parents with me; how difficult it would have been if they hadn't had their passports and visas ready to travel or if they had everything ready to go but could not afford to pay for an emergency international trip. Looking from that perspective, I had a lot of reasons to have a very merry Christmas. Although this was not an ideal Christmas, I was still able to celebrate time with my family, and that is what mattered the most to me.

I realized that I was no longer the same person who had been admitted to the hospital on December 4, 2013. I now had the discernment of what was to be part of two different worlds, the outside world and the cancer patient world. It is not easy to explain, but I was aware that, fortunately or unfortunately, I understood what it meant to belong to two totally distinct worlds. I knew I had gone into a painful and distressing transformation the moment I was diagnosed because once I was admitted to the hospital, I experienced all the physical and mental pain of a cancer patient. I knew the pain of having death so close to me. I began to understand several truths that I could not even fathom until I lived this particular life:

Every moment should be lived intensely, as if it were our last one. We all know that one day our journey will end; we have this false notion that we have so much time to do everything, but we forget we simply have no idea when our time is up. Being in a hospital with death looming makes you remember that life is fragile. These constant and not so friendly reminders happen every single minute that you have a pain, have a fever, sweat, throw up, and when you hear the steady beeping of an EKG. We learn a hard lesson that time cannot and should not be wasted, because we don't know when we will take our last breath. Hopefully, we will not waste our lives focusing solely on material possessions; they will not help us when our time comes.

Family and friends are essential. It was amazing to feel the abundance of love from my true friends. It is a pure and beautiful love that asks nothing in return. It was beautiful to see people giving me love just to make me happy, people who wanted me well simply because they loved me.

Do not expect too much from others! Everybody is fighting their own battles. I also learned that every person gives us what they can; it may sound like an obvious lesson, but I learned that people can only give what they have at a specific moment. Sometimes, I expected certain resilience from some friends who asserted that they would be with me until the end of the treatment, but they did not keep true to their word. At first, I was sad because I thought I was not as important as I thought I was to them; however, with some maturity, I realized that each person brought what they had and in a way they could. If the person did not have time to be there, to text, or show any kind of support that day, week, or month, it did not mean that the person was better or worse than the others who were there with me every day. They simply couldn't demonstrate their love at the time that I needed it, but that did not mean their love was not real. I learned how to respect others' plights and limitations.

Money can afford a prestigious health insurance plan, but it cannot push death away. We all know money cannot buy happiness. However, we also know that some money doesn't hurt anyone, and it could certainly buy a lot of items that make us truly happy. There is one thing that money cannot buy: the desired ticket to immortality. Therefore, holding ourselves back from being happy because we are stressed about not having a better car, brand-name clothing, or an extravagant house is a mistake we must learn from. We become enamored by these possessions, so much so that we do not realize that they cannot heal us when we fall ill.

Gratitude is a blessing! Remember to be thankful for each day you have. A person who has belonged to both worlds knows that every day is given to us as a unique gift, a blessing that we only come to understand when we know that one day we may not be granted a second chance.

Do not procrastinate! When you live knowing that you may not have one more extra day, you simply do not want to waste your valuable time; you live with intention and become more courageous so that you may utter powerful words like "I love you" without a moment's hesitation.

Math, math, and math! It is time for you to put people in categories: positive people in one column, the negative ones in another. Remember the simple math operations you learned in school—addition, subtraction, multiplication, and division? Time to use them! Whoever is not adding up in your life, please do yourself a favor and subtract them as fast as you can. If you don't, your problems will multiply, and you will feel divided about who you really are.

Do not hold a grudge and understand the importance of forgiveness. Oh, this was a difficult task for me, but after a lot of reflection, I came to the conclusion that in order to live well, I had to abandon the pains of the past. To forgive and be forgiven is not a deed we need to do to others but for ourselves, because it makes us lighter. We live better, without having to carry the burden of a heavy heart, anguish, or bitterness; these feelings only bring pain and unnecessary resentment. By forgiving others, we free ourselves.

None of these lessons were easy to learn and hone. However, I needed to own these lessons in order to be a better person.

Reflecting on these lessons while I was on that hospital bed, I looked at my parents lying on the cold floor and felt so loved by them and my friends. I had two options: unhappily go to sleep, thinking about everything that I was missing, or go to sleep with the serenity of knowing the many lessons that that disease had taught me. I took the second path, and in doing so, I felt immense peace as I slept through the entire night.

$\mathcal{C}$hapter 48

To Stay or Not to Stay— That Is the Question

Over the next few mornings, the doctors visited me daily. I got used to my daily routine: breakfast, painful shots, a lot of medication, tests, lunch, many visits from cheerful friends, jokes and funny stories about my childhood from my parents, more shots, blood work, more medication, dinner, and then prayers with my mom. One morning, one of the doctors from the leukemia team came to disturb my routine.

"Well, Mrs. Da Silva, how have you been feeling lately?"

"Very well, thank you!"

"Good news: you can go home within a few days. Do you feel safe to go home?"

"I am not going lie to you. I feel very safe here. The nurses are always very kind to me. They are super helpful, but if you think I'm all right, I trust your call, and I can certainly go home whenever you feel that I am ready."

I kept repeating it, trying to convince myself, "I can go home."

I was in disbelief that I had just agreed to abandon my new routine.

The news that I could leave the hospital sounded great; however, even though it was reassuring that the doctors said I could soon go home, I was scared. Although one side of me wanted to go home and get back to a shadow of my normal life, I felt so protected in the hospital. I had even decorated my room to make myself feel more at home. I just pressed a red button, and the sweetest nurses were right there by my side, helping me with everything I needed. My parents were right by my side, Richard visited me every single evening, and my friends were always present. Why would I want to go home? It sounded crazy to leave such a safe place! Also, I could not help but worry about living without medical support. What would happen to me if I got sick at night at home? Who would I call? I would not have an emergency button to press. The kind nurses would not be there anymore.

Without daily examinations, how would I know if I was doing okay? Many uncertainties began to cross my mind. I told my friend Priscilla and my parents about how happy I was to go home, but I also confessed that I was very afraid about the prospect. I feared that my illness could take a fatal turn in the middle of the night, and no one would know how to help me. It seemed like an exaggeration, but the truth is that for a cancer patient, death is omnipresent. This disease certainly showed me that I was braver than I ever thought I was, but I still feared the Grim Reaper.

After a long conversation with friends and family, I realized that those fears were not uncommon; according to the doctors, many who were hospitalized for a long time had similar concerns. I knew it was illogical for me to stay in the hospital more than I needed to, not just for me but especially for all those I loved. My parents had slept on the floor for almost a month and deserved to have the comfort of resting on a bed. I also knew that Richard was exhausted; he worked all day, and every night, he came to the hospital to see me. All my friends who visited me traveled through the cold, snow, and traffic and then drove around, looking for a parking space, just to make me feel loved—including the pregnant ones, Priscilla and Kate. I could not do that to them; it would be better for everybody if I went back home.

I was determined if I did not want to leave the hospital for me, I had to leave for all those who I loved so much and who had shown me so much love and support. I owed it to them. Gradually, I got used to the idea of going back home. Even if I would not have all the help that I had in the hospital, I would still have the comfort of home. I went on, day after day, trying to convince myself of how happy my parents, my husband, and my friends would be once they found out that I could go home. If the doctors thought I could go home, that was a good sign; it meant I did not need so much care. I trusted my doctors' decision, so within a few days, I would be a stranger stepping back into the world where I had once belonged.

Everyone was so ecstatic with my speedy recovery that their happiness started to change my fear of going back home. Gradually, I began to tell the nurses that soon I would go home. I always saw the same reaction: a wide smile. They kept repeating how much they liked me, and one of them kept saying that she felt that I did not belong in that hospital anymore; according to her, it was time for me to be free again. Some said they were already praying that all would be well. That encouraged me so much! I did not know them in the world outside the hospital, but I will always be grateful for all the love they poured on me, always giving me the certainty that I just had to have faith and believe that God would take care of everything.

I stopped seeing the return back home as a threat. I had nothing to fear; it was just the next step. I would continue the treatment in the comfort of my home sweet home.

*C*hapter 49

Happy New Year!

T he morning of December 31, 2013, marked the end of 2013 and the first note of good news.

"Ms. Da Silva, according to all your exams, you're fine! What do you think of going home today?"

"Perfect! It will be great to spend New Year's Eve in my own house!"

At that stage of the game, my fear of leaving the hospital was gone, and I was happy to go home with my parents and my husband. I quickly translated to my parents what the doctors said, and we all got excited with the certainty of being able to start the year outside of the hospital. My parents celebrated the great news by hugging each other, and I immediately started calling everyone to let them know that their prayers had been heard. I called Richard, and then I started calling and sending text messages to all my friends and my colleagues. I just felt I needed to share the news with everybody, news that was better than winning the lottery. I called my friend, the school secretary, asking her to notify all of the staff members that I would be leaving the hospital in a couple of hours.

My parents and I were filled with so much joy that we started packing up everything I had in my room; I had accumulated so many items in my temporary house. We were all anxious to go back home, but we still needed to wait to collect all the medication that I would need to bring home. It was a long, long, but worthwhile wait! Finally, at six o'clock, we were dismissed. I still could not believe that I would be able to spend some hours of New Year's Eve at home. My dad wheeled me. My heart was beating so fast when we got close to the door of my room. I felt as if I had been released from a cage. I would have my life back! Everything was new, and the possibility of being able to step outside was a miracle. Breathing the air of the world, which everyone breathed, was a gift. Maybe I had been awarded a few days, months, or even years longer in the world, but the lessons I had learned would stay with me forever. I was determined to teach and share my story with whoever wanted to listen to it. Life is indeed the most priceless present, but we do not realize this until we are faced with the possibility of losing it.

As we entered the elevator to leave the hospital, a nurse who had helped throughout my entire time there held my hands while my dad gripped the wheelchair handle. The nurse's eyes were filled with tears as she expressed how happy she was for me; she was very excited that I would be able to spend New Year's Eve in peace and with my family. She was an angel!

She helped us put all the presents I had received into the car. Many fit in the trunk, and once there was no more space, she waited until my parents sat down and then put other presents and my belongings on their laps. Then she closed the door so that Richard could drive. As my parents were already buried by my gifts, she opened my door again to give me something that could not fit on my parents' lap. I heard the sound of something falling on the pavement, but at the time, I was so happy that I didn't even bother trying to locate the origin of the noise;

nothing mattered more than the fact that I was leaving to go to my home sweet home.

This whole story was beautiful, and it seemed too good to be true. Five minutes after driving away from the hospital, I started frantically looking for my cell phone. I asked Richard, "Do you have my cell phone? I can't find it anywhere. I think I lost the phone you just gave me. I have had it for less than two weeks." To my despair, he just nodded.

"Dad, Mom, do you have my phone?"

"No, sweetie. You were just holding it when we left the hospital."

I wanted to post that thanks to my friends' and family's prayers, I would be able to spend the new year in peace, but my phone was nowhere to be found. It seemed like another drama had just started. The loss of a cell phone was nothing compared to everything we had gone through, but I could not tolerate any issue that would tarnish this blessed night.

I was sure I had entered that car with my phone. That was when I realized that the object that had fallen may have been my phone. The phone was at the car door and must have dropped when she closed the door. After this realization, I blurted, "Richard, stop this car! We need to return to the hospital because I'm sure my phone fell when the nurse closed the door. We must go back to the hospital to get my phone that's lying on the street."

"Do not worry. If it fell, it might be under the seat, so as soon as we get home, I will park the car, and we can check it out."

For a few minutes, the phone drama brought me back to my known world, where a lost phone was my only concern. On the way home, I saw the sign to the East River Parkway and was glad that God was allowing me to see that beautiful view again. When the car stopped, my eyes filled with tears; I just could not believe that I was right in front our apartment building. I kept staring at the building in disbelief. I had finally made it back to my former life, and we would have a cozy place where we could spend our New Year's Eve.

After this emotional moment, we all began to turn over the car to find the darn cell phone. My father was almost lying down on the floor trying to find it, but he didn't succeed. Richard also desperately looked for it, but he thought it would be better for us not to remain outside in the freezing winter air. We all went in the elevator in an awkward silence. As soon as Richard put my stuff on the floor, he said that he would go back downstairs to find my cell phone. Imagine my surprise when, ten minutes later, he was back but without my cell phone. As soon as I saw him, I said, "Richard, I'm sorry, Boo, but you need to go back to the front of the hospital as fast as you can. I know you're exhausted, but you have to believe me. The phone is exactly where you parked the car to pick me up!"

"Fabiana, let's assume you're right and that your cell phone dropped when the nurse closed the door. The hospital is in New York, and many people have passed by that street since we left. Do you think nobody realized that there was a brand-new phone ringing on the floor? I am positive that within this short time, your friends tried to call you. You might have received several texts or Facebook messages. Have you thought about how many times the screen lit up in the darkness? I don't want to be pessimistic, but come on now."

"I know that many people have passed by that street, but I'm sure my phone is right there! Please, just drive by, and you will see!"

Even though he looked very tired, he took the car keys and drove back to Manhattan to retrieve my phone. My parents and I anxiously awaited his return, hoping that no one had picked up phone. It may seem like an insignificant concern, but I was determined to begin the new year without a worry, and we certainly did not need any more expenses. To distract myself, I decided to post the good news to my social network with my laptop.

After an hour, Richard came home with my cell phone in his hand, the screen alight with eager responses to my news. I will never forget Richard's words: "I do not know how it happened, but the phone was right where you said it would be, next to the sidewalk. No one had touched it." It seemed impossible, but it was only the first of many miracles to come.

When my parents realized that our pantry was emptier than the store shelves in Target on Black Friday, they noticed that they needed to save our New Year's supper! They were brave enough to face the winter weather to buy some ingredients so that my mom could whip up a homemade dinner, prepared with a lot of love.

Once I noticed that they were about to leave, I wanted to drive them to the store, but they found my idea absurd, considering I had just left the hospital; they soon left for their shopping journey, on foot, in the freezing night. They didn't even know where to go, but off they went with the hope they would find something open.

When Richard and I were alone, I thanked him for believing in me. I was incredulous when he said that I had nothing to thank him for. An hour later, my parents happily arrived home because they had found an open grocery store in the Bronx. According to them, it was a wonderful store that had everything from pigs' heads to chicken legs. To this day, I do not know if they understood that these items did not sound at all appetizing to me. Luckily, they did not bring home a pig's head but instead potatoes, ground beef, garlic, and onions. Out of these humble ingredients, my mom made our special supper, a very tasty soup. Although our supper was simple, certainly the simplest supper I have ever had in my life, it had been made with so much love that it turned out to be the tastiest soup I have ever eaten.

We watched TV while we waited for the famous ball to drop from Times Square. We counted down every second. As soon as the clock hit midnight, we hugged each other, hoping the year 2014 would wash away the miseries of 2013. That year was certainly behind us, but it left behind battlefield scars, the deepest ones left in our memories and on our hearts.

Chapter 50

Impatient, Outpatient, Inpatient Struggles

I had no idea about the challenges that the outside world would bring, but I knew that I would not spend each day stuck in my home. Since I was out of the hospital, I wanted to explore, even if my initial explorations were tentative. The day after we arrived home from the hospital, I woke up feeling great, and I told my parents that I would drive them to a different supermarket.

At the hospital, the nurses constantly warned me that I should always be careful and mindful of the catheter I had on my arm. All of them instructed that I should not make any abrupt movements so that I didn't end up having the catheter removed from my arm. I would have felt horrible if I had done something that caused the catheter to be pulled out. I would certainly feel guilty and stupid if I did anything that brought me more pain. I knew that in the out-side world, I would have to figure out a way to balance my normal life with my more sheltered hospital life, but I refused to deprive myself of common tasks like grocery shopping and driving.

One of the first challenges I faced as an outpatient patient was getting used to wearing a hospital mask in public; I simply could not stand it. The winter was harsh, so it was important that I stay warm when I went outside. According to the doctors, I had to stay indoors as much as possible to avoid getting any infection or colds. My immune system was low due to the chemotherapy, so it was up to me to keep strong. If I had a simple cold, considering my immunity was akin to that of a baby, only God knew where I would get the strength to survive it. Although I felt like ET, leaving home wearing a mask that covered what I liked most about myself, my smile, my parents always supported me, saying that it was totally okay to wear masks anywhere I wanted to go. They also reminded me that I should not worry about people's negative reactions. I learned that if I wanted to take care of me, I should not care about what others thought about me. My parents stressed the importance of protecting myself by wearing masks and gloves. And even though it was hard, I learned how to deal with people's reactions. For someone who had already been through many trying situations in the hospital, an awkward situation in the supermarket would not stop me from living my life. Although I tried to be understanding when people glared, it was strange to see how people judged me without even considering what I may have been through. Perhaps they feared that I had some contagious disease; they did not even consider that I was protecting myself from their contagions.

Being a cancer outpatient helped me become more aware of people's attitudes toward others. I started observing people's behavior with great attention. I recall seeing a patient arrive in the doctor's waiting room and the cruel impatience he had for his compassionate wife. He was always angry, consistently cursing his existence. He kept mumbling that he was sick and tired of his life. He yelled that everything was going wrong for him on that day: the nurses had not cleaned the catheter correctly, and his wife had allegedly bought a snack that he did not like. I did not want, in any way, to belittle his suffering, because I had some bad days in the hospital, and any small thing may add to the grander pile of our misery. I did not want to judge him for being mad in that moment; he was the only one who knew his pain and scars.

I knew it was weird to see the lives of others going on normally while we had to fight so much to simply live. It was not a matter of living well; at that point in our lives, we just wanted to be able to live. Having observed that man's behavior, I came to the conclusion that as much as I suffered during the chemotherapy treatment, I would try my best not to mistreat my parents or my husband. I knew that those who were closer to me eventually took the same blows, but I thought, *If this disease does not make me a better person, it will not make a bitter person either.* I knew that neither I nor anyone was to blame for this disease; I just had to simply deal with the new situation that life had imposed on me, and I was determined to try, as much as I could, to love life. I was determined to give back the same love that I had received in the hospital and throughout my life. Life was too short to be filled with hate. Hate was certainly not an option!

Another aspect of my new life that I had to learn to deal with were the cramps. After a few days at home, I went nuts, wanting to clean the entire house, but little by little, I started to realize the new limitations of my body, such as the weakness of my limbs and the excruciating pain in my stomach.

After getting many tips from some friends about how important it was to drink vegetable and fruit juice for breakfast, the first opportunity my parents and I had, we bought a juicer. We would do anything to contribute to my speedy recovery. We went to a mall in White Plains in a neighborhood near my house, and there I found my salvation, an amazing machine that would invigorate me and help me recover from the toxins that all the chemo I had put into my body.

Unfortunately, I knew that the lifesaving poison had exterminated cells, both good and bad. After falling in love with the great juicer, it was time to patiently wait in line to pay for it. I was not at all in the mood, especially wearing a yellow mask that people could spot from miles away and with a catheter dangling from my arm. Even though the clerk had noticed that I was as pale as a ghost, she still did not miss the opportunity to make a sale; she insisted on the importance of having a store card. She kept promoting all the advantages that I would have, all the impending discounts. While she spoke about the wonders of the future purchases, I became painstakingly aware of my physical condition. I just kept asking myself if she was blind. A scared, dark voice also asked if I would still have time to use that special card to make other purchases in the remaining moments of my life.

She seemed to have the perception of a gnat as she kept on rambling about the card as if it was the most important thing in the world. Since I could not stand listening to her nonsense for another moment, I gave up and accepted the damn card just to escape the store with my prized juicer. Even after I signed for the card, she still kept blathering about the advantages that the "special" card would bring to my life. I desperately wanted her to shut up, so I could not help blurting out, "Listen, I have already signed the card, and you've won your commission. I know you have nothing to do with it, but I have cancer, and I am in no condition to stand here and listen to all these alleged benefits. Can I please just go? I am really losing my mind, and I am about to cancel this card!"

She, ignoring my outburst, simply replied that the purchase had already been transacted and that I had already won the super 15 percent off my item. At that point, I didn't know if she was deaf or crazy, but when she was about to give me the receipt, she fired out her sales pitch again, like an uncontrollable machine gun, reminding me once again about all the benefits and coupons that I was entitled to since I had just signed up for the card. I could not believe that she was stuck in her spiel; she was so clueless! She said that since I had signed for it, I should also pay a little extra to get the insurance so that I had a warranty for life. It was then that I learned a hard lesson: bureaucracy and capitalism have no sympathy, because there is no disease in the world that can make that process become smoother. Not even a disease as fearsome as cancer could help me cancel the card I had just signed up for.

Apart from the card setback and the surreal pain that I felt in my legs, I was super excited to use our new machine to make some healthy juice, but I continued to forget that my body was no longer the same. I realized that within less than a month of chemotherapy, my body had started to have strange reactions. The first sign of this was my shaky hands.

At the time, I didn't realize the changes that my body had just gone through, and without taking my body's signals into consideration, I decided that after my mother's delicious dinner, I needed to do some deep cleaning in my kitchen. While the rest of the family tried to take a peaceful nap, I felt strong like a bull, as if I was Mrs. Clean, reincarnate. However, my Mrs. Cleaning energy did not last longer more than five minutes.

When I tried to move my brand-new juicer machine to clean up the counter, it slipped from my feeble grip: *catabumba, ploft, plaft, bum!* The noise was thunderous, but I thought it was best to act like nothing had happened. I continued to sing to myself, "Larará larari," when suddenly, my parents and Richard appeared in my small kitchen. Startled, they stared at the broken savior that had not even lasted two hours in my care. Shards of plastic were scattered all over the kitchen, and some pieces were in the living room.

I felt a mix of corrosive feelings; I wanted to pretend that everything was all right, but I felt scared and really upset not only because I had broken the machine, but because I began to recognize that I, an independent thirty-year-old woman, had new limitations that impeded my once strong independence. I thought that breaking the machine marked the beginning of what was coming. I cringed when I realized that the insane salesgirl was right; it would have been smarter to have paid twenty bucks for the stupid warranty.

I learned to be more practical. I noticed that I would have reacted differently in a situation like this before I had been diagnosed with cancer. In the past, the breakage of the machine would have been the worst torment of the day; dramatic as I am, it would have been considered an ecological disaster without any possible solution. But now I saw it differently: it was only a replaceable machine.

In that moment, I realized I had a powerful choice: I could choose to be as dramatic as a Shakespearean tragedy, or I could simply pick up the darn pieces from the floor and face my new reality. We all went to bed thinking about the incident, but we still had hope that miraculously the super machine had survived the accident and would start the process of helping me heal. The following day, we all gathered in the kitchen to plug it in.

Once we turned it on, we heard the most beautiful sound of the week: *vruuuuuuuuuuuuuuuum*! It echoed throughout the entire apartment. What a relief!

Every little joy became a great blessing.

The machine lasted more than six months; once it was damaged, we simply bought another one. And so we led our lives, trying to stress less over the small things and manage our tempers so that we didn't lose our minds and waste our energy. We tend to complain about aspects of our lives that are and are not out of our control: our jobs, the hectic traffic, crowded buses, the rush of everyday life, a lack of time to exercise, pain from excessive exercise … the list does not end. The secret is to find a balance and try to live well with what we have. Complaining about every little annoyance does not make our lives better, so we must find a way to cope.

A question that continued to invade my mind was, Did it make sense to stress over things that were out of our control? I started trying to live according to my present philosophy. I certainly did not know what would happen to me five minutes into the future, but my present would be a little better if I did not compare my current routine with my past routine. I decided that I should not focus on future problems; I simply did not know if I would be alive to solve them. Of course, all this sounded beautiful in theory, but in practice, I had to keep reminding myself to simply allow life to lead me.

My new existence brought with it another new experience, in-somnia. At night, it was so weird, listening to everyone breathing peacefully as I was the only person in the room wondering if I would be able to open my eyes the following day. It was a strange feeling because none of us, healthy or unhealthy, knew for sure if we were going to wake up the next morning, but that thought was certainly one of the thoughts that disturbed the peace of a cancer patient: *will I see the ones I love again?* These thoughts are ampli-fied at night, when any drop of tap water sounded like a waterfall and any shade became an ET from Mars. Some weird thoughts crossed my mind, and every time I realized that evil thoughts were starting to invade my mind, I sat up in my bed, followed by my dad whispering, "Good night." He, who had always been a light sleeper, always happily said, "Good night," and giggled. Those simple words meant so much to me. It was a way to remember that I was still alive and, most importantly, that I was not alone. If the negative thoughts persisted, I frightened away the evil thoughts by thinking about God or listening to some meditation music to calm myself. After reflecting on the uncertainty of my future, I always ended up falling asleep, ready for the next day.

I learned how to deal with other symptoms that turned me into a binging Tasmanian devil from Brazil. It was something I simply had no control over; I could not stop eating! Because of the abundance of steroids I was prescribed, I ended up eating not only a typical Brazilian dinner—rice, beans, salad, and some kind of meat—but as soon as I put my plate in the sink, the first thought that came to my mind was, *What else can I devour?* Ah, dear reader, I ate everything in the kitchen, ranging from popcorn to soup, canned beans, all types of chips, fruits, and basically whatever I found in the fridge or in the cabinets. My stomach was an empty bag; it felt as if the more food I put in, the emptier the bag became. I continued to binge eat whatever was in front of me, so much so that within a month, I had gained a lot of extra weight. The concerns that the doctors had about me slimming down ended.

On top of the binge eating, I also had to contend with nausea. Everything I saw in cancer movies came to light in my reality. Smells, mostly emanating from food, turned my stomach. My nose became so sharp that it could outdo any dog's sense of smell. For example, if my mother drank coffee in another room, far away from me, I felt as if I was the one drinking coffee, not through my mouth but through my nostrils. The most coveted fragrance became a poison to me and anybody undergoing a cancer treatment; smells made us vomit whatever we had ingested.

In addition to these side effects, I had to endure the side effects of the chemotherapy. I will never forget the night I paid for all my sins (or almost all of them)! Although I had not eaten anything fancy that day, my sensitive stomach was still irritated. I threw up seventeen times over the expanse of the night. I quickly became friends with this porcelain throne. It didn't matter if I had eaten something or not; Mrs. Chemo simply did not care. Her motto was to expel any food particle, even if it was imaginary.

*C*hapter 51

That Fabulous, Fancy Scarsdale Wig

Dad had barely finished shaving my head, and I was already as bald as Uncle Fester from the *Adams Family*. Some questions began to crawl through my mind: How could I possibly go outside without having even a tiny thread of hair on my head and still feel good about how I looked? Would people laugh at me? Did I want people staring and feeling sorry for me or trying to wonder what type of cancer I have? The questions and wandering thoughts continued to escalate. While my dad was carefully and joyfully shaving whatever hair I still had on my head, Richard was sleeping like a log; however, to my despair, the hum of the sadistic razor eventually woke him up. Once I saw that Richard was walking in my direction, I felt sick to my stomach; my heart started racing, and I tried to hide as fast as I could behind my dad. All I knew was that I did not want my hubby to see me bald. I remember friends trying to encourage me, saying that I should not worry about it because it was "just" hair and that it would grow back. I truly appreciated their kind words, but I didn't know how to express that it was much more than "just" hair to me, and perhaps many cancer patients feel the same way. It was part of who I was; it was part of my identity that I felt that I was losing little by little.

Dad shaving my head

My father, very proud of his unknown talent of shaving women's heads, insisted on cheering me up. He kept saying with a squeaky voice, "You look b-e-a-u-t-i-f-u-l! I do not think you have anything to worry about. Besides, you have a pretty face, so being bald will not stop you from being beautiful."

I feel blessed for my dad's good sense of humor; it helped lighten the sad moments when I wanted to cry. While I was laughing at my dad's attempt to make me laugh, I started sobbing when I saw my hair slowly falling like a waterfall of feathers, coating the floor in a pool of black. It was deeply saddening to see my mom gently picking up the piles and putting them in a plastic bag. So many images came to my mind while I watched them help me.

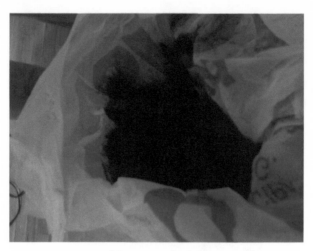

No more hair!

I kept thinking about my curls when I was a baby and my braids when I was a little girl. I also thought about all the different hairstyles I had had for thirty years and the hours I had spent blowing and drying it strand by strand. All gone. No more care needed!

I desperately started looking for the wig pamphlets that the nurses had given me. As soon as I found them, I scanned the address of the nearest wig store. I didn't want to waste any more time sitting at home. I was still sad and concerned about what people on the street would think when they saw me so vulnerable, but I knew that I had to restart my life from somewhere. With the address in my hands, we went to the place closest to my house, a wig store in Scarsdale. I kept crying while I was driving to the store; I simply couldn't believe that such a disgrace was happening to me! It is one thing to watch people fighting a cancer battle; it is entirely a new experience to have to fight it yourself. My parents supported and assured me that nobody would know that I was bald because, luckily, it was still winter, and everyone was wearing hats to protect themselves from the harsh cold. Despite their huge effort to assure me, I still had the impression that everyone was staring at me as if they had just found a crying ET driving around Westchester! I drove the car to the parking lot. The place was so fancy that I had barely turned off the car when the valet was already opening the door of my old Yaris. Still feeling uncomfortable with my new bald head, I kept pulling down my brown hat so that the man, who I had only known for a minute, did not see the unevenness of my bald head. As soon as I gave him the keys, I ran to the front door as fast as I could to avoid any judgmental looks, and like Kramer from *Seinfeld*, I simply burst into the front door. The startled receptionist, who had silky, flowing hair like in those shampoo ads, asked me, "May I help you, madam?"

In a mix of wiping my tears and taking off the mask to not scare the wealthy customers, I answered quickly, "Yes! I need a wig, now!"

"Oh, sure! Please go to the establishment next door!" As if everything I was going through was not enough, I ended up bursting into the wrong store.

When I entered the right establishment, with a little more confidence in myself, I did not wait to be asked what I wanted but instead screamed, "I need a wig, honey! Who can I talk to?"

The receptionist, without asking any questions, directed me to an aisle where I came across everything I wanted to see—wigs! I looked around and realized that everyone in the store had wigs on, and I found this to be divine. We were all alike; however, no one seemed to be sick. The customers who were there looked healthy, and I believed they were just striving to have thicker or longer hair.

I looked at my parents, who did not seem to understand why I was getting so upset over being bald. Even though they did not say it, I could read their scared faces. *Why is she so scared, knowing that this was coming?*

The attendant of the establishment was very polite and gave me several tissues so that I could wipe my unstoppable tears. He took me to a private room where the specialist would see me. There, I felt more at ease, and soon the attendant began to calm me down.

"So, gorgeous, how can I help you today?"

Gorgeous? I thought he could only be mocking me, but I accepted the pampering of someone who seemed knowledgeable about beauty and who appeared to have experience in a situation like mine.

"I'm undergoing chemotherapy, my dad just shaved my head, and I feel awful! I look like a bird without feathers! I need something to put on my head; anything will do!"

"Look, I know this is a terrible time of your life, but do not cry. Remember that you lost your hair because you are getting the proper treatment to be cured."

Well, well, well, I knew that he wanted to comfort me, but I honestly did not see much sense in what he was saying because although I was happy that I was getting the best treatment for my diagnosis, I still would have loved to keep my hair. Who wouldn't? Soon our conversation shifted from emotional to pragmatic. I call this the Uncle Sam part of the job. At that time, I did not know anything about wigs, but I was convinced that I deserved a wig that was 100 percent natural. Not 99 or 98 but 100 percent! That certainty lasted until he informed me about the price for natural hair.

"Well, sir, I'm here today because I want a wig that looks like my hair, and it needs to be 100 percent natural. How much does it cost?"

"Okay. We have one that is fifty-fifty, 50 percent human and 50 percent synthetic."

And he dropped the bomb: "It costs $600."

That sentence sounded like a thunderstorm on a beautiful summer day at the beach. Though it sounded surreal and deafening, it seemed to be a necessary investment to me. However, I still weighed my options.

"But how much more would I have to pay for one that is 100 percent human hair? Is it way more than this?"

"The price of the human one is $1200, but it's magnificent! We measure your head to ensure that it fits your head well, and we trim the wig as you wish. Your hair will look great! Take a look at mine," he said, tapping a higher forelock than Elvis Presley. "I'm using a natural implant, and no one knows."

And I have to admit, his forelock looked real. I almost convinced my dad to buy a wig for himself as well. Even though I wanted that natural hair more than anything in the world, I was aware of my financial situation, so I settled for the first option: half-natural and half-synthetic.

"That's it! I will take the half-and-half one! Where do I pay for the wig, sir? And where do I pick it up?"

"You can pay for it at the front desk, and you will pick it up next week."

When I heard that, I started crying again.

"Are you kidding, me? I need something to cover my head right now, at this very moment! How am I going to leave this store bald? How am I going to have no hair for a week?

He quickly yanked a medium-sized brunette wig from one of his mannequins, which stopped my tears. As soon as he put the new wig on my head, I got up from the chair and said, "Oh, what a relief!" I felt like a woman! I was feminine again! I simply could not thank myself enough for having spoken up and not leaving that store without something on my head. The young man advised me not to get close to any flames because it was only a temporary wig, and I would get my own in seven days.

He took me to the counter, and with my new wig, I felt a little better. I gave my credit card to the secretary, who wanted to verify if my insurance would reimburse some of the expense. I told her that I would call them later. Honestly, at that moment, nothing mattered. All that mattered was that I was leaving that store with my head covered. It felt good to know that anyone who looked at me would think that I was just like the others, even though I knew that I was not myself anymore.

While I was driving back home, the wig was the conversation of the ride! My father, always very playful, made fun of my new hairdo, saying that I was pretty hairy and that I looked prettier without the "hairy wig." Upon arriving home, I ran to show my new wig to Richard, and to my surprise, I found out that he too had shaved his hair to show some empathy for my situation. My heart was filled with love and passion. I knew I had married a man who could love me for inner and outer beauty.

I wore my new wig only on Saturday. On Sunday, I began to look at my bald self in the mirror, and the idea of being hairless did not hurt as much as it did when I initially looked at myself in the mirror. I even started to like being called "a shaved bird" by my dad. Richard was also essential in making me feel good about myself. He continued to look at me with the same passion he used to when I was his bride. Nothing had changed; I knew that by my side I had a good man who admired me not only for my outer beauty but also, more importantly, my inner beauty. He would certainly have to count on the inner beauty for a while because I still felt different without my hair.

On Monday, I woke up determined to make some important decisions. I called my insurer and asked them to confirm that they would reimburse the cost of the luxurious $600 wig I had bought. To my surprise, the operator said, "Unfortunately, we have no agreement with this store, so we cannot reimburse any payment that you made." I simply could not believe what I had heard. I had gotten that list from the hospital. Why on earth would they give me a list of places that were not covered by my insurance? The cancer world was a complicated one to navigate, and I just did not have the mind-set to follow its intricacies.

After a long conversation with my parents about the ridiculous cost of that wig, I made a tough call. We needed to be refunded for the expensive wig ASAP. One of the advantages of living in a first world country is that the customer is always right! I shamefully called the place where I had bought the wig to explain what had happened, and the receptionist said that I would be reimbursed once I presented the receipt and that no questions would be asked.

As soon as we arrived at the store, my dad said that he would wait for us in the car. I knew he was embarrassed. In Brazil, if you buy something and you change your mind, you do not return it unless you find a defect in it. We rarely return what we purchase, especially if we have already used it. If we try to return something that we don't like, the salespeople hassle us so much that we end up keeping whatever we bought just so that we don't have to deal with the inconvenience of returning it.

Since my dad stayed in the car, my mom decided to go with me to encourage me to return it. I was embarrassed having to face such an odd situation. My hands were shaking, and I was so nervous that my voice barely came out of my mouth. With the wig in my hands and wearing the same hat I had on two days ago, I started talking to the same secretary who had welcomed me the first time; she was discreet and did not ask anything. She simply picked up the wig, credited the money to my card, and told me that everything was fine.

With the refund from the wig, my parents and I went to one of the wig stores that my father kept telling me he had seen during one of his adventures in the Bronx. Once we got there, I found one wig that was just what I was looking for. The faux hair was silky and soft, and it wasn't even as hairy as the one I had just returned. I bought the one I wanted and left the store as happy as if I had won the lottery. With the money I had saved with the reimbursement of the expensive wig, I could buy at least a dozen wigs of all shapes, sizes, colors, and styles.

Over time, and with the frequent use of wigs, I also learned that a simple wind was never just a breeze anymore! To a woman undergoing any cancer treatment and wearing a wig, a gentle breeze was more like a tornado, an earthquake, any terrifying natural disaster one could imagine, but not a simple breeze. Every time I had to face a windy day, I thought, *What am I going to do if this wig falls on the ground?*

a. Chase down the wig if no one saw what had happened.
b. Kick the wig with all my strength and scream, "Gooooal!" Then go out to hug the crowd that would hopefully confuse me with Ronaldo, since he is also bald.
c. Firmly secure the wig on both sides and run to a corner where the threat was less dangerous.
d. Do whatever came to my mind when the unfortunate situation happened!

My trips to the hospital made me change my mind about the wigs that were 100 percent natural. After observing some patients in the waiting room, I began to realize that our stubbornness in wanting to have real wigs could have a high price. One day, while I waited for my doctor to call me, I saw some lice walking freely in some friends' wigs. It was then that I knew that 50 percent false would guarantee a healthier scalp.

Meanwhile, on my social network:

> And as I always try to turn a negative situation into something positive, I would like to introduce you to my new hair. As I have always wanted to have bangs but never had the time to take care of them, I believe this is the time to use them. If Beyoncé can wear a wig, I can too, lol.

My dad and I

Chapter 52

The Farewell at the Airport

I am so thankful that God sends us angels who we can count on when we need them the most. My friend Priscilla was certainly one of these angels. She kindly took care of something that was stressing my family out a lot: my dad's change of flights to Brazil. Thanks to her great articulation on the phone and her pregnancy hormones that made her even more outspoken than she already is, she managed to find a way to change the date of my father's flight without paying the horrendous fee that the airline wanted to charge him. What would I have done without those angels sent by God?

I certainly wanted my father around, but I knew that our lives would have to get back to normal slowly, whatever *normal* now meant to us. He had to return to São Paulo, Brazil. Over time, everything was going to fall into place. However, before he got to Brazil, we had to face a greater pain: our farewell! I read that airports are one of the places where we find the sincerest smiles and tears in the world, and I agree.

When I left Brazil for the first time to live abroad, I learned that every farewell was awful, but this one had a much more bitter taste. For the first time, I thought about the uncertainty of seeing or hugging my dad again. We had agreed that my mom would stay with me to help me out with my treatment, but I worried about him. I wondered who would wash his clothes and who would cook for him, and I thought about how lonely he would be since his girlfriend, my mom, would not be home waiting for him. Even though I knew I could not blame myself for having cancer, deep down in my soul, I felt guilty for having had the desire to find adventure and live in another country. Wouldn't everything have been simpler if instead of exploring another country, I had stayed quietly in my neighborhood, without asking too much, without venturing too much? However, I soon realized that wasting my time questioning my past choices would not take me anywhere. I had already made my choices, and they were the ones that formed who I am today. I had already traced my path, and frankly, with hindsight, I did not regret any of the actions I had taken so far. I had made the choices that brought me many good things, and I was grateful for all I had done.

At the airport, the three of us stared at each other with despair because we just did not understand what life was doing to us. My father, being the clown of the family, decided to break the dramatic moment, lightheartedly assuring us that everything would be all right. According to him, those tears would go away soon, and that storm was just a dark cloud that the sun would soon toss away. My father had the gift of convincing us that our family was small in quantity but powerful in quality. He always said that our family was based on strong and solid values, which were love and respect for each other. That reminder comforted us, helping us realize what we always knew—that we were stronger than we thought we were.

I knew that no matter how old I was, I would always be Daddy's little girl, and to him, my mother would be his eternal girlfriend.

After many hugs and the endless kisses of the two lovebirds, we had to leave my father at the airport nine hours before his flight because my mother and I had to rush to the hospital. We had a packed schedule—tons of appointments. My day at the hospital would start with a lumbar puncture with methotrexate chemotherapy, a very painful bone marrow biopsy, and aspiration to ensure that no cancer cells were hiding in my marrow. The day would finally end with a huge shot in my behind that could stop me from ovulating for that month. According to the doctors, this shot could protect my ovaries, preventing me from becoming infertile after all the chemotherapy I had taken.

Dad and I at the airport

$\mathscr{C}$hapter 53

Trips to the Emergency Room

Chest Pain

When you are a cancer patient, you start living in an unscripted horror movie. You have to be in a constant state of alert. You have the impression that your life is a fragile thread that can break at any second. Within a matter of seconds, you realize that you can no longer exist—simple as that! According to my doctor, in case I had *any* unusual symptoms, I needed to call the hospital, talk to one of the nurses, explain what I was feeling, and it would be up to the nurses and the doctors to decide if I should go to the emergency room or not.

Nothing was more distressing than waiting on the other end of the line to find out whether I would put on my pajamas and lay down with pain, hoping it would get better, or put on my clothes and go to NYC to undergo some tests and make sure that the situation was under control. To make matters worse, I felt all sorts of pain at night. It seemed like they knew the right time to piss me off. The pain was punctual. Richard would come home after a hard day of work, and after having only a short moment of peace where he would grab some dinner, all sorts of pain would begin, and we all had to rush to the hospital.

I felt really bad for bothering Richard and my mother, but, dear reader, if you knew that a disease could take your life away, you would not care about being polite and courteous. So I always consoled myself, saying it is better to be an alive, annoying wife than a quiet, dead one.

One night, I was at home when I had a strong stomach ache; we rushed to the emergency room and spent about three hours in the hospital. After being poked here and there without any answers, the doctors decided that I needed a CAT scan. Once the results came back, they concluded that it was nothing—or better, to my embarrassment, the doctors concluded that it was only gas. Still, better safe than sorry! That night, Richard slept only three hours and went straight to work. It felt good to have a man who never complained about having a sick wife. I know my disease was not easy on him, yet he dealt with it in his way.

Chemo Side Effects

The doctors warned me that I would need to get ready for the side effects of the new dosage of chemo that I was taking. One of them would be strong stomach cramps. It did not take long until I started calling the nurses again. Several questions came to my mind, but one that permeated had to do with the amount of alarm each pain warranted. How would I know the true severity of my pain? I knew that every time I entered the emergency room, I became poorer and poorer; it was an "investment" that was expensive and uncertain, but what else could I do? It did not take long to convince myself that I needed to be taken to the hospital. In times like this, who cares about money? Every time I had to decide between going and not going, I always debated with myself for half an hour, but in the end, we all knew that I would opt for having Richard and my mom take me to the hospital. All I wanted was to live, despite the financial burden.

After a couple of months in treatment, I knew the step-by-step procedures of the emergency room. Once again, needles in both arms, urine tests, and whatever other exams the doctors requested. Richard and my mom also knew all the steps by heart. This time, I was hospitalized because I felt a sharp pain in my stomach; it felt like somebody was stabbing me. While I was waiting in the halls of the hospital, I tried to distract myself by making phone calls to some of my friends and listening to music and jokes on my iPad. I tried anything I could to forget the sad reality that I was living. After a lot of exams, the doctors found a small infection in my pancreas, but since it had been found in the early stages, they believed that everything would be fine.

Remission or Relapse—That's the Question

I ended up hospitalized because of that infection. On the same day, the doctor would give me the results of my PET and CAT scans. Needless to say, they were very important to me because they would reveal if I was still cancer-free. Imagine yourself going inside gigantic white machines to find out if you are cancer-free, but then, on the day you will get the results, you get an infection. You are four floors below your doctors' office, but since you are stuck in the emergency room, you don't have a chance to know whether or not you are cured. The pain caused by the new infection was certainly distressful, but the doubt of being in remission or not was worse. After a couple of hours of waiting, I was stunned when my doctors called me and assured me that my resonances were clear and that they were very happy with the outcome of my treatment. So was I! I could dream again!

The Allergy

A few weeks after the infection, Richard and I were on the couch when suddenly my legs became red and coated with red dots. I got frightened and said, "Richard, do you see something unusual on me?" (Of course, the bald head did not count as unusual anymore; it was part of what we considered normal.)

And after having had an exhausting day, Richard answered, "No, no. It's okay, hon! I am exhausted. I need to get some rest."

Richard was so tired that minutes later he was sound asleep on our couch. I did not want to bother him, but I knew I was not okay. That's when I decided to take a look in the mirror to confirm whether or not everything looked fine.

Dear reader, when I looked in the mirror, I came across a horrific scene. I was the same person, but I had turned into a monster. In a matter of seconds, I had purple bags under my eyes, and my head had turned into a red popsicle full of polka dots, speckling my entire body. What scared me the most were my lips; they are naturally thick, but with that transformation, they were six times thicker than Angelina Jolie's. It was the only time that I did not want to wake Richard up. Instead, I woke my mom up, called the nurses, described my appearance, and drove myself to New York City at 2:00 a.m. Richard was so exhausted that he did not even hear us packing. Once I arrived at the hospital, the swelling began to subside, and to this day, the doctors do not know the reason I had that reaction.

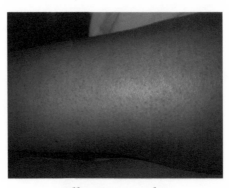

Allergies on a leg

My mother and I suspected that it might have been a reaction to the horse shampoo I had used a few days before. My mom said a lot of girls were using this fast-growing hair tonic in Brazil, and I had the brilliant idea of using it so that my hair could grow faster. I know hair does not noticeably grow from one day to the next, but I think I almost turned into a mare! Neigh! Neigh! Warning: what you are about to see may be the nightmare I incurred after going to great lengths to quickly grow back my hair.

The reality of a cancer treatment! Be strong whenever you can, but do not be afraid to let your
emotions ot whenever you need to!

$\mathscr{C}$hapter 54

The Second Phase of Treatment

$\mathbf{M}$eanwhile, on social media, I posted this:

> What a beautiful day! We are hiking. I hope to go back to Zumba soon, but for now, I'm enjoying hiking with my mother and friends. Some doctors advise me to walk for ten minutes and take a break so that I do not get too tired. Mama and I walked for three hours, and we felt great! Keeping strong! I can't imagine myself walking for only ten minutes. Walking for ten minutes is not even worth putting my wig on.

I had already completed the first phase of the treatment, but I still had a couple more phases to go to finish my first year. Some friends kept asking me where I had gotten such a strong will and fervent optimism. To be honest, I did not know where it came from, but I knew that there was a greater power within me that helped me believe I would live longer than the statistics had predicted, and I blindly believed it. Some days were rough, but I always believed that a better day was about to come. At this stage of the treatment, the second stage in outpatient care, I had to have chemotherapy from Monday to Thursday. The question was, Who would take me to the hospital when I started feeling nauseous? My mother did not know how to drive, and even if she could, she did not have a New York or an international driver's license. Richard and all my friends promptly offered to help, but I knew they all had their lives to live and their commitments. Besides, who would be available to take me to the hospital for days, weeks, and months? No one had this availability. The other option would be to take a subway to New York City and depend on public transportation. I could not forget that I was undergoing chemotherapy, and with my immune system so weak, would it make sense to expose myself to all the viruses and bacteria in the subway? Also, I wondered what people would think when seeing me in one of the busiest subways in the world, wearing a mask and gloves. They would probably think I had a contagious disease, and the trains would empty out. Well, that would be a comfortable ride! But did it matter what others thought? I had to think about what would be best for me. That was a lesson I had to learn. At that time, I stopped putting others first, and I paid more attention to what I needed. What made sense to me was to drive to the hospital. If I felt sick, I would reach out to Richard, and on the days when he couldn't take me, I would reach out to one of my friends who had offered to help.

Trust me, I was a good driver, and I was always very lucky not to get stuck in a traffic jam. I underwent the heaviest toxic chemo treatment and still drove myself for half an hour or forty-five minutes; it was the exact time I needed before I started feeling nauseous at home. Every time I finished the chemo du jour, my mom and I rushed to the hospital parking lot. The attendants, seeing me with my mask and gloves, always thought that my mom was the driver; they handed her the key, and she wisely passed the key to me.

After chemo, my head was always very heavy. I could still taste the metallic flavor of the powerful Vincristine in my mouth, and my sense of smell was heightened. Even though I was not feeling well, we came back home happy, singing Beyoncé's "Drunk in Love" or other upbeat music. I was drunk on chemo, that's for sure! I think those songs were ways for us to escape our reality; it helped us forget all the noise the chemotherapy was making while it slowly killed both my toxic and beneficial cells. Looking at a brighter side: nothing was better than arriving home after chemo. The feeling of a peaceful, quiet house and having fresh, clean sheets to lie down on was priceless.

A few days into this phase, my energy was waning. During the second consecutive week of chemotherapy, I started feeling a lot of pain all over my body but especially indescribable pains in my legs. I had pains that I had never even imagined one would be able to feel and still be alive. I felt like I was squeezed into my own body; my skin seemed too tight, stretching at the seams from holding the chemo and my blood within my frame. I walked like a ninety-year-old granny. Nobody in the world deserved such pain, but I had mixed feelings about my situation. Every time I thought about starting to complain about how life was not being fair to me, I ended up seeing a child battling the same or a similar disease, and that always made me think. *What am I complaining about? I've lived thirty years. I was granted the opportunity to live my child-hood, my adolescence, and part of my adulthood. I graduated high school and college and got a master's. I dated and married a good guy. I already accomplished so much, but these little angels are not even one-third my age and are already fighting this disease. Who am I to whine about fairness?* I felt that I had no right to give up or complain about anything! If I did not try to fight this disease for myself, I had to fight it for the little heroes or for all those mothers who I always admired. Their strength and sweetness when assuaging their children's worries is unfathomable.

One afternoon after having chemo, I was waiting to get my car out of the hospital parking lot when I saw a beautiful little girl who was also a cancer patient. She was about four years old, with blue eyes, rosy cheeks, and baldness that matched my own. She was so beautiful that she resembled a porcelain doll. Since I was wearing my yellow mask, she could not see me smiling at her, but I insisted on smiling. I knew she was fighting the same monster that I was, and if I could bring any happiness to her that day, I would. Her eyes were wet, and I wondered if she had had a rough day. Being an older soldier, I knew that some days were harder than others. That's when, suddenly, I decided to wave at her. I had no hope of getting it back; from her tired gaze, I knew she had had a brutal day of shots, chemo, and scans. However, to my amazement, I saw her slowly turning in her stroller to look at me. I noticed she was moving slowly because she had a catheter in her arm, and even though it was probably very painful for her to move that fragile arm, my wave was reciprocated with a beautiful smile from a princess I will never forget. It was because of this princess, and also because of all the other warriors fighting this disease, that I knew it was worth living and being happy while we were granted a day to smile. I also learned that even though we were going through a lot of pain, we had received the gift of living one more day, and to a cancer patient, one more day means one infinite possibility of being cured. Cancer also made me realize that we were living in a society that distracted us from finding happiness in authenticity. I also realized that sadder than facing such a horrible disease was seeing people who were healthy but living a dull, robotic, and meaningless life because they didn't have a grandiose car, their dream job, a big house, or any other materialistic item that we are taught we must have to find happiness.

Meanwhile, on my social network, I posted this:

Dear Friends,

I'm just writing to thank you all for your prayers and positive thoughts. I just had an exam to check if there was no recurrence of cancer, and the doctors are very happy with my treatments' outcome. I am glad to inform you that they said they had not found any cancerous cells in my body. I just graduated from the second phase of chemotherapy, which was certainly not easy. Today I am in the "Spa" with my mom to start the third phase, and God willing, everything will work out. Hopefully, in a few days, we will be able to be outside again. Thank you from the bottom of my heart for all your love and continuous support.

$\mathcal{C}$hapter 55

White Cookies?

$\mathbf{M}$y mother and I were beginning to prepare for the third stage of treatment, during which we had to go to the hospital four to five days a week to ensure that I took a very toxic chemotherapy (methotrexate) and had no side effects from it. Everything was fine until I went to the bathroom and sat on my potty. To my surprise, when I got up, I came across something I had never seen in my life: white poop. As soon as I saw it, I screamed, "Mooommmmm! Come here; you need to see this!" My mother and I stared incredulously at what has always been, and should be, brown! At that moment, my new horror movie began. I desperately cried, "Oh, dear Lord! Help me, help me! What is this, Mom? Why is it this color?"

"Calm down! There is nothing to worry about!"

"What do you mean, Mom? Have you, in your entire life, ever seen white shit? Let me check on the internet to see what it is."

Needless to say, that this was the worst thing I could have done.

Seconds later, according to Dr. Google, I had my diagnosis: stomach cancer!

Have you noticed that most of the symptoms we look up lead to this awful disease?

I thought, *Oh my God, again, no!* And soon, I was sobbing. I just kept saying to myself, *Oh my God, it's not possible! I barely healed from one. How am I going to have the strength to overcome two cancers at the same time?* I decided to take a picture of the "white cookies," and I called in the nurse, embarrassed to tell her what I had just ejected. Before I spoke to the nurse, I had to go through the shame of explaining to the secretary why I urgently needed to speak with the nurse.

"May I help?"

"Hi, this is Fabiana Da Silva. I need to talk to my nurse, urgently, because I'm not feeling very well."

"Sure, Ms. Da Silva, no problem. May I please know your symptoms so that I can inform our nurse? As soon as she reaches out to your oncologist team, she will get back to you."

I certainly did not want to share such an embarrassing story, but since she insisted, I thought about finding a gentle and polite way to describe what I was going through, but is there a gentle and beautiful way to speak about poop? Like a merciless machine gun, I soon bombarded the listener with the description of the white turds.

I was embarrassed, but I had to include all the details I could. Another lesson I learned from this experience is that being descriptive when you are sick is crucial. I blushed, and my face was burning, but I carried on: "It is not gray. It is white—all white! It has no blood. It came out round, and worst of all, I just read about it on the internet, and it seems that it is stomach cancer."

A few seconds of silence on the other end of the line followed. I knew that after that description, the secretary would not see me as Ms. Da Silva anymore; our relationship had drastically changed! I always arrived at the hospital very well dressed, with beautiful scarves and proper wigs. The secretaries always complimented my outfits or my hairdos, but now they would never look at me as the same woman. After that call, with the detailed oversharing, I was no longer Ms. Da Silva but Ms. White Poop! However, to be honest, in my situation, who cared about what others thought of me? All I wanted was the answer to that puzzle that certainly would change my life again.

To my happiness, my nurse called me a few minutes later to calm me down. She said that I had no reason to worry about the "white cookies." It was just constipation caused by the trillions of chemo toxins in my system. Knowing that it was just constipation, I felt like I was the winner of a lottery. There was still hope!

Chapter 56

The Third Phase of Treatment—Part 1

As we went to the hospital for the third phase, the nurses and doctors at the reception of the fourteenth floor welcomed me with much love. I was lucky to be seen by the same medical team that had taken great care of me in December. I was greeted with joy, and it was very good to see that I was not just one more patient there. I knew I was not just another number. They knew my name, not only my first but my last name as well. When I heard my name pronounced, it sounded like music to my ears. The way they pronounced it made me feel chic! It sounded fancy!

One of the doctors who had taken care of me said he remembered when I was hospitalized. I was surprised that he also remembered details about my case. He remembered that I had a tumor around my heart when I arrived at the hospital in December. He also emphasized that they were all very excited that this children's protocol was working for me. When I was reminded that I had a tumor in such a vital organ, around my heart, a lot of scary thoughts came to my mind, but it was also encouraging to know that the greatest danger had ended. At least that was what I wanted to believe. I already believed it was part of a miracle!

After I was taken to my room, I was immediately introduced to a sweet nurse. According to the hospital regulations, she had to ask me a few questions before we began the procedures. After I had answered several questions about my state of health, we went to the most amazing part of the questionnaire.

"Ms. Da Silva, do you think, or have you lately thought of killing yourself?" she calmly asked.

"No, no! No, not at all."

"Okay. Let's go to the next question. Do you feel hopeless?"

"No, I'm feeling pretty good, thanks! I'm super excited about my recovery, and I am also writing a book and doing everything else that I have to, to stay healthy. If you don't mind me saying, these questions are kind of weird, you know?"

"Yes. I am sorry. We just need to follow the procedures, but I am glad to know that you are doing so well. Ms. Da Silva, but if you think at some point of committing suicide, you can talk to any of us or, if you prefer, you can call this number right here." I understood that it was the hospital procedure; therefore, it had to be done for everyone's safety. However, I kept thinking that they could have someone who had been through hell and had not thought about suicide, and those questions could give some patients ideas, and they could try to execute that plan right there. I also thought, if one was even thinking of killing him/herself, why would this patient call someone who had the sole purpose of not allowing him or her to accomplish what he/she wanted? Anyway, I was happy to be at a place where they focused on the patient as a whole, and making sure that the patients were mentally stable was a plus. The bottom line is the hospital offered the help, and it was up to the patients to make decisions wisely. At night, I was introduced to the new chemo that had the goal of killing any remaining bad cells in my body, but I knew that with the bad, that yellow liquid would take the good ones as well, so I had to be ready for it. As soon as the chemo started dripping, I felt horrible! Honestly, at that moment, I did not care about my appearance anymore. I took my wig off so that I could sleep as comfortably as possible. The same nurse who had taken care of me the night before came to see me the next day. As soon as she saw me, she said, "Have they shaved your hair already? That was so quick!"

And I tactfully replied, "No, no! I just decided not to wear my wig at night so that I could sleep well."

We both smiled at each other with the shared knowledge of the practicalities one undergoes when battling cancer.

Fabiana-3; Leukemia-0

Enjoying life while in a cancer treatment!
Still kicking cancer's ass!

Chapter 57

Easter Bunny, What Will You Bring Me?

Often, a social network may indeed be depressing for those already going through trying times. When I was going through hell and saw my roommates roar in pain, I often logged onto the internet so that I could forget the world of pain and nightmares that surrounded me. However, when I logged onto my social network, I realized that I was living a different reality from everyone else. I did not know which world I belonged to—or wanted to belong to. I didn't have any choice, but I could see a clear distinction between those two worlds: one was the world of real pain, and the other was the exacerbated superficiality of sadness that made no sense, at least not for me.

As I listened to my roommates cry in pain, I watched my timelines fill with pictures of chocolate eggs of all brands, colors, and flavors. I knew that my friends were enjoying all that sugar and having a more pleasant Easter than I was, and I was happy for them. However, I realized that many posts were sad; some were

243

upset about not getting the eggs they wanted, or some, even worse, were upset because they received big eggs but so few.

I saw all that disparity and wondered if I was going crazy or if people had lost their minds with trivial concerns. Did the meaning of Easter morph into a surreal, superficial reality focused on how many chocolates one receives? How about everything I had learned about the crucifixion of Christ and His resurrection on the third day? Did cocoa have so much more value the day of resurrection?

A post from my timeline:

> And my Easter was simple: no chocolate eggs this year. But this Easter was filled with lots of love and affection from my hubby and mom who took me back home on the day of Easter. And these hard times in our lives teach us to appreciate what matters the most in our lives: health, love, and peace. Anything else we will always have time to pursue.

The funniest thing for me was to see that some people did not agree with my post. In fact, some seemed upset and tried to refute my statement, but since everyone uses the internet to express themselves, why couldn't I also give my opinion? Even though I didn't do what everybody else was doing, and perhaps I sounded a bit critical, I was not lying; my Easter was very unusual in April 2014, and many other patients were not even lucky enough to leave the hospital. I prayed that one day the cure to this disease would be found.

Love endures all things!

$\mathcal{C}$hapter 58

Organic or Not Organic?

The truth is that when you have a disease that can take your life away so quickly, everything, and I mean *everything*, results in a reason to worry. One of my biggest concerns was food. I had so many questions, such as, Was there something natural I could eat that would help me recover faster? How could I help my body detoxify from all that chemotherapy that was still needed to kill the bad cells that might have still been living in my organism? How did I keep my healthy cells away from all the toxic chemo that was injected into my body? Was it true that cancer cells were fed by sugar? Was it true that everything I ate would turn into sugar? Would I have a greater chance of living if I became a vegetarian? Every time I went to the doctors, they didn't seem to see any correlation between cancer and food, but every time I read articles that recounted studies that proved a direct connection between the food we ingest and disease, I went nuts because they all described how sugar, and especially processed meat, were factors that increased the risk of having the disease. Coming from a Brazilian family, it would be very tough to become a vegetarian from one day to the next. In my family, anything was a reason to have a barbecue; I did not see how I could save myself from the food that I had enjoyed throughout my life. Anyway, all in the name of survival, and if the price was right, I would eat only greens. I at least wanted to try to do so.

Before I got sick, I found it bizarre that people went to a pricier supermarket just to buy something that did not have any chemicals or artificial coloring and substances. However, after this diagnosis, I did not think it was bizarre at all and took every hint very seriously; any label that said "antioxidant" or "may prevent cancer" was added to my cart. These words meant nothing to some, but they brought me hope! They sounded like the laughter of a Santa Claus in a children's home who had never imagined hearing the laughter of their dad, let alone Santa's laughter. It was a chance for me to survive for a few more days or months.

My mother and I drove as fast as we could to the closest store that sold natural products. We wanted to find all those magic potions that would cure me. We spent hours on the internet researching the best juices and ingredients I could buy. I confess that while entering a supermarket that had only organic food, I felt different, not only because I looked like an alien with my mask and gloves on but because I knew that this place did not fit my pocketbook. I observed the elegance of the shoppers' clothes, their expensive sunglasses and chic ladies' handbags; that green store was built and designed for them. However, to be quite honest, at that stage of the cancer game, I couldn't have cared less about their status. All I wanted was to get the nutrients my body needed; I would pay for anything that promised to help me live a little longer.

I think the saddest moment was when we went to pay for our items and faced the cashier. It was sad to see that my salary was now directed to a private institution that promised their customers that their products were 100 percent natural. I felt happy to feed my body the best products that existed, but at the same time, I felt robbed at gunpoint every time I saw the amount I had to pay for the natural food.

This situation made me reflect on economic issues that I alone could not solve, but at least I was beginning to question what did not make any sense. If it is true that organic food is much better than nonorganic, shouldn't all cancer patients, regardless of their financial conditions, have access to something that would give them better chances to live? It didn't help thinking like Mother Teresa. We live in a society where, if you have money and good health insurance, you can stretch your life a little longer. I had health insurance, and I was fortunate to be able to pay for better food. In short, money always spoke louder than altruism. Whoever had it could stay alive, and whoever did not would not live as long.

I continued eating my vegetables and continued my chemo-therapy prescribed by my oncologist. As far as the organic and all-white meat, I ate these for the first six months of the treatment. My fortress lasted until the day I attended the graduation party of a great friend, Keira. That day, I knew I had to resist the temptation: red meat and sausages! I tried to be polite, and I was strong enough to say no the first time somebody passed by with a serving of meat. However, when my friend offered me meat the second time, I could not resist it anymore! I looked at that tender meat and smelled the aroma of a well-done spicy sirloin with mayonnaise. My mother and I were hypnotized; we started accepting all types of meat that were brought to our table. It was as if someone had told us that all those meats were anticancer plants, and we had to eat them to heal ourselves from a terrible disease: abstinence.

Chapter 59

Different Battles

Mom and I kept practicing our weekly hobby: shopping for healthy food! At this point in the treatment, I was no longer ashamed of the catheter in my arm. I took my wig on and off when we went to get all the organic veggies we could afford. Once we got to the cashier, I realized that the young man who packed our groceries had special needs, and he simply could not stop staring at the catheter hanging from my arm.

Without beating around the bush, as he was a curious child who did not hold back any thoughts, he went straight to the point, "Girl, what's this on your arm?"

Not knowing how to answer, because no one had ever asked me about it before, I dropped the bomb: "Cancer."

Troubled by my dry answer, he started scratching his head and agitatedly replied,

"Oops! I'm very sorry! I shouldn't have asked …"

After seeing him looking at me with despair, as if this were the last time that he would see me, I tried to encourage him while I consoled myself too, replying, "No problem. I will be all right!"

For a moment, we quietly stared at each other. He was probably wondering how I could be so sure that everything would be okay. I had no certainty of anything, but I had faith that I would be okay. While he stared at me, I forgot about my health issues, and I thought about how difficult his life must have been too, but he was working like everyone else; he had not allowed his condition to hold him back from having a normal life. The truth is that although we felt compassion for each other, I did not know what it was like to live a life with special needs, and he did not know the life of a cancer patient. However, I believed what we had in common was the desire to have a sense of normalcy; he was happy not to be part of my reality because he didn't want to die, and I would not exchange my struggles for his. Reflection of the day: be kind to others; everyone is fighting a battle! Empathy is the key for us to understand each other's pain. Do something valuable in life; what is sadder than having cancer or being "special" is to be "normal" and healthy but to have a closed-minded or indifferent perspective.

Chapter 60

Leukemia Awareness

Lia, the principal of the school where I used to work, wrote to me saying that the students had organized a Leukemia Awareness Day. According to her, the student council gathered and decided that on one particular day, all faculty members and the student body would wear something red to spread awareness about blood cancer. I was so touched knowing that all my colleagues and students were doing something to bring awareness about a disease that had directly impacted me and countless others. The students and the teachers baked sugar cookies and cupcakes, and all the money raised would be sent to an institution that is conducting research to find a cure for cancer.

My heart swelled with pride. Imagine a school with six hundred teenagers from around the world stopping to think about those who were fighting the same disease that I was fighting. I knew that they all had their concerns about SAT, TOEFL, IGCSE, and the IB assessments; while studying for these assessments, they still had to learn how to deal with the anxiety and pressures of being accepted by American universities. However, they put everything aside and made my problem their problem too. They were teaching others how to empathize with others' struggles. It brightened my soul to know that the assessments did not cloud their generosity and compassion.

As soon as I heard about the Leukemia Awareness Day, I went to my closet, got out my favorite red shirt, faced the fear of being in a place where I could catch a cold and die, and went to thank my students and the faculty in person. I wanted them to know that what they were doing greatly mattered not only to me but to any cancer patient who was going through the same ordeal. I obviously cried, and they did too!

Fighting leukemia with my students

*C*hapter 61

Third Phase—Part 2

M eanwhile, I posted on my social network:

> What a beautiful day to be at the Spa with my
> mother. They say beauty is in the eye of the be-
> holder, so come on, right? I'm completing the sec-
> ond part of the third phase.

The view from my room—rainy day

My room's view was a warning of what was to come.

I knew, more or less, what I was to expect at this stage; at least that was what I thought. According to protocol, I would be all right for the first part of the third stage. I would have to take another very strong chemotherapy treatment. The doctors would monitor me for four to five days, and then I would be free to complete the remaining phases: fourth, fifth, and sixth—and the final—phase. Then everything would get back to normal, right? Wrong! To my despair, I got to know a little more about my treatment. In the morning, Doctor D.D., who seemed very happy with my results, came to see me.

"So, Da Silva, how are you feeling?"

"I'm fine, Doctor D.D. I'm very excited because we are already in the middle of this long treatment. From what I understand, I only have three more stages. And, Doctor, what happens after I finish the sixth stage of the induction phase?"

"Oh, it gets better! You go into the best phase: maintenance."

"Um … what?"

"As soon as you get to the sixth phase, you will start what is called the maintenance phase. It is a much better phase because you will take chemotherapy pills every day at home. Then the treatment gets easier because you only have to come to the hospital for Vincristine every month."

My eyes filled with tears. "How much longer will I have to take this chemotherapy, Doctor?"

He crushed all my dreams when he calmly answered, "Three years. Three and a half to be more precise."

This number certainly was like a death sentence to me. I've always been optimistic about everything, but everything has its limits, right? How could I listen to how my life would be put on hold for three more years and still be happy, smiling like a jester? Doctor D.D. seemed confused by my frustration. I knew the fact that being alive after receiving this diagnosis was such a blessing. The only problem was that I, like everyone else in the world, still had dreams and plans, but it seemed that I had to be contented with the fact I was still alive, and that in itself had to be enough.

I began to ask the doctor about my plans and dreams of being a mom. How could I put something toxic in my body for three more years and still be able to conceive my children? If I could still have them, would they be healthy or was there any chance that my babies would also have leukemia? The more I interrogated Dr. D.D. about my chances of being a mom, the more I realized from his responses that I was lucky enough to have reached that stage of the treatment. I realized that the disease was not called acute for any simple reason; it could take your life away, or it would allow you to live but would kill your dreams. Unfortunately, from what I understood, my diagnosis was one of the most serious types of leukemia that existed, and every day, all I could do was be thankful for any extra day I had. I certainly thanked God for every day, and I hoped that God, destiny, and the universe could take charge of what was predestined for me. One more time, I was reminded that I had no control over my life.

It took me some time to absorb everything the doctor had told me, but I believed in a higher power, God, and only He had the power to help me find peace.

Hours after I had the infertility conversation with the doctor, I had a visit from a volunteer at the hospital. She, a polite lady who was tall and had dark hair, looked like she was in her fifties. She had a motherly face, and I felt that she had good intentions. She seemed excited to listen to my story. I told her that I had just married my husband in May and that I had been diagnosed with leukemia in December. Because of that, I had not had the time to freeze my eggs, and the doctor had just told me that my treatment would last three years. The woman looked at me in disbelief. I could see that she was unsure about what to say to comfort me in this unfortunate time. Uncertain about what to say, she attempted to console me.

"You are feeling very angry at God, aren't you?"

I admit I was expecting to hear other forms of consolation, and I was taken aback by that question. People usually spoke optimistic phrases like "God does not give you one cross that you cannot carry" or "Everything happens for a reason!" or "A leaf does not fall from a tree if it is not the will of God." Some of the consolations were catchy phrases, but they did not console me. Some made me feel guilty for having this disease, but I understood that some of the visitors had no idea what to say, so they said what they felt was okay, and I was happy that they were trying to comfort me. However, that new utterance about being angry at God had not been said to me before. I found it quite unusual for several reasons. First, because I felt I had a very close connection with God, and I always imagined our relationship was pure love, not hate. Second, I never felt that my relationship with God was like a human relationship, in which suddenly one person gets angry and turns to the other friend and says, "We are not friends anymore! Go away!" However, the visitor insisted on hearing my response to this perplexing question.

"You can open up with me. You're feeling very angry at God, aren't you?"

I looked at her, frightened, and without knowing what to say, I replied, "No, actually I'm not! I would love to be in a different situation, no doubt about it, but I know that focusing my energy on being angry at God would be an enormous waste of my time."

Although genuine, my answer did not satisfy her, so she started trying to convince me that it made a lot of sense for me to be mad at God for everything He had put me through. Since I could not convince her that I was not at all mad, I tried to show her that there were people who were in much worse straits. I did not know how this conversation turned into a debate, but that's how I tried to prove that my horrible situation was not so bad. "Well, I still can be grateful for the good things I have in my life today."

She, not understanding my perspective, tried to dig into my crazy line of thought. "But why do you say that?"

She looked shocked that I still had things to be thankful for.

"Some people surely are suffering more than me. I know I'm in a lot of pain, I am not going to lie, but I think about those innocent children in developing countries who haven't had anything to eat today."

"With all that you're going through, you are still thinking about poor children?"

"Yes, I am. The truth of the matter is that we all have our issues that we are dealing with."

She came to visit me every other day that I was in the hospital. With those visits, we began to understand the obvious: I was not convinced that my life was as bad as it seemed, and she did not convince me to be angry toward God, who I believed would be my salvation. I continued to speak to her, trying to help her realize that my life was not as bad as it looked; it all depended on how one would perceive all the changes that were about to come. It was only up to me to shape my perspective, to learn and come out stronger from this plight. One thing I knew for certain: I would never surrender. If I couldn't make it to the end, I wanted to live my last days happy, never mad!

$\mathscr{C}$hapter 62

An Exciting Fourth Phase

The doctors had already warned me that the fourth phase of the treatment would last six weeks. It would start with an event that I always loved to watch: the World Cup! I had mixed feelings regarding this event. I was not sure if the Brazilian team was ready for it! To make matters worse, the 2014 World Cup was set to be in Brazil, but I could not leave New York to watch the games because I had to finish the chemo protocol I had just begun. Without losing my optimism but being a Brazilian fan, I had my superstitions: I always wore something green and yellow to send luck to the Brazilian team. I also got to the hospital early so that the nurses could help me find the right channel so that I would not miss my soccer game! The cheerful and kind nurses always offered me drinks and crackers.

Without hesitation, I accepted the orange juice that matched my outfit, and I used my imagination to picture myself at a lively pub in São Paulo. There, I did not have orange juice but a cold beer. While undergoing chemotherapy, I watched the game of Brazil vs. Croatia anxiously. I am not a soccer fan, but when it comes to the

World Cup, something inside me changes. My heart starts beating faster, and my emotions go through the roof. I watched it without knowing that my blood pressure also rose every time the Croatian players came closer to our goal.

With every dribble, I moved my legs too, living the moment as if I were in the stadium in Brazil. As soon as Brazil scored a goal, I screamed, "Goooooooooooaallll!" I quickly stood up and danced samba, spinning around the room without worrying if my chemo bag and the pole would fall or if the chemo would detach from my arm. Since the nurses couldn't determine why I was screaming, they all came to my room to see what had happened. Once they discovered why I was screaming, they started laughing. With Brazil's second goal, they already knew that the scream was mine and that Brazil had won. I heard one nurse saying to another, "I heard someone screaming. Who is it?"

"On, no, worries! It's Ms. Da Silva; she is watching a soccer game for the World Cup. She's just celebrating Brazil's goals."

A day before that match, I had a consultation with Dr. D.D., a doctor from Germany.

"So, will you watch the World Cup?"

"Of course, Doctor D.D.," I said, adorned in green, blue, and yellow.

"Who will you cheer for?"

"Brazil for sure! And you?"

"Brazil too. I am German, but I do not like the way the Germans play. They are kind of stiff. I like to watch Brazil, with a lot of dribbles; it is beautiful to watch them! But what if Brazil loses today?"

"Are you crazy? We will not lose. No, Doctor. This thought doesn't even cross my mind."

Mom and I wearing Brazilian shirts

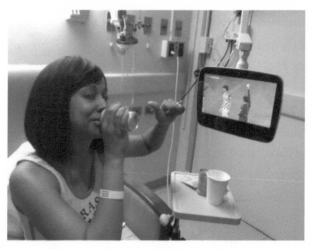

Having a good time at the hospital, drinking some juice while having some chemo and watching Brazil play a good match!

*C*hapter 63

Be Bold! Be Bald!

My friend Crislaine and I decided to visit our friend Caroline, who lives in New Jersey. Caroline had recently had a little boy, and I was excited to meet him. Having cancer was rough, but one thing I enjoyed was that when I didn't have to go to the hospital, I loved having a free afternoon to share happy moments with my friends. Crislaine and her little boy, Kelvin, my mother, and I happily drove to New Jersey. Once we arrived, Caroline introduced us to her handsome boy. It was so great to see her so happy, now a mother of two boys. Caroline had prepared a delicious lunch, and while we ate her delicious penne ala vodka and drank red wine, we listened to the sweet voice of Maria Rita. We had so much to catch up on, and the focus of our conversation was how our lives had changed so much in just one year. It was a day of great joy until we had to leave. That's when my friend Crislaine said, "Fabi, can you help me get Kelvin's pants on? He is jumping all over the place. I can't get a hold of him. I am exhausted!"

"Sure, Cris, no worries!"

Without knowing that it could be a very delicate situation, I sat next to the super-excited two-year-old boy with the mission of putting those pants on, when suddenly the unexpected happened: he pulled off my wig!

We both stared at each other. Verily, I think that everything happened so fast that neither of us understood how all that hair had fallen off of my head. I did not know where to hide! They had never seen me bald. I gaped at my friend with dismay. Her little boy tightly held my wig in his tiny little hands. I had no idea how in the world I would get my wig back. I was so embarrassed; my hair had grown back already, but my wig had become like another layer of clothing, so without it, I felt naked in front of my friends. I carefully took my wig from his cute little hands, and I changed his dirty diaper. As I desperately ran to the bathroom to throw away his diaper, I secured my wig to my head.

Although I thought I handled the awkward situation well, as soon as I looked at myself in the mirror, I noticed that my eyes were inundated with tears. I struggled to compose myself. I knew he was only a child, a handsome angel who I loved very much. I started calming myself down, saying that everything was fine. I kept wiping my incessant tears, and for the first time, I felt ashamed of my wig and putting myself in such embarrassing situations. How could I come out of the bathroom now that my eyes were so red? How could I explain to my friends that I was not hurt because Kelvin had taken my wig away but because life had entrapped me in the side effects of having this stupid disease, and I only felt pretty if I had someone else's hair on my head? I felt stupid that I was crying because a baby had taken off my wig. I simply did not know how to explain to them how that situation made me feel.

I wiped my tears and was ready to leave the restroom and face my reality, but then I heard my friends commenting on what had just happened. They laughed—which was normal because I admit the situation was very funny—but their laughter was depleting my resolve to leave the bathroom and face them. I did not want them to think that I was upset with Kelvin or with them. Listening to them encouraged me to face them. It was as if someone had just taken off my clothes, and I had walked naked in front of my friends. I blushed a little, and suddenly, I wore my clothes, and everything went back to normal. Finally, I pulled myself together and went down to say goodbye. As soon as they saw me, they realized that I had been crying in the bathroom. They understood that this was a delicate situation for me, and they also understood that cancer patients are very strong, but at times, we become so fragile that things that are innocuous to them could be a deadly tornado to us. I was grateful for having friends who were like sisters, and they did everything they could to keep me happy. As soon as I saw them, we spoke about the incident. I explained how I felt, and they understood. Once everything was clear, I quickly changed the subject to my mom's departure. Since she had a tourist visa, she would be here for only four more months. My mom's departure was certainly something that I would genuinely cry about; this made more sense to them because I had to face my new me without my mom by my side, and for this, I cried all over again.

Chapter 64

The Trip to Cape Cod

My boss and friend, Kate, had asked my family and me to spend a few days at her house at the beach. I was ecstatic. I knew I could not go in the water because of my catheter, but I was sure the sea would bring me great vibes and renew my hope. The first thing I did was to consult my doctor to make sure I had his okay, and once he approved, I knew that nothing would stop us from traveling.

After all, my mother, Richard, and I needed a refreshing scene; anything that did not look like a hospital would be fantastic.

Once the doctor approved our mini-vacation, we got home and began to prepare everything. We packed up our clothes, sheets, towels, and bathing suits. We researched the directions to find the fastest route to her house. I Googled sites to explore in Cape Cod as well as scenic pathways where we could walk around. I was thrilled with our escape from the hospital!

Although it was a short trip, spanning from Friday to Sunday night, nothing took away my excitement about being free—free from the white walls of the hospital and its smell. I could not believe that after so much struggle, I could have a few days of summer and joy. However, I have learned that life is too often a balance of joy and disappointments. When I went to the hospital to receive my blood results on Thursday, a day before our trip, the doctor asked to speak to me.

"Da Silva, I do not know what to say, but you will not be able to travel."

My first thought was, *Not again*. It was déjà vu—a doctor advising me not to travel.

"What? What happened?" I asked.

"I know I authorized your travel, but unfortunately, it is too risky for you to travel so far when your white blood cells are so low. It is not safe for you because your immunity is really low, and you could get any infection, and we wouldn't be able to help you."

"But, Dr. D.D.! I have been packing for a week. I have been doing this treatment for seven months already, and I have not gone to any place apart from this hospital."

"I know, Da Silva. I understand your frustration. Do you want me to advise you as a doctor or as your friend?"

To his surprise, I replied, "As my friend! I'm joking, Doctor. You can make the decision that you think is best for me."

The two nurses felt sorry for me because there was nothing they could do to stop my heart from breaking; there was no bandage or medicine that would stop the pain that reminded me that at that time of my life, any freedom I thought I had was a delusion. One of them even tried to intercede on my behalf and said that if Dr. D.D. authorized my trip, she would be in Cape Cod that weekend, and if I got sick, she could refer me to some qualified doctors in the area. With the pressure of having to give the final verdict, the doctor said, "I'm doing this for your own good. Do not travel, rest as much as possible, and when the time is right, you will be able to travel often."

Unable to hold back my tears, I stared at him with gratitude and anger. I felt like I was a child who had just witnessed my ice cream fall from my cone to the ground without having taken a first lick. I was not crying because I could no longer travel but because I understood that at that moment I had no control over my life. I had lost one of the simplest pleasures in the world, the ability to plan for the future, even if it was only the very immediate future. How many times would I have to cancel dinner with friends, parties, or trips because somebody had a tiny cold and I could not be around them? I had to adapt to this sterile life one day at a time and be thankful for each of them.

When I left the doctor's office, my mother noticed that I had been crying, and with a concerned look, she asked, "Why are you crying, sweetie?"

"We cannot travel!"

I heard a pained silence. When I looked at my mom, I saw that she was also crying. She understood what that little trip meant to me and knew that I was tired of getting my hopes up and getting frustrated. My pain was her pain, and I know she was saddened by the fact that life was knocking me out every time I tried to stand up for my happiness.

Once again, life had tried to defeat me, but it was not long before I pulled myself together and began to dream again. After all, I could not travel far, but of course, I could use my free time and vivid imagination to travel to Brazil, Barbados, Italy, France, and many other places that I could and eventually would explore. Dreaming was still possible, and it was free! So, I used my imagination to go to São Paulo, where I was born. Some days, I saw myself walking on the beautiful beaches of Barbados, and then I would find myself transported, eating the best pasta in Italian restaurants, and then drinking the best French wines at a table close to the Eiffel Tower!

$\mathscr{C}$hapter 65

Birthday Party

$\mathbf{M}$eanwhile, on my social network, I posted:

> Today is a happy day, but my heart is very heavy ...
> My doctor who took care of me for months with Dr.
> D.D. told me that today would be a happy and sad day
> for her. She told me that she decided to move back to
> California where she is from, and she reminded me
> that the next time I would see her would be on my
> birthday and also the last time that we would see
> each other, and that day has arrived! I was glad that
> she will be with her family, but I am also sad because
> she will no longer work at the hospital where I was
> being taken care of. We hugged and cried because
> there is no way not to get attached to our doctors
> after spending so much time together ...

On my birthday, I woke up happy and determined to get my
chemo-birthday! I wore a beautiful pink dress, put on my high heels,
and off to the hospital we went. As soon as I arrived at the hospital,

I had a lot of wonderful surprises. The doctor who was moving to California had bought me Melissa cupcakes, and she gave me a beautiful birthday card in which she described how she admired me. It was so thoughtful of her! The second great piece of news I received was that the chemotherapy that was scheduled for that day had to be canceled because my red cell count was low, and the doctors decided to give me one more week to recover before they started the chemo treatment. However, the best news of all was that the party that I had already planned weeks ago would happen, and I knew I would not be throwing up because I would not take chemo on that day. Sorry, chemo, but you could not ruin my plans, at least not this time!

Our birthday party was great! I say ours because Eliane and I had our birthdays only two days apart, and we had celebrated our birthdays together a few years ago. Celebrating another one with her was great. All our friends went to a restaurant in White Plains that we used to go when we were all single. It was truly special for me to see all of them gathered together, celebrating such an important moment for us. My thirty-first birthday had a whole different feel. Now I felt the need to celebrate not only the years of my life but also the months and days that I had been granted the most precious present—to be alive. While my friends were singing "Happy Birthday," a film of my life passed through my mind. It was scary how my life, in such a short period, had changed since my thirtieth birthday. I had told my friends not to worry about giving me any presents. I asked if they could give any small donation to a cancer institution; that would be the best present anyone could give me. Who knew what researchers could do, given the funds? Perhaps they will find the cure for cancer in our lifetime. It is still free to dream, so why not? I was grateful for those six months "extra" that I had survived. Deep in my heart, I hoped to be able to celebrate at least another thirty years. Was it too much to ask to live for only another thirty years? Thirty more years seemed like nothing and everything.

Chapter 66

Cancer Hammered Me!

Meanwhile, on my social network, I posted:

Germany 7 vs. Brazil 1!

Chemotherapy 7 vs. Fabiana 1!

Yes, my friends, this message is for you who have been faithfully following the World Cup and also have been sending me good vibes so that my treatment has a good outcome. The above results seem horrible, but that's exactly what happened! I remember watching the Germany vs. Brazil game, and I simply could not believe my eyes; the "best" Brazilian players were being defeated as if they were playing blindfolded or were amateurs. While I watched it, I had the impression that the Brazilian players were eleven disoriented rag dolls that were running away from something, and in that case,

they were running away from the championship of
2014 in Brazil!

After a week and a half of chemotherapy, "she"—the darn
chemotherapy—began to hammer me as well! The doctors, up to
today, jokingly claim that it was that awful game that made me
sicker. Some days after I watched that shameful game, I began to
have a lot of pain that seemed to be destroying all the cells in my
body.

I woke up in so much pain that I decided to drive to the hospital. The pain was so sharp that I could barely feel my legs; it felt like
I had one thousand needles poking me every second. With the beat
of my heart, I felt a needle. With every breath I took, I felt a needle.
While I was driving, I was afraid I could not make it to the hospital
without crashing my car. All I asked was that God protected my
mom, me, and whoever was driving close to us on our way to the
hospital in New York City. My poor mom kept looking at me, and
in her low and soft voice, she prayed to God that we would get to
the hospital safely. As soon as I got there, the doctors decided that I
would have to be hospitalized, and after five days, I started feeling
painless and like myself again.

I had never felt so much pain in my entire life. Before I was
hospitalized, I felt like my legs had been crushed and smashed
slowly by a big train. My legs hurt so much. My skin felt tight, and
suddenly it seemed that my body was too small for my skin. The
cells and veins had created their own lives; they were forcing their
way out of my skin. It is weird to describe it, but I had so much
pressure coming from my legs that I felt that my body was about to
explode; it was probably rejecting all the chemo I had in all those
months.

Chemotherapy was not easy on me during this phase of the
treatment. The doctors and nurses tried their best to give me
something that could stop that sharp pain, but everything they

tried didn't even tickle the stabbing pain. As their last resource, the doctors decided to give me some morphine, and after having morphine and chemo on the same day, I ended up having a seizure, which made me stay in the hospital until Sunday night.

On Monday morning, I felt blessed and excited to be out of the hospital. I have never been in jail, but I imagine that the feeling I had might be similar to the feeling of freedom that a prisoner who has been in jail for years feels once they have been told it is time to go home. After being hospitalized for a long time, we start appreciating every single thing, like being outside. Only those who lose the ability to be free understand it!

That Monday would be the day my father would arrive from Brazil, and since I would be out of the hospital on Sunday night, I would definitely pick him up. I told him that I would pick him up from JFK and celebrate his birthday with him. That Monday, I was still feeling under the weather, but I woke up early in the morning, and my mom and I excitedly went to the airport to pick him up.

When we were leaving the airport, I asked him where he wanted to go. When he said he would love to go to Central Park, I realized that we deserved to have a little celebration. I could not reject my birthday boy/daddy's wish! We walked around the beautiful pathways, but I felt so weak that every time I saw a bench, I quickly ran and lay on it without any concern for what anyone would say.

Since I had just been released from the hospital a couple of hours before picking him up, I did not have much strength, but I pretended that I was strong because I wanted to spend some quality time with them, and that meant not in a hospital bed. I wanted Dad to think that I was feeling good because I didn't want him to be worried about me, at least on his birthday. Even though I tried hard, I could not pretend for too long; soon I started getting yellowish, and my parents, who know me well, noticed that I was not okay.

The doctor, who had seen me the previous day, said, "I am letting you go, but if you get a fever, run to the hospital." When I got home after a wonderful day in Central Park, guess what? I had fever. The doctor also said that I had to use my intuition, and if I didn't find it necessary to go to the emergency room, I could try to control the fever with some over-the-counter medication.

Dear reader, I do not know what you would do if you were in my shoes, but after spending five days in the hospital and one day in Central Park with my family, all I wanted was to be free and to be home with them. So I did not call the hospital, and I started to monitor my fever. Unfortunately, the fever was swinging from high to low every hour. It started getting higher on Tuesday, and it got worse on Wednesday. To make things worse, I started getting some other symptoms like a black spot on my tongue. That was a red or a black flag. I only got to spend two days with my parents, and I had to go back to the hospital.

There I was again. Cancer did not give me a break and did not care if I wanted to be in the hospital or not. According to the doctors, I would get better from the cold that did not seem to want to leave me alone.

I knew chemo had given me a chance to live, but it had also destroyed my immune system. I had mixed feelings about chemo; not being able to fight a cold on my own showed me that the darn chemo had destroyed not only the bad cancerous cells but also the healthy ones.

I have to confess that when I arrived at the emergency room on Wednesday, for the first time, I was deeply saddened and felt hopeless. Cancer is no joke. I was not happy to be back. How could I feel happy if I was in pain *again*? How could I still smile if I was back in the ER in less than a week? How could I be happy knowing that my dad had just flown nine hours to be with my mom and me, but I had to be secluded in that hospital?

Well, I am grateful to have so many good friends who ended

up calling me in those weeks and who sent me messages after finding out that I was in the hospital. They also dealt well with my bitterness. My parents and Richard had to deal with my despair as well. For the first time, I was upset with God. I could not understand why I was back in the hospital, while everyone else was out enjoying their summer in New York or a cozy winter in São Paulo. That was all I wanted, just a normal life.

Thank God my bitterness lasted a day and a half, and I was able to find good in the bad situation. I started focusing on the blessings that I had: *I still have faith in God. I have a great mother who takes good care of me, a funny and loving father who makes me laugh all the time, and a patient and loving husband who has supported me even though we were married only seven months when I was diagnosed. I am responding well to a treatment that causes patients to lose a lot of weight, and I'm very fortunate that I get to have my mom's food, which is making me fatter and fatter every day. Some clothes don't even fit me anymore, and as a cancer patient, the last thing you want is to lose weight. I have friends, I mean really special friends, from around the world who are praying for me. I have wonderful students who I miss so much every day! I'm in a hospital that is considered one of the best for this type of treatment. The doctors are very professional, and the nurses are so caring that I always feel they are angels in uniforms. I still have a job, and my colleagues are so close that I consider them part of my family!*

After being bitter for a day and a half, I realized that all my complaints and negativity were not helping me. I became tired of being bitter and became the Fabi I was used to being!

What I learned from the fourth phase was that even though I'm full of life, sometimes I would not be able to live everything I wanted to, not because of the illness but because the intensive treatment brought a lot of limitations that I was not used to.

My friends reminded me that all the suffering was temporary

and that I was almost done. I had two more phases, and then I would be into maintenance! Dear friends, thank you for reminding me that I had only three more months of that crazy battle. Since I had already completed eight months, three more would not knock me out—and then life would take its course again.

Chapter 67

The Adventures of the Unexpected Hospitalization

When my father left Brazil, he had no idea that he would travel so far and would spend almost every day of his vacation in a hospital again. I felt bad for ruining his vacation. It was not the vacation he deserved, but as always, he used his optimism and saw the best in every situation; he did not allow the sad moments to destroy the precious moments we had together. No matter where we were, at least we were together. Since the hospital was in New York City, he spent most of his time with me, but he also ventured into the city that he loves the most by himself, his beloved Big Apple. This hospitalization lasted eighteen long days, all because I caught a cold and had no immunity to fight the darned cold since the "blessed" chemotherapy had destroyed some of my good cells.

We had yet to decide what to do about my cousin's graduation party. While we were talking about it, I saw my cell phone blink, and Amanda had just sent me a text message: "Hi! I cannot wait to see you! Quick question: would you mind if I put your name on our cake, saying congratulations to you too? I'm just asking because I am very proud of you, and I would love to share this special moment with you."

Dear reader, where would I find the courage to tell her that I could not be there with her on her graduation day after getting that text message? We were very upset that I could not go, but I wanted my parents to be there for her. My parents were on the fence about what they should do; they wanted to go to show her how proud we were of her accomplishment, but they also wanted to stay because they were afraid of leaving me. After a lengthy debate, I convinced them that they needed to go. I could not go, but they should definitely go and honor her for such a beautiful achievement. So, Olie came to visit me, and she helped me buy the bus tickets so that they could go to Massachusetts on their own. Everything was sorted out. They would walk from Seventy-First to Thirty-Fourth Street, and from there, they would take the bus to go to my aunt's house. It was my parents' first adventure in America!

Would it be too crazy to send my parents to another state in a country where they did not speak the language? Yes! To make matters worse, I guess they were so baffled about traveling on their own to unfamiliar territory that they ended up traveling without a cell phone and without my aunt's phone number or address. They were in a pickle, and they would have to have a lot of flexibility and courage to forge forth in their new exploration.

Since it seemed they didn't have enough troubles to deal with, they got one more. Once they arrived at Thirty-Fourth Street, they started looking for a silver Jaguar that I told them to find. I kept telling them that there was no way they would miss it. Oh, well, I was wrong! Once they finally found the Greyhound silver Jaguar, they were informed that they had to go to Forty-Second Street instead. You can imagine how long it took them to understand that they had to go somewhere else; they were so sure that they were at the right place, and so was I.

Thankfully, most New York City streets are numbered, so it was easy for them to know where to go; they just needed to walk eight more blocks, and they would be off on their little trip that ended up being a voyage. When they finally found the place where the buses leave to Boston, they got on the bus, and the driver told them that they were not going straight to the city where my aunt lived. They would have to transfer to another bus. Since some passengers noticed that my parents could not understand what the driver was saying, the kind passengers started rounding my parents up and started speaking loudly in English, and others tried speaking with them in Spanish. The bus had turned into a very loud Tower of Babel where nobody understood what the other was saying! Can you imagine my parents' despair when trying to understand what the loud crowd was trying to say? After a lot of loud voices and nonsensical gesturing, they were able to get where they had to go, from Hartford to Framingham. Phew! Their travels were like trying to get a perfect score on the SAT without studying.

They appeased each other and kept comforting themselves, saying that they would get somewhere, and if they couldn't find my aunt, they would come back to New York City. Once they arrived in Framingham, they felt so lost that when they reached the station where my aunt would pick them up, they tried to get a taxi to the address that Olie had written down. The driver said, "I am sorry. I cannot take you guys to this place because you are already here."

At first, I was a bit worried about sending them on their own and had no idea how difficult it would be for them. To a degree, I was happy because at least they would not have to spend their weekend in the hospital. It was good for them to have a mental break from our hospital routine. I was glad that they could get some fresh air, meet new people, and see old friends. I was glad they made it okay and were able to be there for Amanda!

Chapter 68

My Roomies

I was still in the hospital, and since I was there for a long time, I met many interesting patients, and each one of them taught me a lot. I will call all of them "Mary."

The first Mary was from Jamaica and was about sixty years old. She was such a pleasant person to be around. Every time we talked, she gave me great advice and always stressed the importance of eating well and drinking natural juices. Also, she had such beautiful faith that every time she talked about it, it gave me peace and strengthened my own faith. She was always cheerful, and her small part of our room was always packed with at least twenty people. People would come and go; it looked like a great Caribbean party! Her section of the room was always decorated with lots of colorful flowers, balloons, and loud laughter. Since I could not be at my cousin's graduation, I loved crashing my roommate's Caribbean party from my bed. Her visitors were not worried that it was late at night. Some nights it was 11 p.m., and they were still popping in from all over New York. Some told funny jokes and continued to celebrate and make her laugh, and even though they didn't know I was listening to all their jokes, I enjoyed having a room full of life. It reminded me of the happiness at our parties in Brazil.

The first Mary went away, and the second came in: a woman who seemed to be in her forties. Contrary to the first Mary, this one was moody. She did not like any noise, and she did not like that I wanted to have my lights on. The side of her room had dim lights, and she enjoyed the silence of the hospital that, in my opinion, would cause anyone to lose their mind. I sometimes overheard her talking to her mom, and she sounded a little bitter. Since we were in the same room, I could not help but listen to her conversations over the phone. For some reason, I was afraid of getting closer, but I felt that perhaps a conversation could help her a bit, or at least cheer her up a little. So I went to her side of the room and realized she no longer had a sparkle of life in her eyes. She seemed so hopeless. I tried to cheer her up as much as I could. I told her about my diagnosis, how I was slowly recovering and was hopeful to get my life back. But when she told me about her case, I understood the reason for her sadness. Not only did I understand, but more importantly, I respected how she felt about her diagnosis. We were on the same floor, in the same room, but our cancers were very different. This Mary was in terrible pain, and she could not be alone, but she told me that none of her family members could be in the hospital with her. If she needed to use the restroom, I would run to her section of the room so that I could walk her to our bathroom. She told me she had been diagnosed with two cancers, melanoma and rectum. After our conversation, I understood that Mary didn't feel that she had anything to be thankful for. She had left two kids at home with neighbors, and she was not sure if she would go back for them or who would take care of them if she did not come back. That was her true pain, her concerns, and it was not my place or the moment to cheer her up. What she needed was somebody to listen to her, and that was what I did.

The second Mary was released the next day. When I asked her

who would pick her up, she said she had nobody to pick her up, but she was glad that she would go home even if it was by subway. She had gained her freedom back. I was happy that she would be able to be with her kids. While I was there, I saw people coming in and out but had no sign that I would be released. I had hope that my white cells would increase and my immune system would get stronger. Once my white cells started increasing, I would kick that cold, and then, one day, I would go home too.

For a few hours, I had the room to myself, but that was a luxury that did not last long. A third Mary arrived, a woman in her seventies. She was blonde with short hair and had so many pounds of makeup on that she could be easily mistaken for a clown that had come to cheer us up. Her fancy jewelry and clothes announced that she was well off. I, of course, went to her side to start a conversation and realized she refused to look at me; she looked like she had just seen a creepy ghost. I did not know why she was looking at me like that. After all, we all had cancer, and we were all fighting the same stupid disease. At first, I thought it could have been a misunderstanding. Maybe she was not scared; it was just my impression. However, as soon as I left her side of the room, I heard her desperately press the emergency button several times. As soon as one nurse picked up, she whispered to the nurses that she demanded to leave our room immediately. I could not believe what I was hearing. Why did she want to change rooms? Was it because I was wearing a mask? That couldn't be it! I had no contagious disease; I was only wearing a mask to protect myself. The crabby old lady started calling her nurses desperately. She did not mind whispering anymore. She started screaming, "I want to change my room right now! Please help me! I insist that I be transferred right now. I can pay for a private room if it is necessary!"

On the other side of the curtain, I quietly listened to her desperate request to be away from me, and I started crying. I felt so small; it had never crossed my mind that one day someone would be afraid of being around me. That rejection from someone who knew what the pain of having cancer was hurt my soul deeply. I felt like I was a beast who was a danger to the entire hospital. I left my room and went walking around the hospital hall. As soon as I saw a nurse, I said, "Excuse me, young man, I noticed that that lady is making a big fuss to leave our room. Do you know why she wants to leave?"

The nurse did not know how to explain it without hurting me. He tactfully said, "Look, Da Silva, please don't worry about it! She's a little concerned because she saw that you are wearing a mask. She just had pneumonia, and once she realized that you have a cold, she requested to go to another room."

"But can I infect someone else?"

"No. You're wearing a mask to protect yourself. If you could pass any disease to anyone, the team of doctors would have put you in a separate room alone. Try not to think about this incident."

"But if she just had pneumonia, I should be the one afraid of catching something from her. Anyway, never mind!"

It was the second night that I slept without my parents, but Richard would soon come to spend the night with me. I kept thinking about Amanda's party and followed every moment of it through the photos that my friend Bela, from Portugal, posted on social media. I was happy to see pictures of my parents in a setting different than the hospital. They so deserved to have a good time!

I thought about how contradictory my life was. On the one hand, I was so loved by my friends. On the other, I was rejected and felt so hurt by a woman I had never met before and who I would probably not see again. I had only one option: carry on with my life and not think about the ones who make me feel negatively about myself. To my happiness, the old lady was taken to another room. As soon as Richard came from work, he had to listen to all my blah-blah-blah about my former roommate who thought I had Ebola or Zika or some other type of contagious disease.

The peevish Mary left my room, and the next morning, the fourth Mary checked in. This one was a blessing, a woman whose look would make anyone feel empowered with peace! She had come to my room because her roommate was a little disturbing and talked too much. All the fourth Mary wanted was a peaceful room to rest. It seemed we had found a match! The nurses told her about me and what had just happened with my former roommate, and she told them that she wanted to be in my/our room. She was such a lovely lady. Mary looked about forty years old, and her eyes and her sweet voice transmitted peace. She was an angel! She was the balance I was looking for; I did not need a party girl or a gloomy person that could bring me down. She told me how she had struggled with her previous roommate because the woman wanted to talk to her the entire night, and she kept repeating that she was very happy that she was sharing the room with me.

When she was on the phone, she always told her friends that she was happy that she had finally found a roomy who she could bond with and trust. After having the Mary witch in my room, it made me feel good to have somebody who wanted to be close to me again. It was something so little, but it made me feel good to know that I had been "chosen." Even though the third fancy Mary had rejected me, it turned out great because that was how the fourth Mary ended up moving to my room. Being rebuffed was a blessing in disguise!

Unfortunately, after a few days, the fourth Mary started having some severe pain. She cried all the time, and it hurt to see her suffering without being able to do anything to help. I wondered quietly, *Why, God? Why does such a good woman have to go through so much suffering?* I did not know how to help her. I prayed softly to God to alleviate the pain she felt in her stomach. Whenever she asked me to, I used my emergency button to tell the nurses that she was in excruciating pain again. Mary started getting worse. Her skin had turned tallow, and she kept begging the nurses to give her more medicine for her brutal pain. I felt hopeless; I knew she was suffering so close to me, and there was nothing I could do to alleviate her pain. From the other side of the curtain, I begged God that the doctors could help her. They put a tube in her nose, and from her scream, I could tell that she felt a lot of pain. The doctors kept trying to calm her down and explained that that tube was needed so they could remove any feces that was blocked in her stomach. I listened to their conversation, horrified about what would happen to her.

"Doctor, I beg you! I need you to remove this tube from my nose!"

"You need to stay calm, Mary. We will do everything to help you."

"Please remove it! I cannot put up with this pain anymore!"

One of the nurses said, "Mary, it is okay. I want you to try to talk to me. Let's talk about you. Do you have any pets?"

I, on the other side of the curtain, thought, *Who wants to talk about a pet when you have all this pain?*

"Yes, I do," Mary murmured.

"What color is it?"

"White."

"What else can we talk about to calm you down?"

"Florida."

"I want you to think and imagine you are in Florida. What color is the water?"

I heard that and thought, *This nurse is crazy!* The fourth Mary took a deep breath.

"Have you ever taken your puppy to Florida? I want you to listen to the noise of the sea. Are you listening to the birds?"

With a quieter voice, she replied, "Yes!"

And believe it or not, the doctor's technique worked! She was calmer. But the calmness lasted for about a minute. She soon began again.

"Take it off my nose now! For God's sake, I cannot put up with this pain!"

"The nurses are doing everything to help you. Let's go back to Florida."

Meanwhile, the nurses kept extracting stool from her nose.

"I want to go home! I want to go home! Get this out of my nose!"

"You cannot be spewing feces. We need to remove more so that you do not feel more stomach aches. Let's go back to Florida."

I listened to everything, terrified. Would I also have to go through this kind of pain? There was so much pain, agony, and grief in her screams that you did not need to be a medical practitioner to know that something serious was going on. By listening to her begging for help, I could certainly say that she went through levels of pain that not everyone could take, and I feared for her life. When I woke up, the fourth Mary was no longer in our room. Neither her flowers nor her pictures were on her side of the room anymore. I noticed that in my corner of the window, there was one of her little vases of flowers. I was too scared to ask the nurses where the fourth Mary was. I was scared that their answer would be, "I am sorry, Ms. Da Silva. Unfortunately, Mary has succumbed to her disease."

To my delight, after a few days, as I was walking in the hospital halls, and who did I see coming my way? I could not believe my eyes. The fourth Mary! We hugged each other when we saw that we were both okay. We did not need to say a word; we were just happy that we were both alive. That hug said it all!

Chapter 69

The Lawn—Reflection on the Second Maria

A reflection I posted on my social media:

> Is the neighbor's grass always greener than ours? Not always! But what is our reaction when the lawn of another is not as healthy as expected?

> Well, we always hear that saying that the grass is always greener on the other side of the fence, and I agreed with it. However, the last time I was hospitalized, I began to have some other reflections about it. Why do we have to wait until we look at a neighbor's lawn that is all burned and without flowers to start appreciating our lawn more? Why would we have to wait for the lawn of another person to become worse than ours to be thankful for ours, sometimes even yellowish but healthier?

The reason I wrote that was because I also found myself looking at the lawn of one of my roommates in the hospital and thanked God that her grass was not mine. I noticed that her lawn was more damaged than mine because she had two types of cancer and was not in remission. And the lesson I learned was that we should not always wait to see something worse than our problems before we become grateful for what God has given us. The day to be grateful for the situation in which we are in is today, not only when we see that someone is struggling for something that is (or appears to be) more difficult than our battle.

Chapter 70

Fifth Phase—Part 1

The doctor had already told me that this phase would be similar to the third. I would have to spend four to five days in the "spa," and after that, I would have my freedom again. This time my roommate was a Russian woman in her seventies. She spoke broken English but certainly could get her message across whenever she wanted to. The fifth Mary was very funny, and when I understood what she was saying, I always burst into a good laugh.

She was quiet for a couple of days, but suddenly, something magical happened, and she began to show her strong personality. One day, I woke up with Mary calling me.

"Hey, man, can you come here?"

"Excuse me. Are you talking to me?"

"Yeah, man! You put this catheter in my arm, and it hurt a lot, dude!"

I had no clue what she was talking about. I remained laying on my bed. I kept thinking, *Why the hell is she calling me dude? Maybe because my hair is short and she thinks I'm a man?* I decided to remain silent because whoever she thought I was, was not in good standing with her. I did not want to give her any reason to fight, and from her tone of voice, I could tell she was ready for a good fight. Suddenly, I heard someone abruptly opened the curtain that separated our room. I knew it couldn't be her because the nurses said she hadn't walked in weeks. When I opened my eyes, there she was on my side of the room, staring at me. Her angry face showed that she was ready to attack someone.

"Damn, man, why did you hurt my arm twice last night?"

"Ms., I am sorry, but I don't know what you are talking about. First, I'm not a guy. I am a woman! Second, I did not put any catheter in you. Look at me! I am patient like you. I also have a catheter," I said, showing my catheter to her.

The poor fifth Mary seemed confused with all that information and went back to her side of the room, scratching her head and mumbling things I could not understand. As soon as she left, I rushed to the phone to call the nurse's station.

"Hi, guys! This is Da Silva. I'm sorry to bother you, but someone needs to come here and talk to Mary. She is a little confused. She just came out of my room! She thinks I am a man and that I put a catheter on her arm last night."

"Don't worry, Ms. Da Silva. We're sending a nurse there to take care of the situation." The nurses came in and calmly explained to her that I was not the nurse who had put the catheter into her arm. It took her a while to understand what they were saying, but she finally understood that I was a girl.

The fifth Mary was gradually showing her personality more and more, and I thought the way she dealt with the formalities of the hospital was pretty funny. When the nurses came at night, they asked her several questions to ensure that she was lucid. The questions were as follows:

"What is your date of birth?"

The fifth Mary answered correctly. The nurse then continued.

"Great! In what country are you?"

"The US."

"What season are we in?"

"No, I do not know," she answered, showing some signs of impatience.

"Very well. Who is our current president?"

"Ah, stop bothering me with these stupid questions! Shit, I just want to rest and get some sleep, and you come here every hour to bother me. Every night, you are asking me questions, doing blood work, measuring my blood pressure, giving me medicine. What do you want from me? Leave me alone! For God's sake, when can I sleep? Let me sleep!"

Her responses reminded me of my grandma's straightforwardness.

She had a sharp tongue that could intimidate any diplomat who speaks seven different languages; she was not intimidated by her lack of formal vernacular. Every time I heard her talking fiercely, I burst out laughing. I do not know if she had dark humor or if she was just very real with them. I admired her for being so outspoken and for having the ability to say whatever came into her mind without worrying about what others would think of her. Whenever she had any crazy thought, she spit her words like an angry mom who needed to scold her child for getting bad grades at school. I had to agree with the fifth Mary that it was hard to get a good night's sleep in the hospital. We knew that as soon as we lay down, either the machine would start beeping or it was time to take shots or medicine, or they had to measure our pressure. However, I felt sorry for the nurses. I knew they were only doing their job, and we needed them to do their job so that we could survive.

Finally, the fifth phase of my treatment went well, and in four days, I was back to the place I loved the most: home.

Chapter 71

The Unwanted Correspondence

After spending eighteen days hospitalized, I deserved to go home and have some peace, right? Wrong! We got home and found a letter from my health insurance that stated I could contest a hospital bill in the amount of $238,000. According to this letter, I owed this amount for the five days I was hospitalized right after I was informed I had cancer. According to my health insurance company, since it took five days for me to have my first chemo, the five days I was waiting for chemo were not medically necessary.

Dear reader, as soon as I read that letter, my head began to spin. How did they come to the conclusion that I had to pay for a medical procedure if I had medical insurance? Besides, it was over $200,000! I could buy a house with that money—certainly not in Westchester, but at least a condominium in Westchester! To my knowledge, I hadn't joined Big Brother 2014 and won the top prize. If I had, perhaps I could afford it, but why would I put my prize money toward an expense my insurance should cover?

That letter drove me nuts for so many reasons. First, the absurd amount of $238,000! The math that five days in a hospital equaled almost 300k did not sit well. Is there any teacher who has this money sitting under their mattress? I certainly did not! Being a newlywed, a teacher, and a former cancer patient, I was more broke than those who were impacted by the housing bubble bursting in 2008. I believe the 1929 Stock Market Crash would accurately depict the state of my bank account. Second, the doctors recommended that I remain stress-free as much as I could. How could I remain tranquil now that I knew that I would probably have to sell my pants or my parents' house so that I could finish my treatment? Third, they claimed that I should not have been hospitalized when I was informed I had cancer. Excuse me? How can anyone be diagnosed with cancer and simply say: "Thank you so much for having me today. Now that you revealed that I have one of the deadliest diseases in the world, I'm going home! That's it; I do not need to stay here. After all, cancer can be cared for at home with teas and some apples!" We were talking about freaking cancer!

I hope I don't need to tell you that my first reaction was to cry, do I? I hope not, or I will think that you, dear reader, got bored with so many sad stories and skipped a few chapters! Well, I did not know what to do, so I called one of the social workers from the hospital. She always called to check how I was doing mentally, so I thought it would be a great idea to let her know that at that point of my life, I had the same level of sanity as a dog who had contracted rabies. As soon as she picked up the phone, I started spewing all the sour news I had received, and I think between the sobs and words, she understood that I was broke, not only monetarily, but I was mentally in pieces.

She listened to my concerns, and she tried to reassure that everything would be just fine. First, she said it could have been a mistake, but if it was not a mistake, she reiterated that the hospital could offer me good payment terms, and I could pay that bill in thirty years. Thirty years? Did the world just turn upside down while I spent some time in the hospital, or was I hearing that it was normal to pay for a hospital bill over the expanse of thirty years? I usually do not lose my temper that often, but the poor social worker had to deal with the angriest side of me. After repeatedly telling the social worker that I wouldn't pay for it because it did not make any sense, I arrived at a conclusion: either the hospital had given me the wrong diagnosis, and I did not need to be hospitalized, or my insurance had made a mistake, and I wouldn't have to pay that amount of money. Simple as that! Those were the only options I would consider; unfairly paying all that money would not be one of the options.

I could not think of anything else! However, some scarier thoughts began to creep into my mind: *if they do not believe I had to be hospitalized for five days when I was diagnosed with cancer, how much are they going to charge me for staying eighteen days because of a common cold?*

After a lot of thought, I began explaining to my parents that we would probably have to sell their house to pay for my hospital bills. I called Richard, and I explained that we needed to think about where we would live because we clearly would need to sell our apartment. At this point, who needed a house? The Brooklyn Bridge would be a great address, or we would go to a homeless shelter. Whatever! Whatever solution I could think of would still not even be close to the amount needed to pay that enormous bill.

I called my friend Priscilla, who listened to me complain about the monstrous value, crying and screaming that the world was not fair. It may be cliché, but I will repeat: one who has friends has it all. They are like those soft blankets on a harsh winter day that you cuddle up with, and you realize how lucky you are to have a warm place to live. She patiently assured me that it could only be a mistake, which I did not need to worry about it. Priscilla not only listened to me, but she even asked her husband, Brian, to call me, and they convinced me that at that moment, I should focus only on me. Brian told me to bring the bill to the hospital when I had my next appointment, and they would help me. That's exactly what I did.

I took the letter to the nurse who took care of me the whole week; she laughed and said that it was ridiculous. She calmed me down, saying that the hospital would contest the bill, that they had enough proof that I did not stay in the hospital because I wanted to take a break from home. After a few weeks, I received a letter of agreement saying that I did not need to pay anything; it was just a mistake. All my tears and unnecessary stress were for no reason. A lesson I learned that day was that it is not worth stressing over little things—although that bill appeared to be quite large, at least for me. When you find yourself at the end of the tunnel, do not give up. Things will get better!

Chapter 72

Surprise!

My mom, my dad, Richard, and I were invited to have lunch at Olie's home on a Saturday. My immune system was very low, and even though the doctors advised me to stay away from people, I wanted to see my friend. To my surprise, when I opened the door, I came across a house full of friends who were instrumental in this troubled phase of my life: Priscilla, her baby, Peace, and Brian; Crislaine, her baby, Kelvin, and her husband, Elvis, also joined. Even my friend from Florida, Fabibella, her baby, and her husband, Dustin, were there! Caroline, her babies, and her husband, Francisco, were also present. Olie, who had offered her house, and Vanda cooked a stroganoff that tasted like an expensive steak from an upscale steakhouse in Manhattan.

I was very happy to be there with them and with my family. This is what has real meaning and value in life: family and good friends. I was delighted to see my father worry-free, drinking his beer, laughing out loud in an energizing environment. I was at peace to see my mother not worried about how I was feeling for a few hours. I was happy to see the happiness of all my friends, to be able to follow the next stages of their lives, and I was glad they were part of mine. It was the first time in one year that cancer was not the main topic of our conversation; we talked about everything but cancer. We talked and laughed, and we didn't see when the afternoon came! Children's giggles and noise filled the atmosphere of happiness, and I was thankful to be able to be present in a joyful moment. It was tough saying goodbye to those people who I loved very much because I did not know if I would meet them again. Unfortunately, a diagnosis like this gives you the constant reminder that everything that you do can be the last time you do it.

Great friends

Finally, in the evening, we came back home. My father continued with his ultimate goal: learning English. He was determined. His first strategy was to take his *English for Dummies* book wherever he went. It helped, but he felt that he needed to improve his English skills faster. He began a new strategy. It consisted of sitting close to a church and smiling nonstop. He knew that somebody would soon stop by and start preaching to him, so he always looked thirsty for wisdom. He allowed them to give the greatest sermon ever and listened attentively so that he could pick up some new words. Then, in the end, he would finish the conversation with, "I am sorry. I do not speak English." I am not sure how the brothers and sisters took this new strategy, but no one would deny that he was doing everything he could to learn English.

A few days after his English training, it was time for him to go back to Brazil again. As much as I had already done farewells for seven years, I never got used to saying goodbye to him yet. Airports taste like chocolate cake when you are there to pick someone up, but they taste like rotten strawberries when you need to drop them off.

Chapter 73

Fifth Phase—Part 2

I was excited about this stage because it was the last one that required staying in the hospital. It made me feel positive that the same team of doctors who took care of me in December were with me again one year later. They had taken care of me with so much love that seeing them again reminded me that there was hope.

As soon as I got to the reception desk, one of the nurses screamed, "Guys, guys, Da Silva has arrived!" Dr. Hernandez, who I was very fond of, hugged me and kept repeating how amazing I looked. She seemed thrilled to see me. She had the look of a mom seeing her daughter come back home from college for the first time. She was always positive and truly believed that I would survive. The nurses kept complimenting me. I did not know if it was to make me happy, but it worked; all compliments were welcome.

When I went to my room, I was excited to learn who my roommate would be. As soon as I arrived, I realized that it was the worst room I had been assigned to. The room was pretty small, and since I did not have a window on my side, I could barely see the street. To use the bathroom or get out of my room, I would have to go through my roommate's side. Since she seemed like a cool woman, and I wanted her to remain cool, I felt it would be better to avoid disturbing her, so I spent most of the time inside my room. After all, I would be there for only a few days, and I was looking forward to being free again.

This was how my night went:

10:00 p.m.

I took a chemotherapy pill, Prednisone. The doctors had warned me that this drug would keep me up the entire night and would give me a lot of energy. As soon as I heard this, I knew I was in for a challenging night. I already had a lot of energy without taking anything. I would need a nightclub in the hospital so that I could rock with some other patients who did not want to waste their nights staring at a ceiling and counting sheep.

11:00 p.m.

Intravenous chemotherapy: Methotrexate. It was because of this darn chemotherapy that I needed to stay in the hospital. The doctors wanted to make sure that the majority of chemotherapy was released from my body; they needed to monitor if the toxins did not stay in my body.

12:00 a.m.

Urine collection to check whether the chemotherapy was being released or not.

1:00 a.m.

The nurses needed to check my blood pressure, temperature, and heart rate.

2:00 a.m.

One doctor, who was wearing a sweet, stinky perfume that

would make any cancer patient nauseous, said that my heartbeat was very low. He said it was only forty beats per minute and reminded me that normal is sixty when a person is sleeping. So he decided to make an urgent electrocardiogram. I thought, *Really? An electrocardiogram now, at two in the morning? Something serious must be happening to me.*

2:30 a.m.

The doctors did the electrocardiogram, and we needed to wait for the results.

4:00 a.m.

Eating myself up inside, I could not stop thinking about the electro. Would my weak heart get back to full speed? *Let's work, buddy!*

5:00 a.m.

The nurses woke me up to check my blood pressure, temperature, and heart rate. My adorable nurse—and I'm not being sarcastic, she is one of my favorites—told me that everything looked fine on my electrocardiogram and that the reason my heartbeat was too low may have been because I was asleep and they had given me medicine that lowered my heartbeat.

6:00 a.m.

Wakey, wakey! Weighing time! I was happy because I had not lost even a pound, but I was still sleepy.

7:00 a.m.

My nurse stopped by to say goodbye and introduced me to the new nurse who would be with me all day.

8:00 a.m.

Exhausted, with one eye open and the other closed, I listened as a group of doctors came into my room to tell me that I was doing very well, but they noticed I looked a bit tired. *Oh, really? A bit tired?* I was a zombie. I had not slept the entire night! The dark circles under my eyes were so deep that a panda would have lighter shading than I had. Anyway, to compensate for the hectic night I had, I slept all day and woke up feeling brand-new and ready to play a tennis match, but since I could not, I wrote a few more chapters of this book.

$\mathcal{C}$hapter 74

Weird Things That People Said to Console Me

In horrible circumstances like a cancer diagnosis, people do not usually know what to say, so they end up saying whatever comes to mind. Below, you will find some attempts people used to comfort me, but they didn't work because they felt awkward or out of touch. To some of them, I felt like saying: "I know you mean well, but try another one because this is just not working!"

Person A: I do not even know what to tell you, but I think God wants you. He needs you!

What I felt like saying: Yeah! I also wanted to be close to God, but not so close. If He does not mind, I will postpone our meeting for thirty years. Is that too much of an ask?

Person B: I was doing some research on your disease, and I found out that out of ten people diagnosed with leukemia, only one is black and that this disease is more common in men than in women, and it is more common in children than in adults. You are not white, you are not a man, and you are not a child! You are so unlucky! What are the odds? I think you should play the Mega Million!

Commentary: Okay, the spirit of Sherlock Holmes is among us! Thank you for deductive reasoning and extensive Wikipedia research, but this is actually not helping anyone! Besides, a little sensitivity would be welcome!

Person C: Girl, if I were you, I would have killed myself already, you know!

Commentary: So encouraging and uplifting, thank you, but no thank you! If I dared to do it, I would leave a note saying that you inspired me!

Person D: You should not think about death. If I walk down the street, I can get hit by a truck and die at any moment.

What I thought of stating: Really? Me too! Unfortunately, cancer has not made me invisible to cars. If I cross a street and a car hits me, it is not going to be good either. As much as I understood that people wanted to warn me that anyone could die at any moment, people needed to understand that having a cancer diagnosis put me a little closer to the Grim Reaper.

Person E: I do not believe that you were not eating properly! Why didn't you eat well? Anemia is pretty serious!

In the back of my mind: First of all, it is *leukemia* and not *anemia*! Second, I always ate very well. I did not get cancer from not eating my fruits and veggies. However, I did learn that leukemia causes anemia and not the other way around.

Person F: At what stage are you now? Is your cancer terminal?

Commentary: I dismiss these types of comments!

Person G: Just out of curiosity, tell me everything that happens when you're undergoing chemotherapy.

Comment: Let's agree that the "out of curiosity" was used at a bad time.

Person H: You should not worry about your hair! Hair doesn't matter! The most important thing is your health.

Commentary: Of course, if given the choice between my hair and my health, I choose health, though a little hair wouldn't hurt, would it? Only those who lose it know how much it hurts to be without it.

Person I: You had this cancer because you needed to learn a lesson!

Commentary: What lesson is this? Please tell me! I am a teacher, and I love lessons.

Person J: You had it because you have too much resentment in your heart!

Commentary: It was weird to think that I could be the one who had brought this disease into my life. I started reflecting on it, and I took the time to forgive all the people who had hurt me in the past, those I knew had a dark place in my heart. I have to confess it was a great exercise; I did not how much time I had left, and I did not want to spend the rest of my life holding grudges. However, I thought it through, and I remembered that leukemia is a disease that affects children as well. If we follow this resentment premise, then we would assert that kids are unable to forgive others, which is why they have cancer, so we've resorted to blaming children—even innocent infants—who have not had the time to create a grudge for their own disease?

Person K: Do not be sad! And do not cry. You have to be strong all the time!

Commentary: Yes, I agree, I need to be strong to be able to cope. However, if a cancer patient needs to cry, please allow us to do it without feeling guilty for being sad. We live in a world that demands a lot from us, so people feel that they have to be resilient all the time. With this disease, I learned that crying does not indicate a weakness. I also learned that being sad is part of the maturing process. Being sad at sad moments was acceptable; I just needed to watch it so that sadness did not consume me.

Person L: God forbid I ever have such a disgraceful disease like yours! I know you are receiving a lot of love and everything, but I cannot envy you having cancer.

Commentary: Hello? I hope that you do not envy me having this disease either! Envy itself is not a good feeling, but if you want to envy something, please envy something that makes sense. If you need to envy somebody's cancer, I suggest you look for a psychiatrist because something is just not right in your head!

Person M: Wow! You change your hair more than Chris's mother. Which Chris? In that program *Everybody Hates Chris.* You are not going to put on a blonde one, right?

Comment: Please do me a favor. Stop paying attention to my wigs! If I want to wear a blonde one, yes, I definitely will.

Person N: This disease has to be bad karma from your previous lives.

Commentary: How do you know? If I had other lives, I do not want to know what I did in them to deserve it. What the hell did I do to deserve it?

Person O: Remember that you studied hard; you need to use what you studied in college and go back to work.

Comment: This can only be a joke, right? Of course I wanted to get back to work, but I could not. I would rather work from Monday to Monday, from 7 a.m. to 7 p.m. for free than have this disease and fight for my life by enduring such a long treatment.

$\mathcal{C}$hapter 75

My Thoughts

- You know the danger of a windstorm when you leave home wearing a wig.
- Worse than being a cancer patient is seeing a lot of healthy people vegetating, complaining about trivial things.
- Only those who spend some holidays, such as Easter, Christmas, and New Year's Eve, lying in a hospital bed know that celebrating holidays is a gift that a lot of people do not get to do because they are hospital bound. Life is composed of moments; live each one of them as if it were your last one!
- Being diagnosed with this disease made me realize that I would do everything I could to be alive. I would eat healthy foods, drink a lot of water and my green juices, pray, meditate, and be positive. However, I had no control over the end of my story. So it was up to me to believe that whatever happened was for my own good, regardless of the outcome.
- I learned that I would never complain about having a bad hair day. Every hair becomes beautiful and wonderful when the poisonous chemotherapy takes it away from you.

- You learn to celebrate each hair that is born, be it on the head, armpits, or legs. This is a sign that your body is functioning well.

- Work and fatigue are no longer super problems. Seeing people complaining every Monday that they have to go back to work makes us reconsider what real problems are. Do something that you love and stop wasting your time on earth being a victim of everything and everyone.

- I learned to appreciate the gift of going and coming back when I was no longer in charge of my schedule. Spending weeks and months in the hospital allowed me to perceive daily miracles.

- In the darkness of the night, I wondered if it was fair that I was worried about the possibility of not waking up the next day while everyone else cherished a peaceful night of sleep.

- Sometimes it felt weird that some people believed very strongly in my recovery and at the same time forgot to believe in the solutions to their simple problems.

- Some lies make us feel better! Hearing "You're beautiful!" when you feel your worst can be empowering.

- "You're much more beautiful now!" My goodness, if I am more beautiful bald, what did people really think of me when I had hair and did not look like an ugly, chewed lollipop?

- The worst is that I felt beautiful! First, I used a wig that I loved. Then, when my hair began to grow, I started using scarves, and for me, they were "colored hair." Every day I put one on, it always matched my clothes. I thought I was a Barbie with permission to change my hair color on a whim.

Chapter 76

The Sixth and Final Phase and Three and a Half Years of Uncertainty

The sixth phase lasted forty-three days. And I underwent six weeks of intense chemotherapy. After, my immune system began to fall, fall, fall. I had 0.1 white blood cells when the normal is 4.0. My platelets reached ten when a healthy person has 160. Even with all these obstacles and having to have a lot of blood and platelet transfusions, I managed to finish the sixth stage, and that meant that I had completed the first stage of treatment. There were still three and a half years of chemo and many other painful exams to do, but I did it!

With the completion of this phase, my life was starting to get back on track, and I celebrated every small win. My catheter was removed, and I was free to take a shower without having to cover my arm with plastic. For the first time in a year, I enjoyed the water cascading on my head without worrying whether or not my catheter would get wet; it was a new baptism, and the removal of the catheter symbolized that I was a new me. The scar will always be on my arm to remind me that I had a fight and that I did my best to overcome the beast!

Most importantly, I managed to finish my first year of intensive chemo treatment, and I knew that from the day I was diagnosed, until my last day on earth, I would fight leukemia with faith, optimism, and good humor.

However, this first year was certainly not the end of this experience and journey. I would have to dedicate at least nine years of my life to medical checkups to ensure I was healthy.

After three years and a half, I reached a profound cancer milestone: the last chemo treatment. As with everything, I faced this moment with positivity, vitality, and of course faith. I had faith in my journey, faith in my strength, and most importantly, faith in myself to accomplish anything.